Y'all come &
see us. soon!
Best wishes John Ehrhardt
3/21/97

AUSTIN

LONE STAR RISING

TOWERY PUBLISHING, INC.

AUSTIN

LONE STAR RISING

BY JOHN T. DAVIS AND J. B. COLSON

CORPORATE PROFILES BY LAURA TUMA

ART DIRECTION BY BRIAN GROPPE

PRODUCED IN COOPERATION WITH THE GREATER AUSTIN CHAMBER OF COMMERCE

IN 1839, THE FLEDGLING REPUBLIC OF TEXAS' FIRST LEGISLATIVE SESSION WAS HELD IN AUSTIN. HOWEVER, IT WOULD BE 50 YEARS BEFORE THE CURRENT PINK GRANITE CAPITOL BUILDING WAS COMPLETED. LIKE ALL THINGS IN TEXAS THAT ARE BIG AND GRAND, THE STATE CAPITOL WAS INTENTIONALLY BUILT SEVEN FEET TALLER THAN THE U.S. CAPITOL. AFTER NEARLY BEING DESTROYED BY FIRE IN THE EARLY 1980S, THE AUSTIN LANDMARK UNDERWENT A MASSIVE RESTORATION REVEALING THE INTRICATE BEAUTY AND CRAFTSMANSHIP THAT YEARS OF "GOVERNMENT EFFICIENCY" HAD COVERED OVER.

IN MAY OF 1839 WHEN EDWIN WALLER AND A GROUP OF SURVEYORS MAPPED OUT THE ORIGINAL CITY OF AUSTIN, THEY DECIDED CONGRESS AVENUE WOULD BE 120 FEET WIDE. BUT NEARLY 10 YEARS WOULD PASS BEFORE THE CITY TURNED THE MUD-RUTTED THOROUGHFARE INTO A PAVED STREET. MORE THAN A CENTURY LATER, A BUILDING CRAZE IN THE EARLY 1980S ONCE AGAIN TRANSFORMED THE APPEARANCE OF AUSTIN'S FAVORITE AVENUE.

▲ LARRY KOLVOORD / AUSTIN AMERICAN STATESMAN

▲ BILL KENNEDY

LIBRARY OF CONGRESS CATALOGING-IN-PUBLICATION DATA

Davis, John T. (John Terry), 1955-
    Austin : lone star rising / by John T. Davis and J.B. Colson ; corporate profiles by Laura Tuma.
       p.   cm. — (Urban tapestry series)
    "Produced in cooperation with the Greater Austin Chamber of Commerce."
    Includes index.
    ISBN 1-881096-08-4 : $39.50
    1. Austin (Tex.)—Description and travel.   2. Austin (Tex.)—Pictorial works.   I. Colson, James B. (James Burton)   II. Tuma, Laura, 1957- . III. Title. IV. Series.
F394.A94D38   1994
976.4'31—dc20   94-14484
                                       CIP

TOWERY Publishing, Inc.
1835 Union Avenue
Memphis, Tennessee 38104

PUBLISHER: J. Robert Towery
EXECUTIVE EDITOR: David Dawson
SENIOR EDITORS: Michael C. James, Ken Woodmansee
ARTICLES EDITOR: Stinson Liles
EDITORIAL CONTRIBUTORS: Brenda Thompson, Michael Kardos
COPY EDITOR: Carlisle Hacker
ASSISTANT ART DIRECTOR: Anne Castrodale
TECHNICAL DIRECTOR: William H. Towery

URBAN TAPESTRY SERIES

TOWERY
PUBLISHING, INC.

Contents

PRESERVING NATURE IN AN URBAN SETTING HAS BEEN ONE OF AUSTIN'S PERENNIAL CHALLENGES. WHEN THE CONGRESS AVENUE BRIDGE NEEDED IMPROVEMENTS, THERE WAS ONE CATCH: THE WORLD'S LARGEST URBAN COLONY OF MEXICAN FREE-TAILED BATS TAKES UP SUMMER RESIDENCE UNDERNEATH THE STRUCTURE. THE RESULT WAS A COMPROMISE THAT IMPROVED THE BRIDGE WHILE LEAVING INTACT THE UNDERCARRIAGE DESIGN THAT SERVES AS HOME TO THE TINY CREATURES. (FOLLOWING PAGES)

GARY LOCKHART / BLIMP PHOTO / VIDEO

"The city lies against and below two short, spiny ribs of hills. One of the little rivers runs round and about, and from the hills it is possible to view the city overall and draw therefrom an impression of sweet curving streets and graceful sweeping lawns and the unequivocally happy sounds of children always at play. . . .

"Occasionally through the trees, and always from a point of higher ground, one can see the college tower and the Capitol building. On brilliant mornings, the white sandstone of the tower and the Capitol's pink granite dome are joined for an instant, all pink and cream, catching the first light."

BILLY LEE BRAMMER,
The Gay Place

BILLY LEE BRAMMER WAS A POLITICAL aide to Lyndon Johnson who found a higher calling when he poured his life into a single novel. He penned those words in the late 1950s, when Austin, Texas, could fairly be described as a place where the University was a credit to its football team, and the State Legislature thought "High Tech" must be the name of a new style of modern art. Though the Capitol and the Tower still figure in the city's skyline and command much of its attention, the Austin that Billy Lee wrote about has passed largely into memory. The city which supplanted it is vibrant where the old college town was sleepy, diverse where 1950s-era Austin marched in the lockstep of conformity, and compelling in a way that no other city in Texas can quite match.

But still, in the mind's eye of those who love her, there is an enduring vision of Austin—the Southwestern pastels of pink and white that Brammer wrote of set against the green contours of the hills—that lingers pleasantly in the collective imagination. Everyone who lives in Austin, or even tarries for a visit, takes away a vision.

From sunrise until dark, the joggers make their circular peregrinations around Town Lake. The lake itself is the lowermost of a 150-mile-long series of seven lakes created in the 1930s and 1940s by a succession of dams along the Colorado River. Beautification efforts, spearheaded by Lady Bird Johnson, have laced the lakeside trails with gazebos, flowering trees, and thousands of small horticultural grace notes.

The same plentiful dose of sunlight that nourishes the lakeside greenery also catches the men working the high iron around the peak of downtown's Bank One tower. There are no designer sweats or matching shar-peis up here. One of the city's first new generation of skyscrapers, built in the early 1970s, the bank tower once dominated downtown in haughty, Bauhaus-inspired splendor. Clad entirely in gold glass, the building was Austin's declaration of independence from its university/capital legacy. It presaged the current preoccupation with economic diversity and high technology which characterizes the city today. But it, too, is yoked to changing times. The workmen are busy replacing the gaudy gold panels with more austere smoked-glass panes and dark granite accents.

Yet the commuters begin flocking into town before the sun has even made its initial appear-

TOWN LAKE IS A MAGNET FOR AUSTINITES—WHETHER IT'S SITTING ALONG THE BANKS, ENJOYING A MEAL OVERLOOKING THE WATER, OR BEING LUCKY ENOUGH TO HAVE AN OFFICE WITH AN UNOBSTRUCTED VIEW (PAGES 8 AND 9).
RICHARD REYNOLDS

FOR A CITY WITH A WELL-DESERVED REPUTATION FOR BEING LAID-BACK, IT'S SURPRISING HOW MANY DIFFERENT ACTIVITIES AUSTINITES ARE INVOLVED WITH. MUSIC, ART, WRITING, ESPOUSING A CAUSE, OR RUNNING A BUSINESS ON THE SIDE KEEPS MANY ON THE GO WELL BEFORE DAWN AND LONG AFTER DUSK (OPPOSITE).

THE MAJESTIC UNIVERSITY TOWER HAS COME TO EMBODY, ALONG WITH THE MASCOT LONGHORN STEER, THE SPRAWLING UNIVERSITY OF TEXAS (LEFT).

BY JOHN T. DAVIS

ance. They come from the bedroom communities of Round Rock, Cedar Park, and the piquantly named Pflugerville, bound for the glass-fronted headquarters of Austin's collection of shiny, high-tech industries.

Tracor, the original high-technology pioneer, established itself in Austin in 1967. Even before (and especially in the wake of) the 1985 oil field bust, the city aggres-sively recruited a consortium of high-tech and R&D companies, including Motorola and IBM (the city's two largest private employers), MCC, Lockheed, 3M, Texas Instruments, Advanced Micro Devices, the Pharmaco pharma-ceutical research firm, Radian, and others. But not all of the new 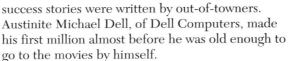 success stories were written by out-of-towners. Austinite Michael Dell, of Dell Computers, made his first million almost before he was old enough to go to the movies by himself.

The city habitually offers large tax-abatement packages to lure out-of-state "clean" industries and, for their part, most of the immigrants prove willing to adapt themselves to the city's low-impact ambience. The 3M Company, for instance, built its Austin headquarters west of town, in the pristine hills near Lake Travis. But in doing so, they bought several hundred acres elsewhere in the vicinity and set it aside as a habitat for endangered bird species. That spirit of give-and-take is what the city seeks to engender in its corporate citizens. Ideally, a business' investment in Austin is emotional as well as financial.

Like much of the rest of Texas, Austin was riding high, wide, and handsome during the late 1970s and early 1980s. The price of oil kept going up, and land parcels flipped like flapjacks on a truck-stop griddle. The art of the deal turned into a grown-up version of Toys R Us on steroids; private helicopters, cellular phones, and a goodly amount of Texas-style ostentation became the order of the day. On the plus side, the city finally opened some good Italian and Vietnamese restau-rants, as a nice counterpoint to the perennial and ubiquitous Number-Two Tex-Mex Dinner and chicken-fried steak.

Inevitably, the entire, over-inflated scenario collapsed in a welter of over-valued real estate and bad paper in the mid-1980s. Even former Gover-nor John Connally, the epitome of the Texas high-roller, went belly up. Banks and savings-and-loans went Dixie with breathtaking rapidity. Once, the bumper stickers on the wheeler-dealers' BMWs read, "Let the Yankees Freeze in the Dark." Now, humbled, they replaced them with a new epigram: "Please God, Just Let Me Have One More Oil Boom and I Promise Not to Piss It Away This Time."

Everyone, of course, should have known better. In hindsight, everyone did. But there was a payoff of sorts. Years later, memories of the bust spurred Austin's determination to diversify its economic base. Today, that strategy is paying large dividends as the city and the state climb out of the trough of the 1980s.

And we got to keep the restaurants. Hours before lunchtime, down on the decidedly low-tech end of things, the fires are lit under the oak wood stacked in the smoker of Sam's Bar-B-Que, over on the city's east side. The first of the day's installment of mutton, ribs, and sausage sits waiting for their transformation into the stuff that a carnivore's dreams are made of. Despite the proliferation of mesquite-smoked tofu, post-Impressionist designer pizza, and goat-cheese-and-prosciutto nachos, many Austinites still share an enduring reverence for the Holy Trinity of grub: Tex-Mex, barbecue, and Southern homestyle cooking, specifically chicken-fried steak. Which is a good thing since, as Texas writer Dan Jenkins noted, "Grease got us through the Depression."

As these first fires are being stoked, the city's legions of musicians, playwrights, actors, filmmak-ers, and authors begin to drag their collective, sleep-starved bodies to an array of "day jobs." All over town, they toil as paralegals, shade-tree mechanics, bookstore clerks, waitresses and bartenders, carpenters, and receptionists. One musician, currently enjoying national renown, was once summarily fired from her receptionist's gig. "They said I wasn't *perky* enough," she explained dryly.

It is all in the service of Art, and especially music, that elusive muse which has taken root in Austin to such an extent that the City Council had "Live Music Capital of the World" incorporated into the city letterhead.   ➤

IN THE EVENING, AS THE DAY BEGINS TO dim, the great tidal shift of commuters reverses itself. Some folks eschew the rush hour to wander down to the Congress Avenue bridge, which spans Town Lake, to witness a migration of another sort.

When the city remodeled the venerable bridge a few years back, the architects of the project did not have much more in mind than speeding motorists on their way from one side of the river to another. Nobody was thinking about bats. But migrating Mexican free-tailed bats discovered the crevices underneath the renovated bridge, and evidently considered them the chiropteran equivalent of Park Avenue, the Playboy mansion, and Club Med, rolled into one.

Today, between April and October, something like one-and-a-half million of the wee beasties—the largest urban bat colony in the world— make their seasonal home beneath the bridge. As the sun declines each evening, they come streaming out in great dark Gothic columns. It is a hell of a spectacle, and an irresistible draw to tourists and citizens alike.

In the fall of 1993, the daily paper, the *Austin American-Statesman*, helped sponsor the construction of a bat observation area near the paper's headquarters on the south bank of the river. The project was cosponsored by Bat Conservation International, a research and conservation organization. Proclamations from the mayor and governor were read, and elementary schoolchildren in attendance sang "a little bat song," according to the BCI spokesman. No one thought this odd.

A few blocks away, on Sixth Street, another nocturnal creature is stirring. . . .

Sixth Street, originally named Pecan Street, has always had an after-hours identity distinct from the rest of the city. One of the neighborhood's residents, William Sydney Porter (who later attained fame as short-story maestro "O. Henry") in 1895 pronounced the strip "bold, bad, and hard to curry." For those with thirsts that whiskey could not quench, Pecan Street pointed an arrow-straight path to the city's red-light district.

By the early 1970s, Sixth Street's gorgeous Victorian and granite-faced buildings housed gin mills, shabby-but-friendly *conjunto* bars, fast-buck finance companies, and secondhand thrift shops. The grand old Driskill Hotel still cast an imposing vista, but she loomed over a population that ranged from local shopkeepers and working people to winos and drag queens.

Today, Sixth Street sits at the center of a web of complex and diverse distractions. College kids from San Antonio to Seattle recognize the downtown strip as an open-air party buffet, home to the soulless cover band and the two-for-one kamikaze. But *real* music making goes on, too, in dark Sixth Street storefront bars like the Black Cat Lounge and intimate listening rooms like Chicago House. Nearby, for those with more eclectic tastes, are the gay bars over on Seventh Street and an array of alternative/ dance clubs, offering everything from smart drinks to trash disco, near the burgeoning arts district near Fourth Street. Sixth Street, in its current incarnation, occupies some indefinable niche between Bourbon Street and Disneyland. ➤

EACH DUSK, BETWEEN APRIL AND OCTOBER, THE CEREMONY COMMENCES. FIRST, ONE OR TWO EMERGE FROM UNDER THE CONGRESS AVENUE BRIDGE. BUT SOON THE DOTS BECOME A STREAM, AND THEN A RIVER THAT UNDULATES FOR HOURS AS THE WORLD'S LARGEST URBAN COLONY OF MEXICAN FREE-TAILED BATS MAKES ANOTHER FORAY INTO THE NIGHT TO FEAST ON INSECTS (OPPOSITE).

WHERE TO GO, WHAT TO DO, AND WHOM TO SEE IS NEVER A PROBLEM IN AUSTIN—THERE'S SOMETHING FOR VIRTUALLY EVERY LIFESTYLE AND TASTE. AND A LOT OF IT GOES ON AT NIGHT (LEFT).

THE MAGNIFICENT GRANITE BATHOLITH KNOWN AS ENCHANTED ROCK HAS BEEN A POPULAR SPOT FOR HUNDREDS OF YEARS—NATIVE AMERICANS CONSIDERED IT TO BE SACRED. A FEW YEARS BACK, WHEN A CELESTIAL HARMONIC CONVERGENCE WAS EXPECTED TO OCCUR, ENCHANTED ROCK WAS OVERRUN BY "NEW AGERS" SEEKING AN EXTRA JOLT OF COSMIC ENERGY. THE SITE IS APPROXIMATELY 640 ACRES IN SIZE, AND ITS 500-FOOT HEIGHT PROVIDES A COMMANDING VIEW OF THE HILL COUNTRY (PAGES 16 AND 17).

RICHARD REYNOLDS

"She said, If you're from Texas, son,

Where's your boots and where's your gun?

I smiled and said, I got guns

No one can see"

BUTCH HANCOCK,

"SHE NEVER SPOKE SPANISH TO ME,"

1977

THERE IS A PLACE IN AUSTIN, DOWN ON the river's edge, where you can reach out and touch the face of the West.

It is a tall cliff that erupts out of the willows and live oaks on the south bank of the Colorado River. From a distance the cliff, which is but one of many cliffs in a chain that winds a sinuous path through Central Texas, resembled a series of balconies to the Spanish explorers who first entered the region sometime in the 16th century. "Los Balcones," they called them. That done, they forded the river, surmounted the cliffs, and marched on. Visions of golden cities danced in their eyes.

The golden city, which would one day arise along the Colorado, sits astride what has come to be called the Balcones Escarpment or, more familiarly, the Balcones Fault. With more exactitude, but less poetry than the conquistadors employed, the authoritative reference work, *The Handbook of Texas*, describes it thus:

"Several miles wide, the escarpment, which appears from the plains below as a range of wooded hills, separates the Edwards Plateau in the west from the Coastal Plains. The Balcones zone was formed under conditions of strain during the Tertiary time when there was a down-warping near the Gulf Coast and a moderate uplift inland. Water-bearing formations passing beneath the plateau to the plains are broken by the Balcones fault group, and much water is forced to the surface by artesian pressure."

The dichotomy which the Balcones Fault punctuates is an important one to understand. It is the place where two American cultures collide.

In Austin, on one side of the Colorado, the land begins a slow descent towards the alluvial bottoms, the rich black farmland, the placid, level landscape which finds its denouement at last on the balmy shores of the Gulf of Mexico. The first loblolly pines and the first Spanish moss appear only 30 or so miles east of Austin. Sharp-scented pines, gracefully dangling moss, warm coastal breezes; these are the icons of the Gulf Coast, bayou country, the Deepest South you'll find. And the South is what the land extending from the river's lower bank portends. East Texas—that is, the region where the West bleeds almost imperceptibly into Dixie's final vanguard—has few cattle or cowboys; rather, it has the blues and grits and a perspective that is inescapably rooted to its decidedly Texan but decidedly *different* way of going about living.

But the other side of the river, atop the Fault, is another story. In some ways, it is another country. There you will find Western Swing and *huevos rancheros* and the yearning that a distant and beckoning horizon inspires. The land rises towards the Texas Hill Country, and the soil becomes thin and miserly, poorly concealing the sharp spines of limestone and granite that lie beneath. Springs and rivers gush joyously forth from hidden aquifers. Chase the horizon line long enough, and it will lead you to the Rocky Mountains. This is the rim of the West of the imagination, still full of promise and unredeemed dreams.

And in the middle sits Austin, the Texas capital, 500,000-odd souls making their private and sometimes uneasy peace between Southern nostalgia and Western idealism.

Austin's past—barely more than 150 years of it—is hardly past. Its future, the city's citizens will tell you, still holds out promise. And the promise beckons: *Money* magazine, for instance, regularly cites Austin as among the nation's 10 most livable cities. Still, it remains a Lone Star anomaly, eternally restless, turbulent, with gusto and trepidation forever existing in the same moment. In the best and truest sense of the phrase, Austin stands apart. ➤

THE COUNTLESS LIMESTONE ROCK FORMATIONS PREVALENT IN THE AREA NOT ONLY CREATE BEAUTIFUL NATURAL WONDERS, BUT ARE ALSO BENEFICIAL TO THE CITY'S BUILDERS AND DEVELOPERS. LIMESTONE IS A GOOD BUILDING MATERIAL, AND A NUMBER OF LARGE QUARRIES ARE WITHIN AN EASY DRIVE OF AUSTIN (OPPOSITE).

SUCCESS IN CATTLE RANCHING HAS A LOT DO WITH LOCATION. WEST OF AUSTIN, THE HILL COUNTRY IS A SCRUBBY, SOIL-POOR REGION THAT REQUIRES LARGER AMOUNTS OF LAND TO RAISE BEEF. TO THE EAST, THE LAND IS FLATTER AND RICHER, AND PROVIDES RANCHERS WITH AN IDEAL LOCATION FOR GRAZING THEIR HERDS (LEFT).

F OR ALL THE CHANGES, THE CAPITOL Building and the University Tower endure as the city's two abiding symbols.

The Renaissance Revival-style Capitol, built largely by convict labor in 1885-88, is Austin's raison d'être. It is the second such building constructed on the site, after its predecessor burned in 1881. And it represents an effort of deliberate hubris, consciously constructed so as to be the largest state capitol, and fully seven feet taller than its federal cousin in Washington, D.C.

For its part, the Tower is the signature structure of the University of Texas, which was founded in 1839 when the Congress of the Republic of Texas ordained the establishment of a "University of the first class." Construction on a 40-acre site just north of the Capitol did not commence, however, until 1882. (Though today the biggest, UT was not the first institute of higher learning in the city. Tillotson Collegiate and Normal Institute, a senior college for black students, which was the precursor to the modern Huston-Tillotson College, opened with 250 students in 1881.)

The Tower itself, which houses one of UT's many superb libraries, was designed in the 1930s by architect Paul Cret. Folklorist, professor, and author J. Frank Dobie, who was often at war with the anti-intellectual nabobs who frequently occupied perk spots on the Board of Regents, openly despised the thing. But the Tower survived the critical slings and arrows (and a certain tragic notoriety engendered by its use as a sniper's perch in 1966) and has come to embody, along with the mascot longhorn steer, the sprawling University of Texas.

Together, the Tower and the Capitol represent the magnetic poles around which Austin originally revolved. Were it not for the institutions those two structures represent, the Texas capital today might still be a Hill Country backwater called Waterloo, differing little from contemporary neighboring communities like New Braunfels or Llano.

In fact, Waterloo is what the city was originally called, back when it was chartered in the spring of 1839. Maribeau B. Lamar, the presidency of the Republic of Texas still in his future, passed through the site on a buffalo hunt in 1838 and, struck by its inherent beauty, stated, "This should be the seat of future empire." (They talked like that a lot in those days.)

A government commission charged with selecting a seat for the young Republic's government concurred. Waterloo, it was thought, would do nicely. The new city's name was changed to honor Stephen F. Austin, the first great impresario of modern Texas, not long after Judge Edwin Waller, one of Waterloo/Austin's original settlers, began laying out lots.

Waller, Lamar, and their compatriots were not, of course, the first inhabitants of the verdant landscape. Some 16,000 years ago, the pre-Columbian ancestors of the Comanche and Tonkawa bathed at Barton Springs and took in the scenery from the peak of Mt. Bonnell, just as modern inhabitants are still wont to do. ➢

THE SEAT OF TEXAS GOVERNMENT TAKES ON A SPECIAL ATMOSPHERE WHEN THE LEGISLATURE MEETS FOR SIX MONTHS EACH BIENNIUM. LEGISLATORS DEAL WITH LOBBYISTS WHO FLOCK TO AUSTIN LIKE MIGRATORY BIRDS SPORTING ALLIGATOR SHOES AND CELLULAR TELEPHONES. AND, EVERY SO OFTEN, AN OUT-OF-TOWN LAWMAKER TRIES TO HAVE THE CAPITAL RELOCATED, BECAUSE HE THINKS AUSTIN IS TOO LIBERAL (OPPOSITE).

FOUR-YEAR UNIVERSITIES—AUSTIN IS HOME TO FOUR—ARE AN IMPORTANT REASON THE CITY HAS SUCCESSFULLY DEVELOPED INTO A HIGH-TECHNOLOGY CENTER. IN FACT, MORE THAN 32 PERCENT OF AUSTINITES HOLD A COLLEGE DEGREE. OLD MAIN AT ST. EDWARD'S UNIVERSITY SITS STATELY AND SERENE ON A HILL IN SOUTH AUSTIN (BOTTOM). THE UNIVERSITY OF TEXAS' MEMORIAL TOWER IS A FOCAL POINT FOR THE 50,000 OR SO STUDENTS WHO ATTEND SCHOOL THERE (TOP).

"You got to sing like you don't need the money

Love like you'll never get hurt

You got to dance like nobody's watchin'

It's got to come from the heart if you want it to work."

SUSANNA CLARK & RICHARD LEIGH,
"COME FROM THE HEART"
1987

PEOPLE IN AUSTIN WILL PARTY AT THE drop of a hat, and if necessary they will drop the hat themselves. Besides the requisite July 4/Thanksgiving/Christmas trilogy, Austinites of every stripe take nondenominational delight in Cinco de Mayo and Diez y Seis (commemorating two struggles for Mexican independence), Rosh Hashanah, Chinese New Year, Mardi Gras, the Day of the Dead (a Mexican folk holiday falling on November 1 and 2), Juneteenth (aka June 19, the day in 1865 on which Texas slaves were notified of their freedom), you name it.

All this in addition to holidays and ceremonies that are unique to the city, such as the springtime Eeyore's Birthday fete (an alfresco tribute to Winnie-the-Pooh's favorite donkey, which serves as a sort of 1960s-holdover, role-playing paradise); Spamarama (don't ask); the biyearly downtown Old Pecan St. Festival; the Capital 10,000 footrace through the city; the annual South By Southwest music and media conference; the Legends of Golf tournament; the outdoor Austin Aqua Festival; Laguna Gloria Museum's springtime Fiesta; and Carnaval Brasiliero, a local version of Rio's famous Carnaval, introduced to Austin by homesick Brazilian students marooned at UT.

There is a hedonistic side of the city to which

all this merrymaking caters. It has been ever thus. Writer Larry McMurtry, who shared a house with Billy Lee Brammer in Austin in the early 1960s, credited the city with certain "adolescent characteristics," not the least of which is a penchant for the flamboyant and the narcissistic. Folks in Austin love to dress up and gallivant around.

The transitory and carefree social attitude did not appeal for long to McMurtry, but then he comes from austere West Texas stock, who generally take a dim view of hedonism on principle, no matter into whose municipal precincts it may fall. Still, he acknowledged, "Foreigners and Easterners surrender their affections to Austin more readily than to any other place in the state."

That appeal endures. Today Austin, even encrusted as it is with such modern offerings as shopping malls and fast-food eateries and sprawling, generic suburbs, exists in the mind's eye as something different.

Maybe it has something to do with the music. Austin has the usual cultural trappings for a city its size, everything from concert halls to art galleries and theaters, from ballet companies to symphony orchestras. Yet while other cities can boast of great universities and high-tech industries and natural beauty—and while 49 other cities can even lay claim to being state capitals—Austin is known for more than all this. When the words "Austin, Texas" are conjured up, tourists and expatriates do not immediately envision tenured professors or corporate CEOs. They think of Willie Nelson, or the late blues guitarist Stevie Ray Vaughan, or the myriad stars who have plied their trade on the stage of the PBS television series, "Austin City Limits." Despite Austin's diverse mix of business and pleasure, when you mention the city's name, folks tend to think, in short, of music.

No place in the United States can lay claim to the sheer quantity of live music that Austin enjoys. Outsiders often quibble with this claim, but then they visit Austin and find that what has long been an article of faith to city demographers—that the city has more live music venues per capita than virtually any other city in the world—is, in fact, the truth.

Not even Nashville puts so much music on the street. The Tennessee city is the capital of the country music industry, it's true, but, with the exception of the Printer's Alley district and the vast Opryland complex—worthy locales, to be sure—nearly all of its creativity is restricted to the hermetic confines of a songwriter's cubicle or a recording studio.

And despite the plenitude of live music venues in New York and L.A., these cities are simply too seething and contentious to allow any one art form to attain preeminence. Dozens of cultures, each with a host of artistic disciplines, strive for attention, for a space in the spotlight. There is just too much.

Music, on the other hand, has always been an integral part of the social fabric of Austin, and of Texas as a whole. Today, after decades of incuba-

tion, there are scores of clubs, hundreds upon hundreds of working musicians and songwriters, and thousands of people who work in ancillary music business industries, from music stores to booking agencies to independent record labels. The money they generate yearly is conservatively estimated in the millions.

The South By Southwest music and media conference, held each March for nearly a decade, draws hundreds of bands and performers, and thousands of music industry professionals from all over the United States and dozens of foreign countries to the city for an exhaustive round of seminars and showcase performances. The SXSW registrants, in turn, take Austin and its music to the world.

None of this was preordained by design or fate. It wasn't as though the muses did a collective highfive over the Hill Country and shouted, "Strike up the band, by Zeus!" But there is an intangible quality to the city, with its laissez-faire lifestyle, and to the lay of the local Texas landscape—rolling, sensuous, and beckoning—to which the creative mind is drawn. There is, noted Billy Lee Brammer, room enough to caper.

Then, too, Austin lies at the crossroads of several cultures, each of which comes bearing its own vivid and indelible brand of music: Mexican immigrants journeyed up from the Rio Grande Valley to join native Tejanos in search of a better life in *Norte*, packing along fiery *corridos*, and *conjunto*, the delightful and improbable blend of Latin rhythms and Deutsch-Tex waltzes and polkas. Today, *la onda Tejano* ("the Tejano wave") marries Hispanic tempos to rock-and-roll urgency.

Then, too, there were the Anglo-Saxon ballads, imported by the cowboys trailing the herds north, and sodbusters following their clarion call of "free" land West, which became the basis of modern folk and country music.

Black sharecroppers and freedmen brought with them the seminal blues and gospel music (and the seed of what would one day blossom as rhythm and blues, and rock and roll) when they migrated west to African-American enclaves like Austin's Clarksville and Rosewood Park neighborhoods.

There was a rough, wild art to be found in those keening tales of loss and love and hard traveling, and it bred artists who left indelible impressions. One of them, Roosevelt T. Williams, is closing in on 100, but you can still find him

BEFORE THE REST OF THE WORLD DISCOVERED HIS BRILLIANCE, STEVIE RAY VAUGHAN PERFECTED HIS LEGENDARY STYLE WHILE LIVING AND WORKING IN AUSTIN. IN 1990 THE GRAMMY AWARD-WINNING BLUES GENIUS WAS TRAGICALLY KILLED IN A HELICOPTER CRASH. THE FANS WHO TURNED OUT FOR HIS STATUE'S COMMEMORATION ON TOWN LAKE ARE INDICATIVE OF THE PASSION AUSTINITES HOLD FOR THEIR MUSIC AND THEIR MUSICIANS.

playing piano some afternoons in Austin's Continental Club, a black-walled gin mill on South Congress Avenue.

The exponent of a nearly extinct keyboard style called barrelhouse piano, Williams learned his trade in the black juke joints and bawdy houses of Central Texas and western Louisiana. When he got good enough that people would pay to see *him* rather than the drunks or the hookers, he began to make a name for himself.

They began to call him the Grey Ghost. No one ever saw him arrive or depart. He wore a brakeman's coveralls over his gig clothes and hopped freight trains from one town to another. He would alight in the switching yard, tuck his overalls under a bush, and stroll into town to play, unannounced. "They always said I come up out of the ground," he remembered with a sly laugh. "Like a ghost. Grey ghost at that."

But even before the Grey Ghost was born, cowboys riding herd on the Chisholm Trail, which passed near Austin, made their own music out of regional variations on ancient Scottish and Irish ballads and marching songs; "The Streets of Laredo" actually had its origins on the streets of Edinburgh somewhere back in the collective

Gaelic memory. A century-and-change later, it is called country music, and it goes places that the Chisholm Trail buckaroos never dreamed of.

Willie Nelson took his instrumental style from gypsy guitarist Django Reinhardt and his knack for lyrical phrasing from Frank Sinatra. Naturally, Nashville didn't have a clue as to how to handle him. One night in 1971, Nelson's Tennessee house caught fire. He dashed into the flames to save his guitar and a bag of high-octane marijuana, and came home to Texas to take stock and catch a second wind.

Brother, did he. Less than a year later, Nelson was standing on the stage of the Armadillo World Headquarters, just across the river from downtown Austin. He surveyed the crowd: homegrown hippies, who were rubbing elbows with beer-guzzling rednecks with less animosity than anyone would have believed possible in that era. Sumbitch, Nelson thought to himself, I *knew* it could work! He had come home.

The synthesis of rock and country that Nelson envisioned found its natural expression in the musicians of Austin. And why not, there was no one to tell them otherwise. The arbiters of taste were far away on what folks around here call the

THERE'S GOOD MUSIC IN THE WEST TEXAS CITY OF LUBBOCK, AND MORE THAN A FEW OF THAT CITY'S MUSICIANS HAVE SETTLED IN AUSTIN. BUTCH HANCOCK HAILS FROM LUBBOCK, BUT THE FOLK-STYLE SINGER-SONGWRITER OFFERS UP HIS INSIGHTFUL LYRICS — AND ENJOYS SUCCESS — IN THE CAPITAL CITY.

Left and Right coasts. In Austin, the rents were cheap, the climate salubrious, the beer joints accommodating, and the creative ferment irresistible. Rock, blues, everything was grist for the mill.

Take that triumvirate of the basic ingredients of blues, Tejano, and country music, throw in some peppery zydeco and Cajun tempos from nearby Louisiana, a hearty dollop of mazurkas and waltzes from the Czech and German and Polish settlers who staked out much of the Hill Country in the 1850s, and a modern dash of everything else from Nigerian high-life music to Brazilian sambas to alternative dance music, and watch how the blend begins to simmer and spark. It was never about just cowboy music.

One night in October of 1993, Willie Nelson sat in the back of his bus, the *Honeysuckle Rose.* He has owned houses in many places, including far-flung haunts of the semirich like Maui and Boulder, but this customized tour bus is his natural habitat. Still, when he speaks of "home," it is Austin to which he refers.

"If you were trying to describe it to someone who's never been here. . ." he mused. "I dunno, it's indescribable. It's everything imaginable, the people, the weather, the freedom. Those of us who are really touched by it, we don't find it anywhere else.

"Maybe there's a similar feeling that other people have about other places. I'm sure there is, or Austin would be overrun with people. There are other places around that are magic places for me, but Austin is definitely a big one.

"Plus, the sunsets are the best in the world."

As he spoke, Nelson was winding down after a sold-out show at the Bass Concert Hall, the palatial, multitiered showplace at the UT Performing Arts Center. From the PAC and the Erwin Center (the university's arena-sized colossus), Austin's stages run the gamut from the opulent Roaring Twenties-era glory of the restored Paramount Theatre; to the black-on-black *tres*-grunge chic of Emo's; to Antone's, the internationally famous blues club where everything is the color of either cigarette smoke or whiskey; to Threadgill's, a renovated gas station where Janis Joplin first sang for beer and tips; to the unalloyed honky-tonk essence of the Broken Spoke. What would Heaven be without beer joints?   ➤

"We tend to take what we call our 'quality of life' for granted. We know that it is this precise quality that brings people to our town, and we face this prospect with equal parts pride and apprehension. Some of us—but not all of us—sense that what we have here is fragile beyond all comprehension, that it can vanish in a nod or a phrase.

"The University Tower, the beloved Capitol, storied old Scholz Garten—these are landmarks and symbols of our city, but they abide at our pleasure and can be replaced. Not so Barton Springs."

GARY CARTWRIGHT,
Barton Springs Eternal,
1993

GERTRUDE STEIN ONCE LAMENTED OF Oakland, California: "There's no *there* there."

She meant, of course, that Oakland lacked a spiritual center, a place which focused the city's dreams and aspirations and reflected back its best sense of itself. A heart, she might have said. There is no heart there.

Austin does have a heart. It is a living, breathing, glittering blue jewel set in a diadem of greenery in the city's center. It is called Barton Springs.

From time immemorial, rainwater has filtered through cracks in the limestone forms the Edwards Plateau south and west of Austin. There, in the lightless caves of the mysterious underground river called the Edwards Aquifer, the waters mingle and percolate until artesian pressure forces them to the surface, filtered and purified by their journey.

At Barton Springs (which is actually comprised of four separate outflows) the waters pour forth with voluptuous abundance 26 million gallons a day on the average, at a year-round constant temperature of 68 degrees.

By 1946, the Springs had achieved their present aspect: a thousand-foot-long lozenge of gin-clear, bracingly cold, soul-reviving water of surpassing purity, all couched in a setting which perfectly straddled the world between the unspoiled and the urbane. Perch, crappie, catfish, crawdads, and a rare breed of salamander did and do ply the natural rock bottom of the pool. Ducks paddle benignly on the surface.

The Springs' common denominator is, of course, the plunge. Young or old, rich or poor, fit or infirm, the reaction upon diving into the water is the same—shocked sensory overload, followed by a delighted gasp of disbelief. Replaced, in short order, by a rapidly expanding sense of renewal and a limitless sense of ease.

In the past few years, the Springs have become the totemic embodiment of what many see as the natural qualities unique to Austin. Much energy and debate have been given over to what is deemed "the quality of life." The tree-covered hills, the fragile aquifer ecosystem, the interconnected web of flora and fauna have all been evoked in the name of preservation and conservation.

Nor is this a new trend, or a politically correct New Age fad. Roy Bedichek, the state's most famous naturalist, wrote "Personally, if I have to fight for this country, I will not fight for the flag, or democracy. . .or for any other abstractions, which seem cold as kraut to me. (But) I will fight to the last ditch for Barton Creek, Boggy Creek, cedar-covered limestone hills, blazing-star and bluebonnets, golden-cheeked warblers and black-capped vireos, and so on through a catalogue of this natural environment of Austin, Texas. . .everything else is subsidiary, for this love of your native land is basic."

Bedichek penned those words in 1919. ➤

NOW AS THEN, AUSTIN CONTINUES TO grow and thrive and evolve. Some naysayers believed that the public preoccupation with environmental preservation would stymie the city's financial and geographic development. But that seems not to have been the case. According to Alphametrics, an international economic consulting and software firm, Austin's economic growth for the past three years was the highest in the country (Charles Renfro, the company's chief economist, said the city draws its vitality from "technology and a sense of quality of life"); the U-Haul trailer folks cited Austin as the eighth-most popular destination for vacationing families during the summer of 1993; and, in an honor that was as highly touted as its criteria were ambiguous, *Fortune* magazine named Austin as one of its top-five "intellectual capitals."

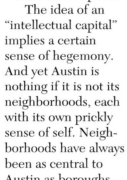

The idea of an "intellectual capital" implies a certain sense of hegemony. And yet Austin is nothing if it is not its neighborhoods, each with its own prickly sense of self. Neighborhoods have always been as central to Austin as boroughs have been to New York City.

Granted, the character of those neighborhoods has changed over the years: The downtown block which is preparing to house the city's new Robert Venuti-designed art museum was once the cradle of Austin's whorehouse district; Clarksville, originally home to the descendants of freed slaves, is now a squeaky-clean, yuppie-gentrified enclave; Hyde Park, the city's first suburb, is ensconced squarely in the heart of the burgeoning city; East Eleventh Street, once a thriving black commercial and entertainment district, is today a tableau of empty storefronts and struggling small businesses—done in, in part, by integration (which siphoned off black consumers to other parts of town) and the construction of Interstate 35 (which erected an intimidating concrete curtain between East and West Austin).

Other Austin neighborhoods retain their essential natures. Much of Travis Heights and South Austin is given over to a certain sort of rough-hewn *je ne sais quoi* which incorporates a lot of garage sales and dogs lolling on porches under spreading live oak and pecan trees. Nationally ranked newspaper columnist Molly Ivins, who makes her home in South Austin, affectionately suggested that the regional motto should read, "South Austin: A Great Place To Buy Auto Parts."

And the Bremond Block, on the western edge of downtown, is a veritable time capsule, containing an array of architectural styles which flourished in the third quarter of the 19th century. How, the summertime visitor may inquire sweatily, did Texans exist in the days before air conditioning? A glance at the shady porches, tall casement windows, and spreading trees with which the Bremond Block recalls a more graceful era provides the answer; quite nicely, thank you.

The Eastside neighborhood around Parque Zaragoza, home to generations of the city's

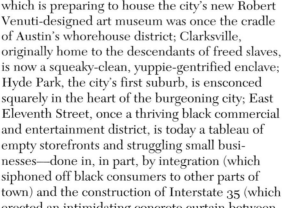

Chicano community, reveals itself in block after block of small and tidy bungalows, each with its ornamental scrim of flowers and hanging plants, and a smattering of Victorian-era mansions. Though financially disadvantaged compared with some other parts of the city, the portion of Austin which lies east of Waller Creek contains some of the city's oldest and loveliest residences (including the French Legation, the Republic of Texas' first foreign embassy). And it boasts the city's most dynamic public art in the vibrant array of wall murals that dot the district like jewels scattered on green velvet.

Murals even decorate the wall surrounding the Holly Street power station, which has attracted the attention of Eastside environmental/neighborhood groups like PODER and EAST for the perceived health risks it represents. The rise of local political entities with real staying power and political clout promises to write a new chapter in East Austin's relations with the city's ruling entities.

The neighborhood organization, in fact, might be said to be the ultimate expression of grassroots (literally, in that meetings are sometimes held in the yard on warm evenings) democracy, Austin-style. People take their relationship to the city very personally indeed. ➤

THE CITY OWNS ITS OWN ELECTRIC UTILITY, AIRPORT, WATER AND WASTEWATER UTILITY, EMERGENCY MEDICAL SERVICE, AND HOSPITAL. GOVERNMENT OWNERSHIP OF SUCH AN ARRAY OF SERVICES HAS BEEN A BLESSING AND A BANE TO AUSTINITES. POLITICS, WHICH RUNS RAMPANT, GUARANTEES EVERYONE HAS A VOICE IN THE DECISION-MAKING PROCESS, AND MORE THAN A FEW AUSTINITES HAVE SUFFERED FROM LARYNGITIS AFTER PLEADING THEIR CASES.

THE PITCH-IN-AND-HAVE-FUN ATTITUDE THAT DISTINGUISHES THE CITY'S RESIDENTS IS DEMON-STRATED DURING CHRISTMAS, WHEN SEVERAL BLOCKS OF HOMES ALONG WEST 37TH STREET BREAK OUT THE LIGHTS AND CREATE A BRILLIANT DISPLAY. EVEN THE ORDINANCE-SPOUTING VOICE OF CITY BUREAUCRATS ALLOWS THE NEIGHBORHOOD TO BEND THE RULES AND HANG LIGHTS FROM CITY POLES AND SIGNS.

ONE OF THE FEW SUBJECTS ON WHICH people from all parts of the city are apt to concur is the Capitol Building. It is, anyone will concede, a lovely structure. Like any city worth its salt, Austin should be seen on foot, and the steps of the Capitol make a grand point from which to embark.

Walk south down Congress Avenue, if you've a mind to. You'll see the glorious old Paramount Theatre on your left, and, near the Sixth Street district, a glimpse of the venerable Driskill Hotel. That's cattleman Jesse Driskill and his boys gazing out from the gables and cornices atop the white structure. On the right lies the old Scarborough Building, Austin's first skyscraper, and, down on First and Congress, the corner lot which once held a three-for-a-dollar taco stand. The owner sold the plot for several millions during the 1980s land rush and promptly retired from the food-service industry.

You won't, unfortunately, see the grand old downtown Woolworth department store, which was torn down to make room for another danged office building. Singer/songwriter Nanci Griffith, who grew up in Austin, recalled changing buses outside the five-and-dime when that was the only way for a teenager to get across town. "I always had just enough time to run into the Woolworth store, get myself a vanilla Coke, dig through the record bin, wink at the boys, and get back on the bus," she recalled fondly.

Stroll north from the Capitol (en route, check out the skylights and underground atrium that are the centerpieces of the landmark's sweeping expansion work) and make your way up to the UT campus. If you happen to walk past the baroque Littlefield Fountain and up the South Mall towards the Tower at the right time of day, you might be treated to the sound of a cascade of lovely voices, as the opera students practice their art beside the open windows of the Music Building.

No matter when or where your college years transpired, the bustle of UT's 50,000-plus student body will seem familiar—a yeasty mix of post-adolescent mystics, button-down grinds, feckless, beefy fraternity kids enjoying the last bloom of youth, inward-looking seekers of truth, and that peculiar Austin breed called "slackers" (after Austinite Richard Linklater's hit cult film of the same name); bright, amiable young people for whom college offers less a horizon-broadening experience, than a monastic cloister sheltered from life's rude tempests.

East of the Capitol lie the sloping banks of Waller Creek which, along with Bull, Onion, Shoal, and Barton creeks, forms the city's arterial system of waterways. Waller Creek was the original eastern boundary of the city. Today, it wanders through downtown, and an array of commerce—everything from an ice factory to gay bars to a four-star hotel to Symphony Square, an outdoor performance space—lines its shores.

The Governor's Mansion, courthouse, county jail, the aforementioned Bremond Block, main library, and the Austin-Travis County Collection historical archives, along with a tree-lined neighborhood of old homes, lie vaguely west of the Capitol's shadow. What was once $100-a-month student housing is rapidly being gentrified into

THE TASK OF GUIDING THE STATE CAPITOL'S *Goddess of Liberty* BACK TO HER PERCH FOLLOWING A RESTORATION WAS ACCOMPLISHED NOT BY TEXANS, BUT BY MEMBERS OF THE MISSISSIPPI NATIONAL GUARD. THE STATE KNOWN FOR HAVING THE "GRANDEST" WAS SURPRISED TO FIND IT DIDN'T HAVE A HELICOPTER BIG ENOUGH TO DO THE JOB.

enovated office space for doctors, lawyers, and other professionals.

Ann Richards, Texas' current governor, ran her 1990 campaign for the governor's chair out of one f the small office buildings that lie just west of the remond Block.

Late in the evenings, when the high-stakes oker game that masquerades as Texas politics

pated somewhat, Richards and her staff would djourn a few blocks south to La Zona Rosa, a estaurant and bar that looks something like what alvador Dali would have painted if he had grown p in Juarez.

There the campaigners would plot strategy ver Tex-Mex noshes, while James McMurtry arry's son, who finds the city far more congenial place to live than his daddy ever did) or Tish inojosa or one of the city's other troubadours ing in the background. For a few moments, ichards could relax into the fantasy that she was st another beehive-haired grandmother lingering ver a plate of enchiladas. . . .

If your peregrinations around the Capitol have spired a certain amount of thirst, stop in for a

beer at Scholz Garten, the city's oldest watering hole (est. 1862). In its heyday as a political hang-out, the spreading pecans and oaks in the beer garden out back bore witness to more legislation than the Capitol rotunda.

Or if you seek refreshment further afield, climb in your car and drive west of town to the Oasis Cantina. Perched hundreds of feet above Lake Travis and comprised of an array of balconies that are Austin's answer to the Hanging Gardens of Babylon, the Oasis offers suste-nance for the body (cold beer and margaritas) and soul (jaw-drop-ping sunsets over the lake). Plus, you get to enjoy the same Austin skyline which once enchanted Billy Lee Brammer as you meander back towards town.

The skyline marks the city, no question about it. The Capitol and the Tower still hold dominion over it, even though their domi-nance is compromised by Johnny-come-lately skyscrapers. The sight of the city, cradled in its rolling green hills on the edge of the coastal plain, is infinitely refreshing.

I have been enjoying that view for almost 20 years. Austin has greeted me upon my return from the South of France, from the desert fastness of the Big Bend, from the wilds of L.A., from an endless array of lost weekends and endless highways.

Something about it beckons. There is a human scale about it which eludes larger cities. And that humanness ignites in one a desire to embrace it whole, the concert halls and the flophouses, the suburbs and the saloons, the works. It is seldom that the heart's landscape assumes such a pleasing perspective.

Especially in Texas.

It's a February night as this is being written, closing in on midnight. Outside, the bluebonnet seeds sleep beneath the frozen ground, awaiting their yearly springtime renaissance. Downtown, the musicians are stubbing out their cigarettes, gutting it up for the last set of the evening. The waters in Barton Springs well up as always, smoking in the moonlight.

Tomorrow, Austin re-creates itself once more.
✭

EAST SIXTH STREET, BETWEEN CONGRESS AVENUE AND INTER-STATE 35, IS THE MUSIC AND ENTER-TAINMENT HUB OF THE CITY. CLUBS, RESTAURANTS, BARS, A HOTEL, AND A COMEDY THEATER OFFER AN ARRAY OF SIGHTS, SOUNDS, AND TASTES. TAKE THE PLUNGE AND STOP IN AT ESTHER'S POOL, WHERE ESTHER'S FOLLIES OFFER A RIBALD REVUE OF COMEDY AND SATIRE.

THE BEAUTY OF THE TEXAS SKY above Austin can turn threatening when a powerful thunderstorm rolls in from the west. The Colorado River, before it was impounded to create Town Lake, was subject to tremendous flooding during Austin's earlier years. The river is now tamed, but one historical note records the Colorado rising 36 feet during one heavy rainstorm.

ASK THE PEOPLE WHO LIVE IN THE area, and they'll tell you the "pot of gold" at the end of the rainbow is Austin itself. The city is unique in Texas. Aside from being the capital, it is a blend of cultures, lifestyles, politics, geography, and unmistakable spirit.

36

THE LOOP 360 BRIDGE SPANNING Lake Austin opened in the mid-1980s, linking the western part of the city and allowing residential and commercial development to occur. With its rolling hills and craggy bluffs as a backdrop, the environmentally sensitive area is a highly desirable place to live.

FIVE MAJOR BRIDGES TRAVERSE Town Lake: Loop 1 or MoPac, Lamar Boulevard, South First Street, Interstate 35, and the Congress Avenue bridge, shown here. During the warmer months, the Hike and Bike Trail that encompasses the lake accommodates a steady stream of walkers, runners, and cyclists—while the daylight quiet of the crevices of the Congress Avenue bridge belies the 1.5 million Mexican free-tailed bats that are settled in for a long day's sleep (OPPOSITE).

THE PADDLEBOAT AND CANOE rental stand is a relatively new addition to Town Lake. Many Austinites prefer that the lake remain uncommercialized, and they have lobbied the city council against other developments.

THE VISION THAT INSPIRED LADY Bird Johnson to beautify Town Lake has resulted in one of Austin's most popular outdoor locations. Thousands of trees have been planted, many of them endangered species, and there are several enchanting overlooks and gazebos where people watch the world go by.

AS IT IS FROM THE GROUND, Austin is also beautiful from the air. Interstate 35 is one of Texas' major thoroughfares (TOP LEFT). West Lake Hills is considered an exclusive area, and it's not unusual for residents of that community to see deer wandering through their yards (TOP RIGHT). Loop 1, more commonly known as MoPac because part of the highway follows the Missouri/Pacific Railroad, crosses over Barton Creek in southwest Austin. The bridge construction was bitterly contested by environmentalists who feared damage to Barton Creek (BOTTOM LEFT). From a wing to a prayer, skydivers take a flying leap high above the city (BOTTOM RIGHT).

WITH THE MENDING OF THE Texas economy in the early 1990s, Austin's downtown has seen a revitalization, a dramatic decrease in high-rise office building vacancies, and a renewed sense of self-confidence (OPPOSITE).

PUT TWO **A**USTINITES IN A ROOM, and you're likely to get three opinions. And that theory holds true for the recently completed convention center. Some love its hodgepodge architecture, while others vilify it. Regardless, its proximity to Interstate 35 and the building's flexibility of use has enabled the city to attract larger conventions and meetings.

44

As RECENTLY AS THE EARLY 1980s, the Capitol Building could be seen for miles around, standing above virtually everything and offering testament to the importance of state government to Austin. Today, the overall importance of business to the city's economy is as real as the visual impact implied by the buildings that now dwarf the Capitol.

AUSTIN'S GRACEFUL "OLD" architecture contrasts with the confidence of the ambitious contemporary structures rising throughout many parts of downtown. In 1896 the city decreed that building fronts on Congress Avenue were to be made of stone, brick, or iron, ensuring the historic street would maintain its dignified look.

Carefully and lovingly restored, many of the older structures like the Littlefield Building (OPPOSITE) reflect the confidence and dreams possessed by early Austinites.

PROUDLY DISPLAYING THE LONE Star of Texas, the *Goddess of Liberty* stands vigil atop the Capitol Building (TOP LEFT). The Lyndon Baines Johnson Library and Museum is one of the most popular presidential libraries in the country. The exhibits and recreated Oval Office showcase the life and times of a man who wrestled with great changes and left an enduring legacy to Texas and the nation (TOP RIGHT). The intricacy of the Norwood Tower may stand in contrast to the clean lines of modern architecture, but its renovation in the 1980s preserved an Austin landmark (BOTTOM LEFT). Proudly looking out over Congress Avenue and Sixth Street, this eagle adorns the southwest corner of the Littlefield Building (BOTTOM RIGHT).

THE SAN JACINTO TOWER, ONE OF the more recent additions to downtown, is at Congress Avenue and Cesar Chavez Street, which was named in memory of the heroic United Farm Workers organizer (OPPOSITE).

GARY RUSS IMAGES ▶

AUSTIN MEDICAL PLAZA

LARRY J. MURPHY / UNIVERSITY OF TEXAS, AUSTIN ▶

DURING THE MID- TO LATE 1980S, the clock ticked loudly for investors who owned newly constructed downtown office space like the 100 Congress Building (OPPOSITE). At one time the city had one of the highest office vacancy rates in the nation. But since the early 1990s, spaces have begun filling and rents are rising.

THE LITTLEFIELD BUILDING, on the corner of Sixth Street and Congress Avenue, stands in stark contrast to a modern-day bank building (TOP LEFT). The separation of church and state seems to disappear as the reflection of St. Mary's Catholic Church bounces off the glass of the offices of the state treasury (TOP RIGHT). In addition to traditional medicine

found in places like the Austin Medical Plaza (BOTTOM LEFT), New Age and exotic medical techniques abound in the city. The George Kozmetsky Center for Business Education on the University of Texas campus pays tribute to a popular Texas entrepreneur and educator (BOTTOM RIGHT).

PERHAPS THE BIGGEST BENE-
ficiaries of the city's building
boom are the window washers, like
this fearless person working at
One American Plaza/Center
downtown (TOP).

The restored Old Main building at St. Edward's University
holds a number of graceful,
attractive elements such as this
spiral staircase (BOTTOM).

AUSTIN HOME-BUILDING BROTHERS Clark and Doyle Wilson have managed to survive the city's roller-coaster building cycles over the years. Recently, the pair have gone into competition with each other, and in 1993 Clark Wilson snatched up 10 Max Awards for building excellence. While they have different philosophies about their respective businesses, renewed residential development in the early 1990s should mean both will prosper.

ADVANCED MICRO DEVICES employs more than 2,700 people in Austin. The semiconductor chip manufacturer has a big stake in the city, and in 1993 broke ground on a $1 billion wafer manufacturing facility that will take silicon wafers like those shown below and turn them into microchips.

THE COMBINATION OF EXCELLENT universities, beautiful surroundings, and an aggressive, long-term recruiting campaign has made the city one of the nation's leaders in the field of high technology. Hundreds and hundreds of industry-related companies occupy glass-encased office buildings where they try to do things like build a better "mouse."

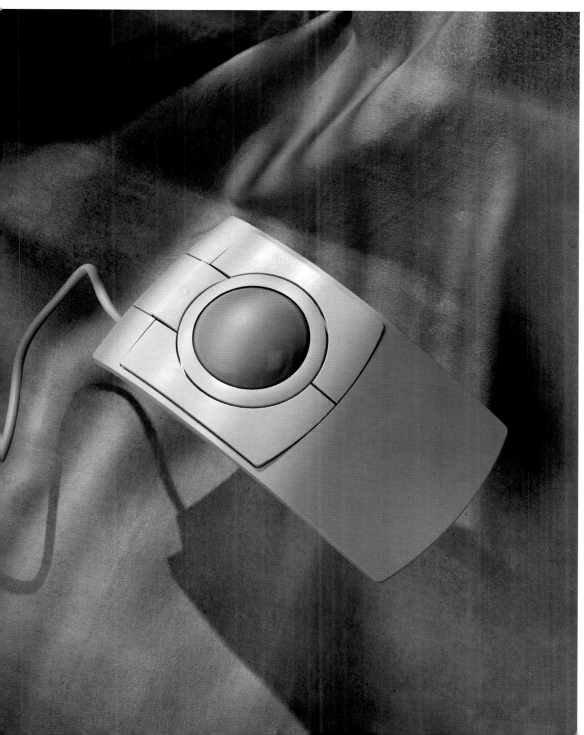

CHANCES ARE THESE TWO MEN ARE
discussing where to eat, whether
their softball team needs a better
pitcher, or the latest version of a
new software program (TOP).

The cutting edge of high
technology is continually sharp-
ened in Austin, where projects like
the IBM automated seeing
computer are put through their
paces (BOTTOM).

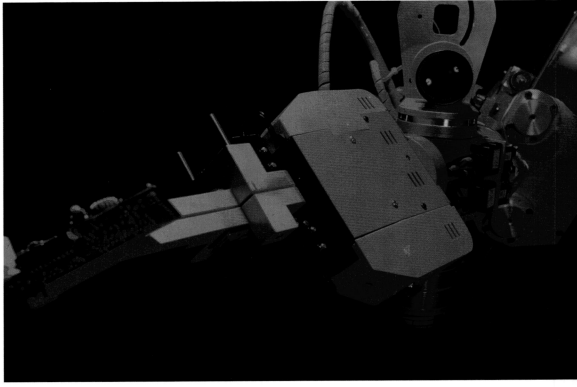

THE BEST IDEAS ARE THE SIMPLE ones, and CompuAdd founder Bill Hayden realized the profit potential of low-priced, high-performance personal computers (TOP).

In the beginning, there was light, and then scientists developed lasers. The pair below study the properties of lasers. The student on the right balances his interest in science with a T-shirt proclaiming his appreciation for folk music.

SMALL ENOUGH TO FIT INTO A lunch box, this computer circuit board demonstrates the worldwide reach of high technology. The computer chips were made by Advanced Micro Devices, Texas Instruments' Malaysia operation, and companies from Japan and Korea (PAGE 58).

RICK WILLIAMS PHOTO

THIS PAIR OF CHIP DESIGNERS would probably agree with Benjamin Disraeli, who said in 1868, "There can be no economy where there is no efficiency." The magnitude of a postage-stamp-sized chip is revealed in this engineering photograph used to check pathways that are measured in microns (PAGE 59).

REAGAN BRADSHAW PHOTOGRAPHY

In the spring, Central Texas is blessed with a breathtaking array of wildflowers. The bluebonnet is the state flower and covers hillsides, along with Mexican hats, Indian blankets, poppies, primrose, and dozens of other varieties. The Texas Department of Transportation defers mowing rights-of-way until after the wildflowers have gone to seed (TOP).

From radios to rocket ships, color-coded transistors and computer circuitry rule our lives (BOTTOM).

THE SWEET TASTE OF SUCCESS IS found in honey production. It's said that consuming locally produced honey will help ward off pollen-related allergies (TOP).

Texas offers a quality work force, so it's not surprising that the small community of Kyle, just south of Austin, helps manufacture parts for the DC-10 jetliner (BOTTOM).

THOUSANDS OF AUSTINITES WEAR the "bunny suits" required in the clean-room manufacture of microchips (TOP). Like any work uniform, they have to be cleaned, but you can't take them to some coin-operated laundry. Jack Brown Cleaners, the city's largest, offers this specialty service. And yes, they'll do your shirts, too.

A human brain is carefully evaluated for possible disease following a session on a CAT scan at city-owned Brackenridge Hospital (BOTTOM).

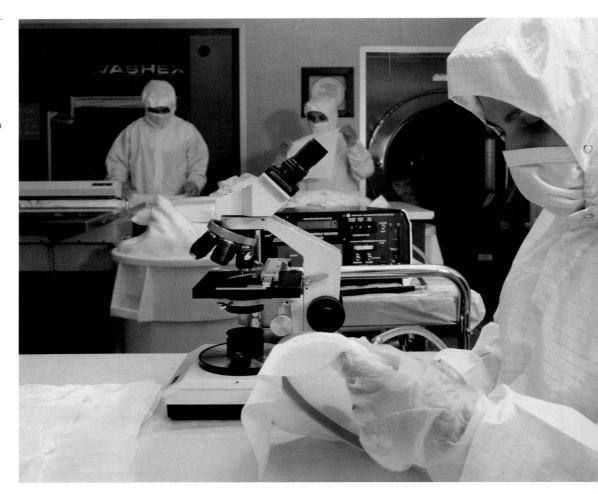

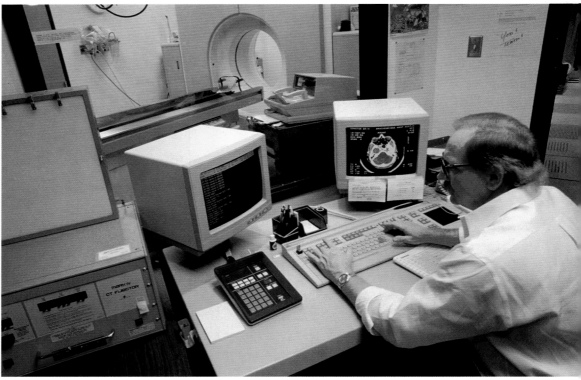

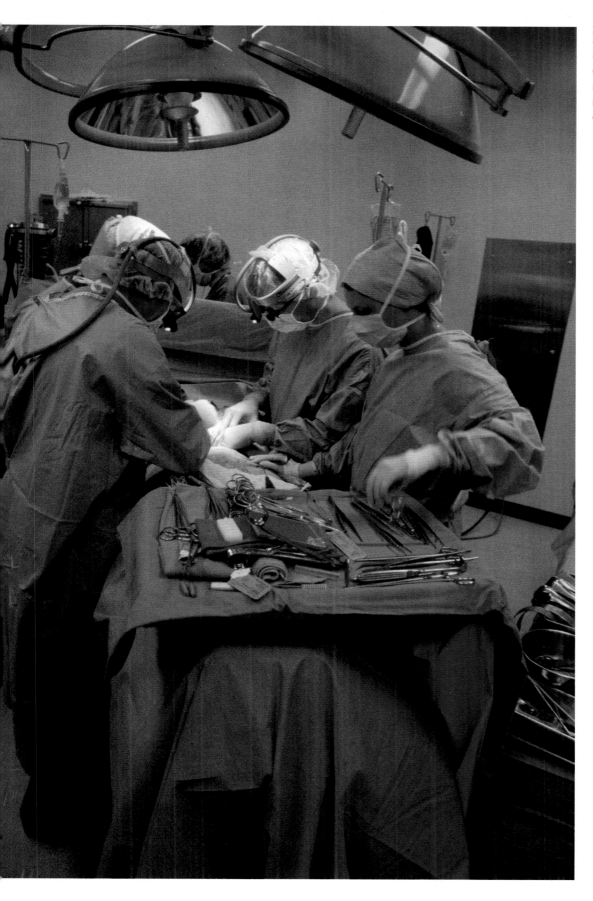

BRACKENRIDGE HOSPITAL SERVES as the trauma center for a 10-county region of Central Texas, and its medical care programs, such as this kidney transplant operation, are first-rate.

If a society can be judged by the way it treats its children, then Austin fares well. Starting at an early age, computers are a big part of the education process (TOP).

The Austin Children's Museum encourages a hands-on, interactive approach to learning that challenges the minds and creativity of young people (BOTTOM).

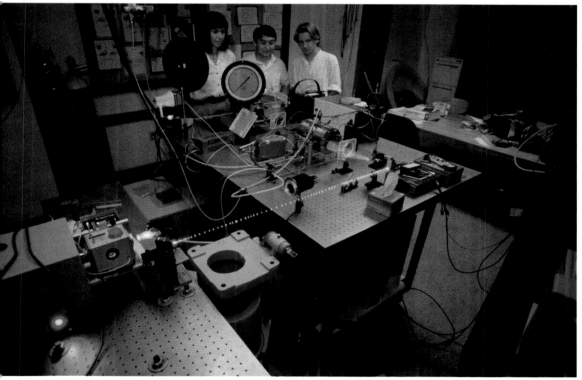

TWENTY YEARS AGO, A LAB CLASS in college might have meant dissecting a frog or mixing things in a test tube. Today, "labs" such as this computer class at the University of Texas put students through the paces of today's computers (TOP).

The properties of light have spawned technologies such as fiber optics, and the development of lasers has opened up new areas of medicine and research at UT Austin (BOTTOM).

▲ LARRY KOLVOORD / AUSTIN AMERICAN STATESMAN

GOVERNOR ANN W. RICHARDS IS adept at the politics of persuasion—she has to be, in a political world still largely run by men. As Richards has said before, "Ginger Rogers did everything Fred Astaire did, only she did it in high heels and backwards" (LEFT).

Now that the doors have been opened by Richards and other women elected to statewide political office, young girls like this pair conducting a telephone poll may also one day be models for aspiring women (RIGHT).

THE CHAMBERS OF THE TEXAS
House of Representatives can be
a hurly-burly world during the
legislative session. However, in
a quieter moment, when the
lawmakers, tourists, and media
are gone, a carpenter takes a
moment to make a repair.

TEXANS LOVE THEIR CARS AND
trucks, but there are still plenty of
folks who love to ride horseback,
like this pair participating in a trail
ride (TOP).

The landscape of the 1992 U.S.
presidential campaign changed
dramatically when Ross Perot
threw his hat into the ring
(BOTTOM).

In Texas, Independence Day is March 2. That's the date when the Republic won its independence from Mexico in a brief battle at San Jacinto, near Houston.

Governor Ann Richards campaigned in 1990 on the platform of ushering in a "New Texas." She won in a squeaker, but has since gone on to wow Texas and the nation with her leadership and skill (BOTTOM).

JAMES MICHENER COULD LIVE anywhere in the world, but he chose Austin as his home during the research and writing of his epic novel, *Texas* (TOP). Mollie Ivins is rarely at a loss for words. Her ability to capture the absurdity of Texas political life has earned her national recognition. In her spare moments, she can sometimes be found at La Zona Rosa in downtown Austin (BOTTOM LEFT). Barbara Jordan's eloquence and intellect make her a Texas treasure. Now a UT professor, she achieved national recognition in the U.S. House of Representatives during the Watergate hearings (BOTTOM RIGHT).

◀ ALAN POGUE

MYSTICS, TREE EXPERTS, ROSS PEROT, and people from around the world did what they could to save the 500-year-old Treaty Oak after a man poured a herbicide around the tree's roots. Despite incredible odds against survival, the historic tree lives today (TOP).

One of Austin's greats, John Henry Faulk passed away in April 1990. Blacklisted during the McCarthy era, Faulk was later vindicated and spent much of his life defending freedom of speech (BOTTOM LEFT). The city has always been a good home to creative people. Writer Dan Quinn was the winner of the first Turner Writing Award (BOTTOM RIGHT).

▶ KEVIN VANDIVIER

ONE OF THE BEST PLACES IN TEXAS to see bald eagles is around Lake Buchanan, part of the Highland Lakes chain. The Texas Vanishing River Cruise is also excellent for bird watching. John Karger of Last Chance Forever releases one of the majestic birds (TOP).

In Austin, anybody can become anything. Just ask Michael "Max" Nofziger, who was once a flower vendor but has since been elected to the Austin City Council. He has proved to be a voice of common sense, and he is respected to the point that his colleagues on the council have elected him mayor pro tem (BOTTOM).

A TIRELESS AND EFFECTIVE WATCH-dog of Barton Creek is Joe Riddell, seen here paddling his kayak along the creek. Riddell is representative of a cadre of environmentalists who are active in Austin's political scene (TOP). In the Hill Country, paradise can be found just around the next bend in the river (BOTTOM).

THE INTRICATE MOSAIC OF PATTERN and light left by this group of waterfowl can be seen in many places along Town Lake. All it takes is a little water, some paddling birds, and a warm Texas sun.

NORMAN MACLEAN WAS RIGHT when he wrote, "Eventually, all things merge into one, and a river runs through it." For Austin, that metaphorical river is a creek, and its name is Barton. It is the touchstone for this community—a liquid line etched in limestone, which serves as a reminder of the city's fragile beauty (OPPOSITE).

WHEN THE RAINS COME AND FILL the streambeds, the deep-toned call of a waterfall reminds us that inanimate things often seem to come alive (OPPOSITE).

THE STEADY FLOW OF BARTON Creek makes its contribution to the Edwards Aquifer, fills Barton Springs Pool, and then empties into Town Lake. But for these two boys, their moment is in the present, savoring the rush of water and oblivious to the notions of hydrology (ABOVE).

THE PRICE OF PROGRESS HAS BEEN
well spent at Hamilton Pool,
where a summertime crowd yields
to relaxation. It was increasingly
difficult to access the pool until
the Travis County Commissioner's
Court invested in walkways and
other facilities (TOP). However,
the fate of the Barton Creek
salamander, who lives on the
bottom of Barton Springs Pool, is
less assured. Environmentalists
cite this small creature as one
more reason to safeguard Barton
Creek (BOTTOM).

IF THERE'S A HEART THAT BEATS OUT the rhythm of life in Austin, it's Barton Creek and Barton Springs Pool. Located inside the confines of 400-acre Zilker Park, the 1,000-by-125-foot Barton Springs Pool has been frequented by people—and the Barton Springs crayfish—for thousands of years. And today, its bracing, pure waters attract swimmers year-round.

WHETHER IT'S IN A NEIGHBOR-hood or a city-owned pool, there's plenty of water to take the heat off a hot summer's day. The city operates a number of pools, some of which are spring fed. Although swimming pools are great, there's nothing quite like taking a plunge at an old swimming hole.

BELIEVE IT OR NOT, THE WATER is as pure as it looks. Occasionally, after a heavy rain, Barton Springs Pool closes because there's little topsoil to filter the runoff. However, the pool usually reopens within a day or so.

WHEN THE WILDFLOWERS COME out in spring, there's an abundance of vivid colors throughout much of Texas. Dozens of varieties wash across fields and hillsides, and the perennials are eagerly anticipated by newcomers and native Texans alike (OPPOSITE).

Very little hay is grown west of Austin because the soil is too poor to support the crop. But to the east, not far outside of town, farms dot the countryside, supplying forage for herds of cattle (TOP).

One thousand one, one thousand two. . .whatever game these boys are playing, it's certain their minds are carefree (BOTTOM).

THE DIVERSITY AND BEAUTY OF Central Texas' flora is just one more reason people love living in Austin. The fragrant rain lily sprouts after a good rain, but the petals don't stretch out full until a day or so before their life cycle is complete (TOP LEFT). The dayflower only blooms for a day or so and then withers (TOP RIGHT). This specimen of a delicate orange gill fungus has made its home on a pine tree (BOTTOM LEFT). Indian paintbrush grows over large portions of Texas, from the northeast to the southwest (BOTTOM RIGHT).

WHATEVER ELSE YOU MIGHT WANT to say about cacti, they are survivors. Most people think they are restricted to the desert, but the prickly pear is a common sight throughout much of Central Texas (OPPOSITE).

POSSUMS AND RACCOONS ARE found in abundance around the Austin area, where there are plenty of wet-weather creek beds for them to travel along. The region around Austin is blessed with an abundance of birds. In fact, Texas is the most popular state for bird-watching. These brown herons are resting in a tree (BOTTOM LEFT). Cardinals, like this male, can often be found in pairs (BOTTOM RIGHT). Watch a pair carefully as they sit near a feeder; the male will pluck a sunflower seed, peel off the shell, and feed it to his mate.

THIS PAIR OF CEDAR WAXWINGS winters in Texas. The bird on the left is about to gobble down a juniper berry (TOP LEFT). Monarch butterflies are just one of many varieties fluttering around in Texas (TOP RIGHT). With the abundance of wildflowers, hummingbirds are a common sight in the Austin area. Many people put out feeders and landscape their yards with native plants to attract them (BOTTOM LEFT). The nodding thistle makes a good feeding station for bees. The plants reach a height of up to three feet (BOTTOM RIGHT).

BLACKLAND PRAIRIE, EAST OF Austin, is known for its rich soil and excellent farmland. This spring crop of sorghum will be used to feed livestock (TOP). All plowed and ready to go, this land may be waiting for a cotton or grain crop to be planted (BOTTOM LEFT). Except for the modern-day watch, this scene could be from a hundred years ago (BOTTOM RIGHT).

▼ JAMES M. INNES

A HORSE STANDING IN A FIELD OF bluebonnets lazily eyes his next bite of forage. The field below, however, is further along in the blooming cycle, as the bluebonnets are fuller and more lush.

THE NINE-BANDED ARMADILLO IS common throughout much of Texas. When startled, they leap into the air, land, and then scurry off. So ubiquitous is the animal that one of Austin's seminal music venues was named the Armadillo World Headquarters.

LONGHORNS WERE A MAJOR factor in establishing Texas as a preeminent cattle region. The breed is tough and resilient, and can survive on a range where other cattle would quickly die. The development of new strains, such as the Santa Gertrudis, reduced the state's dependence on Longhorns, and the breed nearly disappeared. But today its future is assured.

SOME UNIVERSITIES HAVE DOGS
as mascots. Not the University of
Texas at Austin, where the mascot
is a Longhorn named Bevo.
Pampered and well-fed, Bevo
shows up at all the UT home
football games, oblivious to the
screaming of raucous fans.

LYNNE DOBSON

REAGAN BRADSHAW PHOTOGRAPHY

"HOOK 'EM, HORNS" IS THE SIGN fans give as they root for the Longhorns. UT, as it's commonly referred to, takes its football seriously. The huge Longhorn Marching Band always gives a great halftime show. Their precision work is a crowd-pleaser for the 78,000 fans who consistently fill Memorial Stadium each fall.

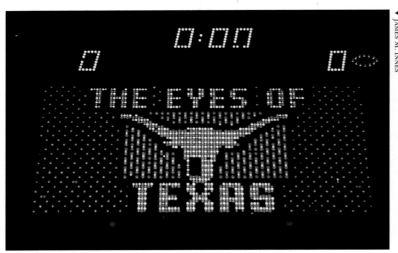

IN AUSTIN, YOU SEE BURNT
orange everywhere—from the
background detail of the Memorial
Stadium scoreboard to the warm
glow of a Central Texas sunset on
game day to the night-time
luminance of a campus pep rally.

THE FRANK ERWIN CENTER, home to both the UT men's and women's basketball programs, is also known as the "Drum." One of the terrific things about Austin is that there's little pretense about anything. Barbara Jordan, former U.S. Representative, is a big fan of the Lady Longhorns and frequently attends games (BOTTOM).

PART OF THE REASON UT AUSTIN excels in so many areas is its huge endowment, backed by the vision and acumen of its regents. Funding is buttressed by the Permanent University Fund, which has been generously replenished over the years by oil and gas revenues collected by the state.

96

An image of a fierce Longhorn is attached to a limestone building on the UT campus. Limestone, which is a popular building material in the region, provides interesting textures, as seen in this hand-carved seal of the University of Texas at Austin.

THE DOME OF THE CAPITOL Complex is made of iron and was cast in Belgium. Many years ago, people could venture all the way to the top to get a spectacular view of the Capitol floor below, but now the seventh level is as high as anyone is permitted (PRECEDING PAGES).

PAGE 98, GARY LOCKHART / BLIMP PHOTO / VIDEO
PAGE 99, JAMES M. INNES

ELIJAH E. MYERS OF DETROIT designed the Renaissance Revival-style Capitol Building in the shape of a Greek cross. The chamber for the 150-member congress reflects one of the most culturally and ethnically diverse states in the nation (OPPOSITE). When the legislature is in regular session, for six months every two years, a seat in the house gallery is an excellent vantage point for watching the show (TOP). Bob Bullock has had a distinguished career in public service. Elected lieutenant governor in 1990, he is renowned throughout the state for his tireless work (BOTTOM).

AUSTI

THE MOST PRESTIGIOUS ADDRESS
in Texas politics is 1010 Colorado
Avenue, the governor's mansion.
The mansion was built in 1855-56,
and Governor Elisha M. Pease,
who selected the site, was its first
resident.

THE OLDEST ORIGINAL STRUCTURE in Austin is the magnificently restored French Legation. Constructed of hand-sawed Bastrop pine, it was built by French Charge d'Affaires Jean Peter Isidore Alphonse Dubois de Saligny. In 1841 de Saligny got into a dispute with an innkeeper, whose pigs kept invading the garden. De Saligny left Austin when the innkeeper refused to corral his pigs. The "Pig War" cost Texas a much-needed $5 million loan.

CONGRESS AVENUE IS ALWAYS A great place to have a parade. This one, celebrating the return of soldiers from Desert Storm, featured a massive yellow ribbon tied around the Capitol Building.

MEMBERS OF THE TEXAS NATIONAL Guard fire a cannon as part of a Veterans Day 21-gun salute (TOP LEFT). On June 19, Texas celebrates a unique African-American holiday known as the Juneteenth Freedom Festival. It commemorates the date in 1865 when slaves in Texas received word of emancipation (BOTTOM LEFT). Chances are, the armadillo wearing shades will not win the Capitol 10,000-meter race. Held each spring since 1978, the Cap 10 draws the serious and the silly to an event that yearly attracts nearly 22,000 participants (RIGHT).

ENCOURAGING YOUNG MUSICIANS is important in a city that bills itself as the "Live Music Capital of the World." These three are giving it all they've got at a fiddling contest at the Broken Spoke, one of Austin's best-loved country-music venues (TOP). The group of youngsters at South Austin's Stacey Park doesn't seem to be quite as sure of themselves, but they get an "A" for effort (BOTTOM).

Diez y Seis celebrates the 16th of September in 1810 when the revolution for Mexico's independence began. It is an occasion for festivities and performances, like this one in the Capitol rotunda, (TOP). Symphony Square is just a few blocks from the central business district. It offers a relaxing and intimate atmosphere to enjoy performers like this group of Mexican folk dancers (BOTTOM).

THERE'S A GREAT DESIRE TO enjoy life in Austin. And when your feet start tapping, the desire to dance is not far behind (TOP). Joe Avila, of Joe's Bakery on East Seventh Street, offers excellent Mexican pastries or a piñata to fill with treats for the children (BOTTOM).

HISPANIC-AMERICANS IN TEXAS, like everywhere, dote on their children. This young girl is the center of attention as she and her friends prepare to perform a dance (TOP). Local artist Mercedes Peña relaxes in her home, showing a confidence borne by success (BOTTOM).

SALSA IS A STAPLE FOR MOST folks in Austin. While the ingredients are relatively simple, the great skill comes in the preparation. For Austinites there's plenty to enjoy (OPPOSITE).

In 1977, the Texas Legislature wisely named chili the official state dish. To achieve perfection, combine the basic ingredients of tomatoes, chili peppers, onions, lots of beef, and a variety of spices and let it all simmer for a couple of hours (LEFT).

THE ARTS HELP KEEP AUSTIN
creative and they continually bring
new participants into the fold.
Bending like willows in the wind,
this class at the Austin Ballet
Academy may produce a future
prima ballerina.

FLOATING DELICATELY ATOP THE water, lily pads like these can be seen in the Taniguchi Oriental Gardens at the Zilker Botanical Gardens, a serene spot for relaxing the day away.

IT'S MIME TIME ON SIXTH STREET, where the nonstop nightlife is anything but silent (LEFT). The place to be for fireworks is Auditorium Shores alongside Town Lake. Spectacular pyrotechnic displays, such as the yearly Fourth of July extravaganza, regularly draw thousands of Austinites (TOP RIGHT). The Paramount Theater on Congress Avenue is preserved in its original decorative style, with ceiling murals and extravagant detailing. The theater is listed in the National Register of Historic Places (BOTTOM RIGHT).

FROM HONKY-TONK TO HIGHBROW, if you're a music aficionado, then Austin is the place to be. Conductor Sung Kwak leads the Austin Symphony, accompanied by the Austin Choral Union, in a performance at UT's Bass Concert Hall.

THE PARKING LOT IN FRONT OF
this retail shop in northwest
Austin is reflective of the city's
low-impact attitude. The trees
occupy what some might consider
prime parking space. However,
preserving the live oaks makes
both a visual and environmental
statement (TOP).

Austinites love a good beer, and
Celis Brewery has been successfully bottling its hometown
product for several years
(BOTTOM).

ONCE THE MAJESTIC DINER, this 1950s-style building has been home to a variety of restaurants, including Peso's pictured here. However, the popular spot has changed names once again, and is now known as Cafe Brazil.

ART DOESN'T HAVE TO BE HANG-
ing on a wall in a gallery to be
considered legitimate. In Austin,
sometimes the wall *is* the art.
Zaragosa Park, in East Austin,
reflects a graffiti style (TOP).

Street art like this mural
located at the corner of Eighth
Street and Congress Avenue,
makes Austin even more of an
interesting place to live (BOTTOM).

MAKING A BOLD STATEMENT OF cultural pride and sentiment, artist Raul Valdez brings his Pan-American mural to life (TOP).

The illusion of this Sixth Street scene is as real as the wall being painted. This distinctive mural is part of the Renaissance Market, an eclectic group of vendors selling handmade jewelry, clothes, and crafts (BOTTOM).

JOSEPH MCMILLIAN, PRESIDENT of Huston-Tillotson College, speaks with a group of students on campus. The school, which is the oldest institution of higher education in the city, is one of the finest predominately black colleges in the nation. It, along with St. Edward's University, Concordia Lutheran, and the University of Texas at Austin are the four 4-year colleges in the city.

LIVING LIFE ON THE STREET IS hard, even in a tolerant city like Austin. This group of homeless men are remembering their friends who have died in Austin over the years. The Salvation Army, Helping Our Brother Out, and Caritas are just a few of the many programs in Austin that provide shelter, food, and hope for the future (TOP).

Stop by the UT campus anytime the weather is nice and you'll find students espousing a variety of causes at tables set up around the mall (BOTTOM).

HABITAT FOR HUMANITY HAS become a great American tradition. The organization is quite active in Austin, building new homes throughout town for many of the city's less fortunate citizens.

KEEPING GOD'S HOUSE IN ORDER is a never-ending task. Just ask the hard-working congregation of this modest African Methodist Episcopal church in Bastrop (TOP LEFT). Barton Springs Baptist Church serves a small but vibrant congregation in South Austin (BOTTOM LEFT). Sterling Lands is the pastor of Calvary Baptist Church (RIGHT).

AUSTIN HAS BOTH BENEFITED and suffered from new construction. In the early 1980s the city was one of the fastest-growing real estate markets in America. But the subsequent savings and loan and real estate disasters sent things into a tailspin. Thankfully, activity has heated up again. The hills west of downtown are coveted as a place to live, but building there is seen as a threat by environmentalists (TOP LEFT). That doesn't stop another lumber truck from making a delivery to a construction site (TOP RIGHT). Davenport Ranch offers expensive homes and commanding views of Lake Austin (BOTTOM).

ONE OF THE CITY'S MOST DESIR-able places to live is Central Austin. It offers proximity, restaurants, and a stronger bond to the Austin way of life than other parts of town. Clarksville is about as central as it gets. Originally an African-American community, this trendy neighborhood reflects a variety of homes and lifestyles (TOP). Hyde Park was the late-1800s brainchild of Colonel Monroe Shipe. In those days, 45th Street, the area's official northern boundary, was considered the edge of Austin's universe. (BOTTOM).

BEGINNING IN THE 1970S, THE
city's downtown skyline underwent
a dramatic transformation from
quiet, one-story shops to a
metropolitan center of business.
The two buildings in the background were some of Austin's first
skyscrapers.

IT'S RARE THAT SNOW FALLS IN Austin, but decorations throughout town let you know the holiday season has arrived.

THE CHRISTMAS "TREE" AT Zilker Park is the cornerstone for the annual Trail of Lights. The tree is actually one of the city's antique "moonlight towers," which were among the first electric lights in the nation. The contract specifications for the towers said a person should be able to read the face of a pocket watch on the night of a new moon, 300 yards from the tower. Thirty-one were originally built, 17 remain, and Austin is the only city in the nation with such structures.

WITH ITS COLUMNS, WRAPAROUND porches, and turrets, the Littlefield House on the campus of UT is one of the city's finest examples of Victorian-style architecture (TOP).

The Zilker Park Moonlight Tower can be seen for miles during the holiday season (BOTTOM).

GERMAN-BORN SCULPTRESS
Elisabet Ney designed and worked
in this home in Hyde Park in the
1890s. Her powerful sculptures of
Texas legends Stephen F. Austin
and Sam Houston are in the State
Capitol. The home was converted
into the Elisabet Ney Museum.

WITH AS MUCH GOOD WEATHER as there is in the city, it would almost be possible to hold UT classes outdoors all year long.

AUSTIN IS A GREAT PLACE TO raise a family, and this young couple in the Brykerwoods neighborhood proudly announces their new arrival.

THE COMMUNITY TAKES PRIDE IN its diversity of religious faiths, and virtually every persuasion can be found in town—even the national headquarters of the American Atheist Society. However, the thoughts of this young girl are on her first communion as she poses in front of a rendering of the Virgin Mary (LEFT). Muralist John Ruiz works on his graceful portrayal of the Blessed Mother displayed on Guadalupe Avenue (TOP RIGHT). Cecil Henniger can sometimes be found downtown using his stentorian voice to preach to passersby (BOTTOM RIGHT).

CLOUDS AND SUNLIGHT ARE WHAT put texture in the sky, and the beauty of the moment gives people reason to pause and reflect upon the magnificent things to be seen in Central Texas.

THE AUSTIN SKY CAN BECOME ferocious in short order. Weather systems often converge in the Central Texas region and produce violent thunderstorms and other mystifying examples of nature. The top of the Norwood Building glows as a shaft of sunlight peeks through threatening clouds.

CITIES ACROSS AMERICA strug-
gle with gang-related crime, and
Austin is no different. But the
local police force takes a creative
approach to preventing problems
before they occur (TOP).

Is that a devil in police clothing
or is that officer just being devilish
during Austin's annual Sixth Street
Halloween event? Tens of thousands
of adults dress up as crazily as they
can for the yearly festival, proving
once again that Austinites love to
party (BOTTOM).

THE COMMUNITY OFFERS A NUMBER of excellent parks, green spaces, and activities for children. This group of kids is giving it all they've got during a tug-of-war event (TOP).

Riding along on his bicycle, this youngster is one of tens of thousands of Austinites who rely on cycling for transportation (BOTTOM). Many serious bicycle racers live and train in the Austin area. There are excellent roads offering first-rate training opportunities as well as a "veloway" in the southwest part of the city.

▼ LARRY KOLVOORD / AUSTIN AMERICAN STATESMAN

WHATEVER YOU DO IN AUSTIN, DO it with style. This coiffed, color-coordinated couple is right at home in a city filled with out-of-the-ordinary sights (LEFT). Even Bart and Lisa Simpson are relatively tame compared to some of the outlandish outfits seen each Halloween on Sixth Street (TOP RIGHT). Needless to say, costume rental companies do a booming business.

Darrell the Clown appears to have a simple answer to car body problems—just stick another ornament on the old beast, and before you know it, it's art (BOTTOM RIGHT).

Throngs of Austinites attend the annual Old Pecan Street Spring Arts and Crafts Festival to eat, shop, listen to music, and while away a lazy day (RIGHT). Vendors like T-shirt artist Grant Sehaubut are out in force and ready to sell their latest creations to festival attenders (TOP LEFT). The entrepreneurial spirit in Austin is rampant, and the Halloween activity on Sixth Street is a good example (BOTTOM LEFT).

BRING THE KIDS, COOLERS, CHAIRS, and blankets and head to Auditorium Shores for any number of free concerts during the summer. In fact, throughout the warmer months, the City of Austin sponsors free concerts each and every week.

▶ PARK STREET

▶ PARK STREET

▶ GARY RUSS IMAGES

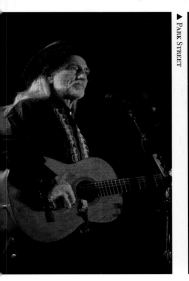

E DON'T CALL IT THE "LIVE usic Capital of the World" for thing. Marcia Ball would likely ve a more profitable career if e had gone to Nashville. Instead, e stayed in Austin and has joyed both critical success and happiness (TOP LEFT). South By Southwest, or SXSW, has developed into one of the most important music and entertainment conventions in the nation. Created by the alternative weekly newspaper, the *Austin Chronicle*, SXSW attracts hundreds of bands hoping to land a coveted recording contract (TOP RIGHT). Willie Nelson is a legend whose story has been told and retold. He turned his back on Nashville in the early 1970s and made his home in Austin (BOTTOM LEFT). Eric Johnson, who perfected his craft in the city's clubs, mesmerizes fans with his unbelievable guitar ability (BOTTOM CENTER). Joe Ely is a Lubbock native who migrated to Austin and firmly established roots in the city (BOTTOM RIGHT).

IN AUSTIN, LOCALS CAN TAKE THE oddest things and make them look perfectly normal. These flamingos, perched atop a bar, fit right in on Sixth Street.

THIS FLOCK OF PLASTIC FLAMINGOS in front of a nursery at the intersection of Loop 360 and Bee Cave Road received national attention when the West Lake Hills City Council anguished over whether to force their removal. A mild media frenzy ensued, however, and the birds were allowed to stay.

LAKE **A**USTIN **IS FAIRLY NARROW**
and unsuited for sailing, so virtually all the boats on the water
are motor driven. This conglom-
eration is enjoying a parade,
though obviously not an orderly
one.

THE BELOVED WILLIE N. FESTUS twirls atop the sign of a local exterminating company. Willie has been stolen, shot with an arrow, and vandalized, but he's one bug that keeps coming back. Artist Vicki Behl does some restoration work (TOP).

Lucky for the technician at the Austin Children's Museum, this dinosaur's roar is worse than his bite (BOTTOM).

LULING, A SMALL TOWN SOUTH OF Austin, has made quite a name for itself thanks to the productive oil reserves located there. The town is blessed with having shallow wells, which are cheaper and faster to operate.

RALPH BARRERA / AUSTIN AMERICAN STATESMAN

IT LOOKS LIKE THE SWIMMER IN lane seven got a jump on the competition during a meet at the Texas Swim Center on the UT campus (LEFT). The UT swimming program is highly rated, and the design characteristics of the Swim Center's pool give it a reputation for being extra fast (BOTTOM RIGHT).

The Austin Aqua Festival, an eight-day extravaganza, features outdoor concerts, boat races, and jet ski events (TOP RIGHT).

Ralph Barrera / Austin American Statesman

AUSTIN IS VERY MUCH AN EQUAL opportunity city. Women have served as mayor, city manager, head of the chamber of commerce, and on the city council. They're even race car drivers and firefighters. The firefighting crew at right is cleaning hazardous materials from protective clothing.

BY THE END OF THE DECADE, Robert Mueller Municipal Airport will be moved to the recently closed Bergstrom Air Force Base. The new facility will offer better runway space in a less congested part of town, providing easier access for the major airlines as well as small charter services like Austin Jet (TOP).

Lack of runway space is not a problem for the pilot of this Apache helicopter. The state-of-the-art aircraft can land on a dime (BOTTOM).

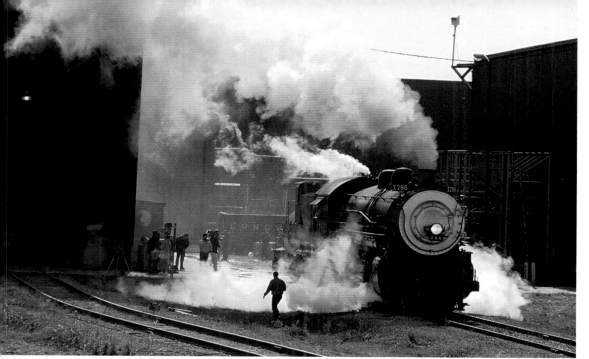

Train enthusiasts can be persuasive, as evidenced when the Austin Steam Train Association convinced the city to let them restore No. 786 to working order. Now serving as the locomotive for the Hill Country Flyer, the popular Cedar Park-to-Burnet trip is packed during warm-weather weekends (TOP).

The Zilker Park train is significantly smaller in size, but loved just as much. The mini-gauge train makes a trek around the edge of the park (BOTTOM).

AT LEAST ONCE IN YOUR LIFE, chop your own load of firewood. It will help you appreciate the strength of nature, and you'll enjoy the fire on a cold winter's night a lot more. You'll also understand the kind of day these men put in and how good it feels when somebody says, "Let's quit for now and have a cold one" (TOP).

These well-pressed "cowboys" are enjoying a longneck at the Schultz Beer Garden (BOTTOM).

NO TELLING WHO THIS HORSE borrowed the hat from during a visit to the Travis County Heritage and Exposition Center (TOP).

The family that choppers together, stays together, though there's some question as to where the dog sits (BOTTOM).

HUNTING IS CONSIDERED A RITE of passage for many in Austin. Lucky Texans who own land where deer graze don't have to spend hundreds or even thousands of dollars to purchase a deer lease, good for only one hunting season.

156

AUSTI

ONE OF THE MOST SUCCESSFUL wildlife management stories in Central Texas involves the deer. Controlling the hunting season, limiting the number of deer taken, protecting does, and monitoring their feeding ranges ensures the population will flourish.

IN TEXAS, LIVESTOCK PRODUCTION
is dominated by cattle, accounting
for approximately 70 percent of
the industry each year. This sign in
Taylor, northeast of Austin, lets
ranchers know where to get their
feed.

PAISANO RANCH, WITH ITS ROAD-
runner gate, was once owned by
Texas writer J. Frank Dobie.
Today, the facility is managed by
the University of Texas at Austin,
and promising writers working
under six-month fellowships live
and write there.

AFTER WINTER HAS MOVED ON, a field of Indian blankets is sure to warm even the coldest of hearts. The prolific, bright flower grows throughout the state except in forests and the driest of areas (OPPOSITE).

EACH SPRING, THE FINEST TRACK-and-field competitors in the Southwest Conference converge on Austin for the Texas Relays held on the UT campus (ABOVE).

IN AUSTIN, IF YOU SEE A GUY with the hair shaved from his legs and arms, it's likely he's either a swimmer or a serious bicycle racer. This group of cyclists whizzing by is practicing at Camp Mabry, part of the Texas National Guard complex at MoPac and 35th Street. The camp has a one-mile oval track that is open to the public.

AFTER THE REQUISITE EARLY-morning workout, these quarter horses at Manor Downs appear to be ready for the feed bag. Until pari-mutuel wagering was approved by Texas voters, Manor Downs, about 25 miles east of Austin, was as much a concert venue as it was a place to stage a race.

THE HORSES ARE OFF AND RUNNING at Manor Downs, but the jury's still out about the future of pari-mutuel gambling in Texas. Long opposed by conservatives, horse racing got off to a shaky start, and then was rocked further when the passage of a state lottery steered potential fans away from the track. It's a sure bet, though, that a day spent at Manor Downs will provide lots of fast action and thrilling finishes.

GOVERNOR ANN RICHARDS purchased her first lottery ticket at Polk's Feed in Oak Hill. (TOP LEFT). One person's junk is another person's treasure, and if you look long enough in this antique shop in Buda, south of Austin, you just might find your treasure (TOP RIGHT). Pick a card, any card, because it doesn't matter to Frost McKee, who's listed in the *Guinness Book of World Records* for card memorization (BOTTOM LEFT). Chester "Jelly" Stewart lives in East Austin and divides his time between preaching the gospel and repairing lawn mowers (BOTTOM RIGHT).

▲ ALAN POGUE

▲ KEVIN VANDIVIER

OWBOYS TAKE PRIDE IN A LOT things, but they spend good oney on only a few. Go see anny Gammage for one of the st hats you can buy (TOP LEFT). arlie Dunn, revered as one of the finest custom boot makers ever, passed on at the age of 95 in September 1993 (BOTTOM LEFT). When you want a sampling of Austin's wit, you might want to chat with Jim Hightower. His one-liner, populist humor helped him get elected as commissioner of the Texas Department of Agriculture in 1986. Hightower's 1990 reelection bid failed, however, and he is now busy with his nationally syndicated radio show (TOP RIGHT). Born and raised in Austin, Cactus Pryor is an author, talk-show host, and raconteur (BOTTOM RIGHT).

THE AREA IS FORTUNATE TO HAVE
a number of excellent golf courses.
Arnold Palmer brought his prodigious
talents to the city and designed
the course at Hidden Hills in
Northwest Austin.

THIS PAIR AT HIDDEN HILLS
enjoys the fruits of Arnold
Palmer's design work. One of the
nice things about Central Texas is
that you can golf almost year-round.

For many Austinites, good health is more than an attitude, it's a way of life. The city encourages exercise with running trails and citywide recreational programs. This runner is about to cross over the Lamar Boulevard bridge.

THIS KITE LOOKS LIKE A GOOD one, but it is nothing compared to the airborne creations that regularly show up at places like Zilker Park. A spring kite contest at the park brings out hundreds of kites and thousands of spectators.

WHEN THE WEATHER WARMS, Austinites of all ages catch a collective case of spring fever. However, this common ailment can be cured with a trip to Lake Travis. Considered one of the best scuba diving areas in the state, Lake Travis is the largest body of water in the Highland Lakes chain (TOP).

Buchanan Dam impounds Lake Buchanan, uppermost in the Highland Lakes chain. The Vanishing Texas River Cruise takes a leisurely half-day journey around the lake to see sights such as bald eagles and waterfowl (BOTTOM).

GET YOURSELF A COLD BEER OR order up a margarita and sit back and watch the sunset at the Oasis overlooking Lake Travis. With more than two dozen decks hugging the hillside, there's plenty of seating, but if you want to sit close to the edge, be sure to arrive early.

THANKS TO THE DEEP WATER and steady winds, Lake Travis is one of the state's best areas for sailing. This scene of serenity gives way to a flurry of weekend summertime activity when the sailboats and powerboats can make things a little crowded (OPPOSITE).

TRAVIS COUNTY OPERATES A PARK at Windy Point on Lake Travis. Sun worshipers and swimmers head there early, play all day, and often stay out until the last rays of sunshine are gone (ABOVE).

WINDY POINT IS THE BEST PLACE on Lake Travis to go windsurfing. It offers easy access to the water, good steady winds, and a place to relax between excursions (TOP).

Town Lake is highly regarded for rowing. It is long and straight, powerboats are prohibited, and its waters are generally calm. Several colleges and universities from the North send their teams to town during the mild winters to get in some extra training (BOTTOM).

A FEW HEARTY SOULS CAN BE SEEN water-skiing in the winter, clad in wet suits as they skim across the glass-smooth water. To beat the crowds in summer, you need to get up early before the boats churn up the water.

THERE IS A NATURAL COMPOSITION to the Austin terrain that helps make it a beautiful place. And, fortunately, the city works hard to ensure that man-made structures—like the Loop 360 bridge—blend in with the natural landscape.

SOMETIMES IN THE LATE WINTER and the early spring, a light, early-morning fog hugs the ground, giving the downtown skyline a dreamlike appearance (ABOVE).

A BRILLIANT SUNSET OVER THE Capitol dome signifies the end of a long day. More importantly, it holds the promise for an even brighter tomorrow (FOLLOWING PAGES).

LARRY KOLVOORD / AUSTIN AMERICAN STATESMAN

▲ James M. Innes

AUSTIN

PROFILES

IN

EXCELLENCE

A LOOK AT THE CORPORATIONS,

BUSINESSES, PROFESSIONAL GROUPS, AND

COMMUNITY SERVICE ORGANIZATIONS

THAT HAVE MADE THIS BOOK POSSIBLE.

BY LAURA TUMA

1871-1970

THE DRISKILL HOTEL WAS ONCE CONSIDERED THE FINEST HOTEL WEST OF THE MISSISSIPPI WHEN IT WAS CONSTRUCTED AT A COST OF ONLY $400,000. TODAY, THE SIXTH STREET LANDMARK IS AS GRAND AND BEAUTIFUL AS EVER (OPPOSITE).

PARK STREET

Austin American-Statesman

S AY "CHIP" IN AUSTIN, AND DEPENDING ON WHERE YOU ARE, IT might mean microchip or tortilla chip or cow chip or blue chip. At the *Austin American-Statesman*, the city's 180,000-circulation daily newspaper, they'll know about all those chips and more. The

American-Statesman's employees understand the diversity of this well-educated, high-tech capital city, but they also recognize the rich traditions of Austin's history.

"Publishing a newspaper carries a lot of responsibility, especially when it is the only daily paper in town," says Roger Kintzel, publisher of the *American-Statesman*. "We must be fair, objective, and thorough. We try to live up to that every day, but we also are proud to be the major source of information about retailing in the Austin area. We give advertisers the chance to reach more than 400,000 adult readers in one day."

For more than 120 years, the *American-Statesman* or one of its predecessors has served the Austin area. Originally published by the Texas Democratic Executive Committee as part of its effort to restore the state's pre-Civil War political order, the newspaper always has cherished its position in Austin.

The newspaper, today under the ownership of Cox Newspapers, a wholly owned subsidiary of Cox Enterprises, Inc., aggressively pursues its mission to serve the citizens of Central Texas through its pre-

sentation of news and advertising and as a forum for lively discussion of issues. The newspaper's operations and editorial content—including its spirited editorial page, which features Pulitzer Prize-winning cartoonist Ben Sargent—are under local direction.

The *American-Statesman*'s circulation climbed to 180,000 daily and 240,000 on Sunday in 1994. The newspaper has the widest reach of any news medium in Austin. It is also the area's leading vehicle for classified advertising, as the 1.8 million classified ads in 1993 prove.

"We are in this business because we love it," says Maggie Balough, who is editor of the *American-Statesman* and supervisor of its nearly 200 editorial employees. "We are committed to making a difference."

Austin's population is among the best educated, most diverse, and most active of any city in the country. As a result, the newspaper provides its readers unique content in addition to extensive coverage of the Austin area and state government. "A newspaper serves many communities of interest," Balough says. "In Austin, we have more

than most—educational, entertainment, high-tech, government, environmental, ethnic, and cultural communities."

She adds, "Our objective is to provide the knowledge people need to understand the world today. We have to turn the issues inside out and upside down to look from all views. But we also have to provide coverage of those uniquely Austin interests."

CLOCKWISE FROM ABOVE: "PUBLISHING A NEWSPAPER CARRIES A LOT OF RE-SPONSIBILITY, ESPECIALLY WHEN IT IS THE ONLY DAILY PAPER IN TOWN," SAYS ROGER KINTZEL, PUBLISHER OF THE *AMERICAN-STATESMAN*.

THE NEWPAPER'S BEST-KNOWN COMMUNITY EVENT IS THE CAPITOL 10,000, WHICH ATTRACTS NEARLY 20,000 RUNNERS TO AUSTIN EACH SPRING.

FROM ITS BUSY PRESSROOM TO STATE-OF-THE-ART PAGE DESIGN CAPABILITIES, THE *AMERICAN-STATESMAN* AND ITS STAFF ARE COMMITTED TO SERVING AUSTIN'S DIVERSE COMMUNITIES OF INTEREST.

Among the nontraditional features of the *American-Statesman* are daily pages that provide information about the breadth of entertainment in Central Texas, from Austin's famed music scene to the burgeoning Texas film industry to visual artists, dancers, and theater companies. A weekly, consumer-oriented environmental section, Project Earth, is especially popular with young readers. Extensive coverage of books and authors, especially those from Texas, serves Austin's book-reading community.

But a newspaper's commitment to its community and its impact on that community reach far beyond its daily editions. No newspaper is more aware of its role in the community than the *American-Statesman*. Each year the newspaper donates hundreds of thousands of dollars of advertising to local nonprofit groups and encourages volunteerism among its employees.

"We are committed to community leadership," says Dan Savage, the newspaper's executive vice president and general manager. "As a corporation, we sponsor about 150 community events and provide thousands of volunteer hours. We also encourage our employees to get involved with groups that are important to them. It's not something we usually boast about in print, but we are proud of the impact our people make in the community."

The *American-Statesman*'s best-known community event is the Capitol 10,000, which attracts nearly 20,000 runners to Austin each spring. The largest footrace in Texas, and one of the 10 largest in the country, the 10-kilometer run raises thousands of dollars for charity and is one of the city's biggest annual events.

Less well-known is the contribution the newspaper has made to another local passion—bat watching. Austin is home to the world's largest urban bat colony. Just before sunset each evening during the spring and summer, thousands of Mexican free-tailed bats leave their perches under the Congress Avenue bridge in search of food. Since the best viewing spot is adjacent to the newspaper's offices along Town Lake, the *American-Statesman* built an observation post there.

The *American-Statesman* is proud of its product and sees a secure future for the newspaper. But it also is positioning itself in the forefront of technological change that is affecting how Americans receive news, information, and entertainment.

Inside Line, an advertising-supported telephone service that allows callers to hear recorded information and request facsimile copies of documents, receives more than 300,000 calls a month. Through Cox Enterprises, the newspaper has formed partnerships with other communications companies to create more technologically advanced information services.

"The field is changing rapidly," Kintzel says. "Newsprint will be around for a long time, but today information can just as easily flow through telephones, personal computers, or television screens. Whatever the vehicle, we are in the business of gathering and conveying information, so we are perfectly positioned to tailor information for people who want to receive it in whatever form. New technology will expand our business tremendously."

Greater Austin Chamber of Commerce

THE GREATER AUSTIN CHAMBER OF COMMERCE WAS FOUNDED April 13, 1877, by business leaders who believed that if they worked together to improve the economy, more jobs would be created, the tax base would be broadened, better municipal services would be

provided at a lower tax rate, and the community as a whole would thrive. After more than 117 years, Austin and its chamber continue to prove that this philosophy is the best strategy for economic vitality and community improvement.

First known as the Austin Board of Trade and later as the Austin Chamber of Commerce, the organization adopted its current name in 1989 to reflect its regional part-

JUST A SHORT DISTANCE FROM THE CENTRAL BUSINESS DISTRICT, THE COLORADO RIVER OFFERS A BEAUTIFUL SETTING FOR CANOEISTS AND HIKERS (ABOVE).

THE CHAMBER HAS BECOME AN ENTHUSIASTIC ADVOCATE FOR DOWNTOWN REVITALIZATION (RIGHT).

PHOTOS BY JAMES A. DUMAS

nership approach. The private, nonprofit business organization represents members throughout the Austin metropolitan area and works to improve the economic climate of the entire region.

Over the years, the chamber has grown into the area's largest business organization, representing a broad coalition of companies and individuals. Out of a membership of 3,000 member firms, approximately 85 percent are small businesses. From Austin's largest employers and public institutions to one-person firms, virtually every industry segment and interest is represented. This level of diversity gives strength and credibility to

chamber decisions and helps promote programs that benefit a broad segment of Austin-area residents.

More than 3,000 volunteers serve on 70 committees and participate in programs designed to improve economic and social opportunities for local residents. Recommendations about the chamber's policies and programs come from its volunteers, and final decisions are made by a 26-member executive board and 50-member advisory board selected from the membership. The annual Program of Work is implemented by a staff of 45 professionals in close conjunction with the chamber's volunteer leadership.

Redefining Economic Development

"This truly is a member-driven organization," says Board Chair Bi Renfro, CEO of Worthen Nationa Bank of Texas. "The organization is here to meet the needs of its members. We listen to our members; we don't dictate to them."

Renfro says the chamber will continue the collaborative efforts forged in 1993 under the leadership of Ron Kessler. During that year, the chamber continued to establish itself as a leading force i areas not traditionally associated with economic development—edu cation, environmental protection, crime, social services, and others. "The functioning of a community

impacts business," Kessler explains. When things go well, the business climate improves. But when things go badly, business suffers. The chamber can and should be a leader in working on these larger issues, but we can't solve them alone." Instead, the chamber has forged collaborative relationships with many other groups in order to play a positive role in solving community problems.

The results have been impressive. For example, an ambitious program to develop apprenticeships and career pathways for young people entering critical industries is being propelled forward by the collaborative efforts of the chamber, private employers, city officials, and local universities and colleges.

While extending into nontraditional issues, the chamber has also reached out to businesses and business leaders who have not typically been represented by chambers of commerce. "This community is very inclusive, and the chamber has become inclusive as well," says Carol Thompson, a network strategist who chaired the board of directors in 1992. "We have reached a critical mass in the number of women who are actively involved in the chamber, so that it is becoming self-perpetuating. We are at the point of reaching a critical

mass in the number of minorities serving. It is gratifying to see how the chamber has been inclusive of new people and viewpoints."

Thompson was the third woman to chair the chamber's board of directors in the past few years, following St. Edward's University President Patricia Hayes, Ph.D., who held the position in 1988; and former Texas Commerce Bank Vice President Dorothy Rowland, who served as chair in 1978. "The strength of the chamber staff and board is that they see economic development in terms of community building," notes Hayes. "That makes the Greater Austin Chamber distinctive in my experience, especially when you consider its bias for collaborating, rather than competing, with other groups in the community."

The chamber has also developed a structure to give direct representation to members in specific geographic areas. The North Central, Northwest, Northeast, South, and Southwest Area Councils initiate member programs and services that meet their specific needs. Monthly meetings and programs offer expanded networking opportunities with decision makers and also provide information about events and activities that affect business opportunities in certain parts of Austin.

A History of Innovation and Insight

Throughout its history, the chamber has looked out for the greater interest of Austin. In its early years, the organization provided a way for business leaders to work together to keep tax rates low, extend utilities, and provide the services companies needed to prosper. As time went on, the chamber began working to attract new companies to Austin to supplement the employment opportunities provided by local businesses, government, and the University of Texas.

By the 1960s, the need for new companies was clear. Native Austinites and UT graduates wanted to stay in Austin because of its charm and natural beauty, but there weren't enough jobs to go around. Parents wanted their children to be able to find work in their hometown, and businesses wanted to keep the educated and talented work force close at hand. But an economy based on heavy industry wasn't what Austinites wanted.

It was then that the chamber made the critical decision to focus its economic development efforts on clean industry—the term "high technology" hadn't been invented yet. These companies would be compatible with Austin, provide good jobs, and maintain the pristine Hill Country environment.

Technology Growth

One by one, technology firms began arriving in the capital city. Some, like Tracor and Radian, were founded in Austin. Others, like IBM, Texas Instruments, Advanced Micro Devices, and Motorola, were major companies that established important branches in town. By the 1970s, technology-based companies were becoming one of the most important components of Austin's economy.

And that milestone actually occurred before the main high-tech growth started. Since the mid-1980s, the city has established itself as one of the nation's leading technology centers. More microprocessors are manufactured in Austin than anywhere else, and the city is a haven for software development. Likewise, Austin probably has more technology entrepreneurs per capita than any other city, and it competes with international cities for new jobs. The Austin Technology Incubator—a collaborative project of the chamber, the University of Texas, and the City of Austin—is a national model for helping technology firms get started.

As vibrant as the local business community has become, it still depends on the chamber's continuing support. The communications and business services divisions within the chamber have developed a clearinghouse of information and contacts to help local businesses grow and prosper. And the division that oversees both governmental relations and community development/education serves as a liaison between the business community and diverse governmental and educational agencies to build dynamic coalitions that work for the welfare of all Austinites.

Today, the city's economy is more diversified than ever and fortified for stable, long-term growth well into the next century. The chamber is not resting, though. It continues to seek out quality corporate prospects in the United States and abroad, always keeping an eye on how Austin can prosper in the long run.

THE CHAMBER'S MUSIC INDUSTRY COUNCIL WORKS TO HIGHLIGHT AUSTIN MUSICIANS AND SUPPORTED THE CONSTRUCTION OF THIS MEMORIAL TO THE LATE HOMETOWN MUSICIAN STEVIE RAY VAUGHAN ON THE SHORES OF TOWN LAKE.

PHOTO BY JAMES A. DUMAS

Diverse Services for Members

The chamber's programs are divided into several fields: economic development, governmental relations, education, community development, business services, communications, and membership development. Through these areas of focus, the chamber represents the interests of its members and the business community, preserves and develops Austin's unique strengths, and creates opportunities for an enhanced business climate.

Area Councils, Austin Adopt-A-School, Business After Hours, School to Work Transition, Buy Greater Austin, Leadership Austin, Austin International Business Council, Austin Quality Council, the Ambassadors, Business Committee for the Arts, and Military Affairs Council are just a few of the chamber programs involving hundreds of volunteers. The organization is an advocate for downtown revitalization and promotes international business development. It also supports the Employers Support Parenting (ESP) program to enhance parental support of children in school.

As Austin's largest private business advocacy organization, the chamber represents an enlightened business community at the local, state, and federal levels on issues such as transportation, education, and the environment, as well as issues affecting the local business climate. It also creates hundreds of opportunities for firms that need expanded business networks, targeted marketing lists, small-business support groups, business workshops, and business referrals.

The chamber serves as a unique resource for its members as well, providing information, research assistance, small-business assistance, and referrals on a wide range of issues. An additional benefit of membership is that all employees of member firms are eligible to participate in chamber programs and workshops.

Several of those programs and services have won special acclaim. The chamber, for example, started one of the nation's first Adopt-A-School programs, providing a mechanism for local businesses to become involved in schools. Today, more than 1,800 businesses participate, providing the equivalent of $4.4 million and 200,000 volunteer hours to improve local schools.

Buy Greater Austin, which was initiated in 1989, is an innovative program that has redirected millions of dollars into the local economy. The program encourages Austinites and Austin businesses to shop locally, ensuring that dollars stay in the economy and are recirculated as salaries, rents, taxes, and purchases of goods and services. The program has been recognized as one of the most successful of its kind in the nation.

Whether it's working for the community, developing valuable services for members, recruiting new industries, or collaborating to solve society's problems, the Greater Austin Chamber of Commerce is setting a new standard for excellence while helping to make Austin a better place to live, work, and do business.

The University of Texas at Austin

SINCE ITS FOUNDING MORE THAN 110 YEARS AGO, THE UNIVERsity of Texas at Austin has grown from a small, 40-acre campus near the State Capitol into a major institution known nationally for the quality of its academic programs, research, and public service.

"THIS UNIVERSITY HAS A HISTORY OF EDUCATING THE LEADERS OF THE STATE," SAYS DR. ROBERT BERDAHL, PRESIDENT (NEAR RIGHT). "IT'S WHERE TEXANS WANT THEIR CHILDREN TO GO TO SCHOOL. THAT IS A POWER AND A RESPONSIBILITY WE TAKE VERY SERIOUSLY."

THE TOWER AT UT HAS BECOME AN ENDURING SYMBOL OF THE UNIVERSITY AND ITS HOMETOWN (FAR RIGHT).

PHOTOS BY LARRY MURPHY

As the academic flagship of the state-supported University of Texas System, UT Austin's 357-acre main campus is home to more than 49,000 students, 2,300 faculty, and almost 15,000 staff members. The University's wealth of human resources, encompassing a diversity of cultures, provides the foundation of its service to the people of Texas.

One of Austin's Greatest Assets

From community outreach to a respected athletics program and from world-class art collections to cutting-edge research, UT is one of the city's greatest assets. "It would be more appropriate to say that The University is *of* Austin, not *in* Austin," maintains Dr. Robert Berdahl, president. "We are part of

UT gives Austinites access to outstanding permanent and visiting art collections. The Archer M. Huntington Art Gallery, for example, houses the James and Mari Michener Collection of 20th Cen-

UT also boasts the nation's fifth largest academic library system. In addition to outstanding general library facilities, the system includes the Nettie Lee Benson Latin American Collection, one of the most

THE UNIVERSITY'S 87 ORGANIZED RESEARCH UNITS, WHICH RECEIVED MORE THAN $223 MILLION IN FUNDING IN 1993, ARE A BREEDING GROUND FOR TALENTED STUDENTS AND FACULTY (ABOVE).

PHOTOS BY LARRY MURPHY

the evolution and development of this community, and we are interested in supporting all aspects of its development."

Through the Neighborhood Longhorns, more than 600 UT Austin students and adult volunteers work with youth who are at risk of dropping out of school. UT Outreach Centers in several Texas cities, including Austin, also help at-risk teens stay in school and prepare for college.

tury American Art, as well as excellent examples of western American and contemporary Latin American art. The Harry Ransom Humanities Research Center is home to a Gutenburg Bible and the world's first photograph. Its collection of British, American, and French literary materials includes approximately 1 million books, 30 million manuscripts, 5 million photographs, and more than 100,000 works of art.

important collections of its kind in the world.

The Lyndon Baines Johnson Library and Museum—the first presidential library built on a college campus—includes the papers of the 36th president of the United States, as well as gifts, memorabilia and rare historical objects illustrating 20th-century American political life.

Culture comes in all varieties at UT—from student drama to oper

reggae. Performances by students, local groups, and world-renowned artists are hosted each year at the Performing Arts Center, which includes several performance venues ranked among the best on any American campus. The 18,000-seat Frank C. Erwin Jr. Special Events Center plays host to more than 250 shows a year, ranging from men's and women's college basketball to concerts by major artists.

The Power of Research

UT Austin has been a significant force in the city's development as a technology center. Its 87 organized research units, which received more than $223 million in funding in 1993, are a breeding ground for talented students and faculty. In addition to generating numerous spinoff technologies and companies, The University has attracted many new companies to Austin. The University's commitment to research extends beyond its main campus. In Austin, UT operates the Brackenridge Tract, which includes a biological field laboratory; Montopolis Research Center, a 94-acre tract in Southeast Austin; and the Pickle Research Center, a 475-acre tract that houses 21 science, engineering, and archeology laboratories. UT Austin also maintains

facilities in other Texas locales, including McDonald Observatory atop Mount Locke in West Texas, the Institute of Geophysics in Galveston, and the Marine Science Institute in Port Aransas.

Beyond cultural outlets and groundbreaking research, The University has given Austin something else to cheer about—the Texas Longhorns. UT's athletics program boasts more men's and women's Southwest Conference and national championships than any other college or university. Beginning in 1996, UT will compete in the former Big 8 conference, bringing new excitement and challenges to its student-athletes and fans.

Outstanding Academic Resource

UT Austin is a magnet for academically talented students. The University annually enrolls more than 200 National Merit Scholars, ranking it among the leaders in the nation. The average SAT score of entering freshmen is above 1,100—200 points higher than the national average for college-bound high school seniors.

As part of its mission to educate students from all segments of the population, The University continues to diversify its student body. More than 16 percent of students are African-American or Hispanic,

and UT has the largest Hispanic student body of any flagship teaching and research institution in the nation.

To serve the varied needs of its students, The University's 16 individual colleges and schools, 53 departments, and 281 degree programs offer 6,700 graduate and undergraduate courses. Many of its academic programs are recognized as being among the nation's best, thanks to a talented faculty that includes Nobel laureates, Pulitzer Prize winners, and members of prestigious scholarly academies. UT's ability to attract and retain outstanding faculty is bolstered by its 1,000 privately endowed chairs, professorships, fellowships, and lectureships.

For more than a century, The University has extended its reach throughout Austin and across Texas, educating leaders for the state and the nation. "UT is looked to in a way that is different from other state universities," says Berdahl. "This university has a history of educating the leaders of the state. It's where Texans want their children to go to school. That is a power and a responsibility we take very seriously."

Brackenridge Hospital
Children's Hospital of Austin at Brackenridge

EVERY CITY HAS A HOSPITAL IT CANNOT DO WITHOUT, BUT Austin has two: Brackenridge Hospital, with a tradition more than a century old of serving the community, and Children's Hospital of Austin at Brackenridge, the only hospital in Central Texas solely

dedicated to the care of children.

Conveniently located in midtown Austin, the 400-bed Brackenridge and 82-bed Children's Hospital are acute care facilities serving Austin and the surrounding 10-county area. Brackenridge was founded in 1884 and is the oldest community hospital in Texas. Children's Hospital opened in 1988 and cared for more than 25,000 patients its first five years. Both are dedicated to providing high-quality, professional, compassionate care to all

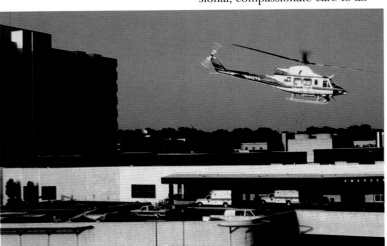

BRACKENRIDGE HOSPITAL IS THE HOME BASE FOR STAR FLIGHT, WHICH PROVIDES AIR TRANSPORT FOR SERIOUSLY ILL OR INJURED PATIENTS (ABOVE).

SKIPPY THE KANGAROO WELCOMES PATIENTS AND THEIR FAMILIES TO CHILDREN'S HOSPITAL OF AUSTIN AT BRACKENRIDGE (RIGHT).

segments of the community.

Staffed by more than 100 physicians and 1,700 employees, Brackenridge provides care in emergency medicine and critical care, maternity services, pediatrics, neurology and neurosurgery, cardiology, orthopedics, and surgery. The hospital is also a teaching facility, with programs to train resident physicians in internal medicine, family practice, obstetrics and gynecology, pediatrics, and surgery.

The Brackenridge Emergency Center is renowned for the care it provides victims of illness and injury. Physicians and nurses specially trained in emergency medicine and on-call surgeons supported by 24-hour laboratory, radiology, and surgical facilities care for almost 80,000 patients a year.

Brackenridge is also the home base for STAR Flight, the emergency medical helicopter service covering 25 counties within a 75-mile radius of Austin.

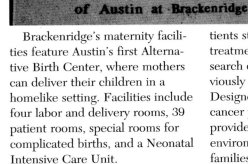

Brackenridge's maternity facilities feature Austin's first Alternative Birth Center, where mothers can deliver their children in a homelike setting. Facilities include four labor and delivery rooms, 39 patient rooms, special rooms for complicated births, and a Neonatal Intensive Care Unit.

Brackenridge and Children's Hospital offer complete cardiac care for adults and children. Services include the use of special medication in the Emergency Center to literally stop a heart attack in progress; advanced cardiac diagnostic laboratories with cardiac catheterization equipment allowing physicians to diagnose and repair defects; and facilities for EKG, stress testing, echocardiography, and nuclear medicine diagnostic imaging.

Consistent with its history of innovative health care, the first open-heart surgery and balloon angioplasty procedures in Austin were performed by Brackenridge, and the only pediatric cardiology program in Central Texas is based

at Children's Hospital.

In early 1993 Brackenridge opened the Texas Cancer Center at Brackenridge. It is the area's first cancer center offering adult pa-

tients standard forms of cancer treatment and investigational research drug therapies not previously available in Central Texas. Designed with the help of former cancer patients, the Cancer Center provides a supportive, therapeutic environment, enabling patients, families, physicians, and nurses to participate in a team effort to manage the disease.

Besides general acute care and surgery, Children's Hospital provides specialized services such as pediatric intensive care and long-term case management for children with chronic illnesses. Complementing the adult cancer care at the Texas Cancer Center, The Park at Children's Hospital opened in 1993 to treat children and adolescents with cancer and blood disorders.

Brackenridge is proud of its reputation for health care excellence. By making a broad array of specialized services available to all Central Texans, Brackenridge continues to fill a critical niche in the region's health care network.

St. Edward's University

ESTABLISHED IN 1885 BY THE PRIEST WHO FOUNDED THE University of Notre Dame, St. Edward's University plays a unique and important role not only in Austin, but also in the state and nation. A private, Catholic university of 3,100 students, St. Edward's provides a solid liberal arts education emphasizing critical thinking, values, and moral responsibility.

"If we're going to educate leaders, we should educate leaders who can speak not just to science and poetry, but also to the kinds of communities we want to live in," says Dr. Patricia A. Hayes, president of St. Edward's. "We help students develop the long-term skills they need to grow themselves and to help their companies and communities grow."

The university offers undergrad-

ate degrees in 33 areas, with preprofessional programs in medicine, law, engineering, and three other areas. Graduate degree programs are available in business administration and arts in human services.

Serving the Future of Texas

St. Edward's University has earned a reputation as a forward-looking institution by developing programs and educating students who will shape the future of Texas. In 1993 the university was recognized by Governor Ann Richards and more than 100 government and corporate leaders as a "model institution" for the state. St. Edward's was cited for its challenging academic standards, for a student body that mirrors Texas' demographics, and for providing innovative educational opportunities to nontraditional students, including working adults.

Several programs are responsive to the changing needs of business.

The Career Planning and Management Program helps students explore career opportunities and develop the skills employers need. In their capstone course, graduate students work with businesses to analyze problems and recommend solutions.

In all of its programs, the university emphasizes measuring results. St. Edward's is one of 30 institutions nationwide using the College Outcomes Measures Program to assess how much students learn throughout their college career.

Recognition for Academic Excellence

Thanks to increasing recognition as a leader in higher education, St. Edward's may be in danger of losing its best-kept-secret status. The Association of American Colleges and Universities, for example, chose St. Edward's as one of 20 schools nationwide to serve as a resource for universities attempting to add a multicultural component to their core curricula. A case study conducted by students and faculty in the St. Edward's School of Business was recently honored by the U.S. Small Business Administration as number two in the nation. Likewise, a reunion of students who graduated from the university's College Assistance Migrant Program was featured on "CBS Sunday Morning" with Charles Kuralt.

Looking Toward the Second Century

The Holy Cross priests and brothers who founded St. Edward's more than a century ago would be proud to see how the university has honored the traditions of the past while embracing the challenges of the future. They would recognize the Main Building, a historic landmark as old as the university. But they

would marvel at the beautiful new campus plaza, the spacious Recreation and Convocation Center, the computerized library, and the state-of-the-art multimedia facilities.

"The philosophy of our founders is evident today, as we give students concrete preparation for their futures while they are challenged to reach beyond achievement and become leaders for the common good," Hayes says. "Our mission is as vital today as it was in 1885."

CLOCKWISE FROM ABOVE: SMALL CLASSES TAUGHT BY DEDICATED FACULTY MEMBERS ARE THE STANDARD AT ST. EDWARD'S.

STUDENTS AND FACULTY USE THE LATEST TECHNOLOGY IN THE CLASSROOM, LIBRARY, AND RESIDENCE HALLS.

DESIGNED IN THE GOTHIC REVIVAL STYLE BY ARCHITECT NICHOLAS J. CLAYTON, THE MAIN BUILDING IS LISTED ON THE NATIONAL REGISTER OF HISTORIC PLACES AND IS A TEXAS HISTORICAL LANDMARK.

Bank One, Texas, N.A.

BANK ONE, TEXAS, N.A. HAS DEEP ROOTS IN THE LONE STAR State. Its Austin origins go back more than a century—to the American National Bank, founded in 1890. ◆ American Bank had a long and distinguished history, surviving the Great Depression

and World War II to prosper in the postwar years. In the 1950s, visitors from out of town flocked to the American Bank building to see its fancy new escalators, the first ones in Austin. In the 1970s, its 21-story, gold-sheathed tower downtown was both the tallest and most recognizable skyscraper in town.

Gaining a New Identity

The early 1980s saw a merger and name change to MBank. The MBank era was characterized by increased consumer demand for convenience, and the bank met that demand by pioneering automatic teller machines, credit cards, discount brokerage services, and insurance. As the '80s drew to a close, the bank on Sixth Street, almost 100 years old, was acquired by Ohio-based Banc One, a bank holding company whose roots date from 1868.

Banc One, with entities serving customers in 12 states, has 1,300 banking offices nationwide. Its net income ($1.4 billion as of December 1993) and Midwestern sensibilities have proved to be a perfect match for the indomitable Texas spirit. Bank One, Texas is now the state's third-largest bank, with approximately $17.4 billion in assets. In Austin, it is the city's second-largest bank, with 16 branches, more than 60 automatic teller machines, and 470 employees.

Focus on Customer Needs

Although Bank One is proud of its market share, customers are its real asset, according to Charlie O'Connell, chairman and chief executive officer. "Talk of buyouts, banking organizations, restructuring, and market penetration means little to the average banking customer, and we know that," he says. "When Banc One came to Austin in 1990, we brought with us a policy of

local autonomy and a strong focus on customer relations. We knew that despite a downturn in the energy and real estate industries, banking talent and commitment to customer service were alive and well in Austin and in Texas."

Bank One's familiar slogan, "whatever it takes," fits the enterprising and entrepreneurial nature of the company. For example, every fall the bank targets special offers to the thousands of new college students streaming into Austin. "We try to make 'student rush' as simple as possible for them," O'Connell says. "Branch personnel take as much care with a college student's first checking account as we do with a professional."

Other special offers are targeted

to such groups as senior citizens and employees relocating to Aust[i] with their companies. Relocation services may include discounted fees on mortgages; checking accounts and credit cards; brokerag[e] mutual funds, and other investment services; convenient accoun[t] setup by telephone; and commercial and consumer loans.

According to O'Connell, Bank One's future, like Austin's, look[s] bright indeed. "Bank One will gro[w] along with the Austin economy," [h]e says. "The prospects are very pos[i]tive as more jobs are created and more opportunities are presente[d] for businesses and families. Our strategy is to compete by doing what's best for our customers."

BUILT IN THE 1970S, BANK ONE'S RENOVATED DOWNTOWN TOWER TODAY BRINGS AN UPDATED LOOK TO AUSTIN'S SKYLINE (ABOVE).

FRONT ROW, FROM LEFT: JULIANNE KING, SENIOR VP/MANAGER, BANC ONE TRUST; PAT THOMPSON, SENIOR VP/MANAGER, RETAIL BANKING DIVISION.

MIDDLE ROW: CHARLIE O'CONNELL, CHIEF EXECUTIVE OFFICER/CHAIRMAN; MARILYN TAYLOR, VP/MANAGER, INDIRECT CONSUMER LOAN CENTER; LEA THOMPSON, VP/AREA MANAGER, BANC ONE MORTGAGE; BILL WHEELER, CHIEF FINANCIAL OFFICER.

BACK ROW: MARIA DANNER, SENIOR VP/MANAGER, RETAIL AND BANK ADMINISTRATION; JOE PETET, PRESIDENT/MANAGER, COMMERCIAL BANKING DIVISION; BRAD TIDWELL, SENIOR VP/SENIOR CREDIT OFFICER.

Steck-Vaughn Publishing Corporation

S TECK-VAUGHN PUBLISHING CORPORATION TAKES THE BUSINESS of education seriously. Thanks to its constant attention to the changing needs of America's students, the 58-year-old Austin firm is one of the nation's most successful and innovative publishers of

educational materials for children and adults.

Steck-Vaughn has a reputation for affordable, high-quality materials that are responsive to evolving classroom needs. Perhaps that's because its products are almost exclusively developed, written, edited, and marketed by people who know the challenges of education firsthand—classroom teachers.

"Our idea is that people with experience in the classroom have the ability to create products that work in the classroom," says Roy Mayers, president of Steck-Vaughn since 1987.

That philosophy seems to be working. During Mayers' tenure as

president, he has seen the company grow from 100 to 360 employees and increase revenues by 20 percent annually since 1988. In 1993, just a few months after becoming publicly owned, Steck-Vaughn was the only Austin company recognized by *Forbes* magazine as one of the "200 Best Small Companies in America."

Innovation for Tomorrow's Classrooms

Mayers sees a new day dawning in American education, as teachers rely more heavily on workbooks and other inexpensive materials to supplement basic textbooks. Tradi-

tional texts, he asserts, cost about $25 per copy, are outdated by the time they are published, and are geared toward average students. "Only one child in a class is average," notes Mayers. "Everyone else is either above or below average. We produce materials for them."

Steck-Vaughn publishes supplemental educational materials that are more economical than traditional textbooks, with most costing less than $5 per copy. The company's materials are also more up-to-date: they are revised frequently and can address topics such as multiculturalism long before they are integrated into traditional texts. Most important, however, the company's materials are geared toward students at all levels, which allows teachers to personalize instruction to the individual. For example, a student with a reading disability can cover the same content as the rest of the class using a workbook designed specifically for his or her skill level.

The company produces more than 1,400 titles in virtually all subject areas for elementary, junior high, and high school students. Steck-Vaughn is also a leader in providing basic educational resources for adults, including materials to help students prepare for the GED (General Equivalency Development) diploma. The company began publishing fiction and nonfiction books for schools and public libraries in 1990 and now publishes nearly 1,000 titles for this market.

"Most of our library materials are nonfiction and curriculum based," explains Mayers. "They are written on grade level, so that if a fourth grader is assigned to do a report about the rivers of the world, he can find a reference book appropriate to his level of understanding."

What links all of Steck-Vaughn's

products is the company's commitment to serving customer needs—from product development to marketing. "We are on the phone with our customers after they buy our products to make sure they are satisfied," Mayers says. "We conduct lots of focus groups during the development stage, and we continue testing products after they are in the market. It's an expensive process, but everything we publish is profitable for the company and meets the needs of the student population."

THANKS TO ITS CONSTANT ATTENTION TO THE CHANGING NEEDS OF AMERICA'S STUDENTS, STECK-VAUGHN IS ONE OF THE NATION'S MOST SUCCESSFUL AND INNOVATIVE PUBLISHERS OF EDUCATIONAL MATERIALS FOR CHILDREN AND ADULTS.

Adams Extract Company

JOHN A. ADAMS
FOUNDER
ADAMS EXTRACT CO., INC.

FRED W. ADAMS
OWNER
SECOND GENERATION

JOHN G. ADAMS
OWNER AND PRESIDENT
THIRD GENERATION

JOHN G. ADAMS, JR.
VICE PRESIDENT
FOURTH GENERATION

DURING FOUR GENERATIONS OF FAMILY OWNERSHIP AND management, ADAMS EXTRACT has produced the finest extracts and spices for over a century. From the beginning, customers have come to rely on the quality of ADAMS products.

Today, with a continued dedication to superior quality, John G. Adams, Sr., and John G. Adams, Jr., are carrying on the family tradition of producing the finest food flavorings, spices, and food colors at a reasonable price. ADAMS EXTRACT currently produces well over 100 extracts, spices, and food colors in a variety of sizes, but the company will always be best known for its vanilla extract—simply called ADAMS BEST.

A Texas Success

ADAMS EXTRACT has traced its beginnings to 1889, when John A. Adams was selling extracts in the harsh Michigan climate. In 1905 he moved his family to the warmer Texas climate for his wife's health. Beeville was the original Texas homestead site for this turn-of-the-century pioneer, his business, and his family.

Most vanilla in 1909 was sold in pharmacies and was often labeled "Do not bake or freeze" on the carton. John A. Adams was a pharmacist whose imagination was stirred by his wife's yearning for a flavoring that wouldn't bake or freeze out. Challenged by her observation, Adams announced that he could produce a better vanilla than the one she currently used. Working with just $6.71 worth of materials on the top of an old icebox, he discovered the formula he wanted.

To test the new product,

Mrs. Adams whipped up a cake for the family to try. "John, this is the best flavoring I have ever used," she announced. "Well, that's old man Adams' best," he responded, meaning it was the best he could do. The name has stuck.

The double-strength extract was sold rapidly door-to-door by sons Fred and Don. At night, by the light of kerosene lamps, the boys helped their father print labels, bills, and envelopes on a hand-operated printing press. The first bottle of ADAMS BEST vanilla was sold with a guarantee that if it was not the best vanilla extract the customer had ever used, the company would refund the money, even if the whole bottle had been used.

John A. Adams had three basic principles:

◆ To make the best extract on the market

◆ Always give the customer the best possible service

◆ To guarantee every product sold.

These standards continue to be the backbone of ADAMS EXTRACT today.

The Austin Move

In 1917 the founder's son, Fred, received the first bachelor's degree in business administration from the University of Texas at Austin. He believed in the growth potential Austin offered and, after purchasing the company, moved its headquarters to the capital city in 1922.

From its new home near the

University of Texas campus, the company prospered during both the Great Depression and World War II.

Expansion and Diversification

Shortly after World War II, ADAMS EXTRACT began diversifying its product line and expanding its operations. In 1945, upon returning from the service, Fred's oldest son, John G. Adams, Sr., continued with the company and received a bachelor of arts in chemistry from UT Austin.

Many of the new formulations created after 1946 were

WORLD'S FINEST
VANILLA FLAVORING

contributed by John G. Adams, Jr., including the development of the first successful household butter flavoring. A longtime industry leader, he was the first Texan admitted to the Society of Flavor Chemists and remains the only Texan ever to serve as a board member and president of the Flavor and Extract Manufacturers of the United States. Responsible for setting the current course of success the company is enjoying, Adams realized that customers wanted high-quality spices at affordable prices, and he spearheaded the spice division in the early 1960s.

Adams, who has served as the company's president since 1971, believes the decision to diversify has definitely paid off. In 1991 spice sales exceeded extract sales for the

1955 HOME OF ADAMS EXTRACT CO., INC.

first time. "Nationally, spices have 10 times the sales of extracts," he says, "and they represent the fastest-growing segment of our business."

WORLD CLASS FOOD COLORS

The Family Tradition

Today, ADAMS EXTRACT still follows the strict standards set by John A. Adams when purchasing its spices and other raw materials. "We have a full line of extracts and spices made from the finest ingredients available," says John G. Adams, Jr., vice president and director of operations. "ADAMS EXTRACT ensures the highest quality in its extracts and spices, purchasing them from throughout the United States and worldwide. We are constantly developing new products to meet the changing taste of consumers. That is why we have introduced products such as ADAMS Fajita Seasoning and ADAMS Cajun Seasoning. This company has existed for over 100 years because we stay in step with the times."

After decades of growth, ADAMS EXTRACT has spread its quality far beyond its home state.

Today, the company sells not only in Texas but to many other states and internationally.

WORLD CHAMPION
CHILI POWDER

1922-1955 HOME OF ADAMS EXTRACT CO.

St. David's Medical Center

S T. DAVID'S MEDICAL CENTER IS THE ONLY AUSTIN HEALTH CAR campus with freestanding facilities for acute, psychiatric, and rehabilitation care. With its two professional buildings and extensiv diagnostic, educational, outpatient, and day treatment programs,

St. David's is one of Texas' leading health care providers and the area's only independent, community-owned, not-for-profit medical center.

The medical center's forward-looking mission is to uphold high standards of health care and to meet the health needs of the Austin area by providing health services, leadership, and collaboration.

Combining Innovation and Compassionate Care

The heart of the medical center is St. David's Hospital. The hospital

the hospital remained for nearly 30 years. In 1955 St. David's opened a new 104-bed facility at its current location on 32nd Street and IH-35 and introduced Austin to such innovations as surgical recovery rooms and private labor rooms.

Today, the 320-bed hospital is one of Austin's major health care resources. Each year, St. David's provides treatment for more than 60,000 patients through over 40,000 emergency room visits, more than 5,000 inpatient surgical cases, and an additional 8,000 outpatient surgery cases.

ogists and specially trained nurses available should complications occur.

Austin's Choice for Comprehensive Care

In addition to St. David's Hospita the medical center campus includes The Pavilion at St. David's and St. David's Rehabilitation Center.

The Pavilion at St. David's is an 80-bed freestanding psychiatric hospital with comprehensive mental health and chemical dependency programs for children,

SINCE 1924 ST. DAVID'S HAS GROWN WITH THE AUSTIN COMMUNITY. TODAY, THE MEDICAL CENTER'S 15-ACRE CAMPUS AT 32ND STREET AND IH-35 ENCOMPASSES THREE HOSPITALS, TWO PROFESSIONAL BUILDINGS, AND OTHER MAJOR FACILITIES AND SERVICES.

LOCATED AT THE CORE OF THE MEDICAL CAMPUS, A FLOWER- AND TREE-FILLED PARK PROVIDES A BEAUTIFUL, PEACEFUL SETTING FOR PATIENTS AND VISITORS (FAR RIGHT).

dates back to 1924, when members of St. David's Episcopal Church and others in the community provided funding and leadership to form a nonprofit corporation to purchase the Physicians and Surgeons Hospital, then housed in a Victorian building at the corner of 17th and Rio Grande streets. But the existing facility was too small to serve the growing needs of Austin, with its population of 55,000. Fund-raising for expansion began, and by 1928 enough money had been raised to construct a new 46-bed building next door, where

St. David's offers comprehensive services in major specialties, including open-heart surgery. The hospital's cardiac catheterization lab and cardiac rehabilitation center combine to treat nearly every aspect of heart disease, from prevention to rehabilitation.

Over 4,000 lives begin each year in the hospital's family maternity center, which features cozy labor/delivery/recovery rooms and private postpartum rooms designed to make childbirth more personal for the entire family. A neonatal intensive care unit staffed with neonatol-

adolescents, adults, and seniors. The facility also provides treatmen for eating disorders and offers spe cial programs in chemical dependency. In most cases, both day an inpatient treatment are available.

The 107-bed St. David's Rehabilitation Center provides a comfortable, therapeutic atmosphere i which patients can regain their independence after strokes, spinal cord and head injuries, related neurological disorders, orthopedic surgery, and other conditions. The center includes a skilled nursing unit, a wheelchair fitness center, a

...in management program, and an outpatient rehabilitation program. These treatment options help patients return to comfortable, productive lives as quickly as possible.

Broad Health Care Services

With a total of more than 500 beds, St. David's Medical Center accounts for one-fourth of all hospital beds in the Austin area. However, because of its numerous related services, the medical center has an even greater impact on the health of the community.

For example, the Central Texas Imaging Center, located adjacent to the hospital, offers modern diagnostic facilities, including two MRIs and a CT scanner. This equipment gives physicians more precise information about the body's inner workings than ever before, making possible more accurate and timely diagnoses.

The freestanding Health Resource Center, opened in 1992, provides community health screenings and health education. The facility also offers mammography screening with the area's most advanced equipment, breast self-examination assistance and information, and post-breast-surgery exercise classes and support groups. In addition, the Health Resource Center conducts osteoporosis screenings to determine bone density in postmenopausal women and patients in St. David's eating disorders program.

St. David's also offers Austin women the most advanced programs for in vitro fertilization and gamete intrafallopian transfer, two processes that give realistic hope to couples who have experienced significant difficulty achieving pregnancy.

Austinites also count on the medical center for its on-site Health and Fitness Center, which is open to members and offers professional health assessments, and for Find-A-Physician, a free referral service that provides information about local doctors. The medical center rounds out its offerings with a variety of specialized support groups, seminars, and educational programs.

As the only community-owned hospital in Austin, St. David's stays close to its roots—providing services that target community needs. In addition to offering several million dollars each year in free care for the needy, the medical center is ensuring that thousands of Austinites have access to free or low-cost health care when they need it. For example, St. David's provides funding to enable nearby People's Community Clinic to remain open five evenings a week, thus extending its services to help ensure access to primary health care for Austinites who do not have health insurance. Through such programs, St. David's reaffirms its commitment to the community—and to high standards of health care—every day.

THE HOSPITAL'S NEONATAL NURSERY PROVIDES PROFICIENT CARE AND TECHNOLOGY TO AID THE DEVELOPMENT AND HEALTH OF NEWBORNS (ABOVE).

OPEN-HEART SURGERY IS AMONG THE COMPREHENSIVE CARDIOLOGY SERVICES AVAILABLE AT ST. DAVID'S (ABOVE LEFT).

LABOR/DELIVERY/RECOVERY ROOMS OFFER A HOMELIKE ALTERNATIVE FOR MANY OF THE MORE THAN 4,000 FAMILIES A YEAR WHO UTILIZE THE HOSPITAL'S MATERNITY CENTER (LEFT).

Young & Pratt, Inc.

PARTNERS J.D. YOUNG, A SHEET METAL FITTER, AND FRANK M Pratt, a plumber and pipe fitter, brought their specialty contract ing firm to Austin in 1929. Already established in West Texas, Young & Pratt moved to capitalize on the building boom spurre

by the growth of the University of Texas. During subsequent years, Young & Pratt installed steam boilers, piping, plumbing, and sheet metal in buildings on the UT campus and around Austin.

Despite Young & Pratt's steady business in unsteady economic times, Frank Pratt decided in the late 1930s that Austin was "godforsaken" and left the company to return to West Texas. J.D. Young kept the business going—and growing—and today it is one of Central Texas' most successful mechanical contracting firms.

Innovation, Experience, and Integrity

One of the 600 largest specialty contractors in the country, Young & Pratt specializes in the mechanical portion of commercial and industrial construction and renovation. The company installs plumbing, as well as heating, ventilation, and air-conditioning (HVAC) systems; performs specialized services for

technology companies; and fabricates various metals and piping. Proof of its success is the fact that Young & Pratt doubled in size between 1988 and 1993, years during which most contractors struggled to stay in business.

President Joseph C. Zern, an engineer who became a co-owner when Young retired in 1967, says there is no secret to the company's longevity. "We find a niche and wiggle into it, stay until it gets too crowded, and then find another niche," he explains. "We also still live by J.D. Young's philosophy of standing behind our work. We've never been involved in a lawsuit, because when we foul up, we fix it. We've been around a long time, and we plan to stay around a lot longer."

Zern, who has been sole owner since 1987, is typical of Young & Pratt's staff of 60; most are long-time employees with many years of experience. "We provide continuity of manpower and experience," says

Zern. "When a customer comes back to us, he knows that the employees who originally built th project are probably still here. We're a union shop, and our folks have experience in their trades. Give them drawings of what you want, and they can get the job done."

Over the years, Young & Pratt has steadily added new services a technologies and industries have come to Central Texas. In the ear days, the company specialized in heating, sheet metal, and plumbin It began installing air-conditionin systems in the 1940s, added engineers to design systems in the 1960s, moved into remodeling an renovating in the 1970s, and bega designing and installing high-tech environmental systems in the 1990

The list of projects the compan has worked on is impressive: Palmer Auditorium, Hancock Shopping Center, Medical Park Tower, Bailey Square Medical Building, Driskill Hotel, Scar-

TYPICAL INDUSTRIAL INSTALLATIONS REQUIRE A HIGH LEVEL OF COORDINATION AND A SKILLED WORK FORCE.

PHOTOS BY REAGAN BRADSHAW

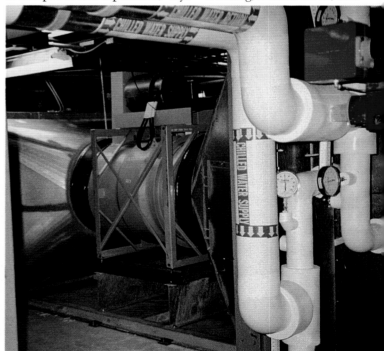

ough Building, Norwood Tower,
d many others, including facili-
es owned by the City of Austin,
niversity of Texas, Southwestern
niversity, and Southwest Texas
ate University.

oving Itself Again and Again
ne arrival in Austin of high-
chnology companies opened a
w chapter for Young & Pratt. For
ample, Motorola chose the com-
ny as its primary contractor for
VAC and related systems during
nstruction of its first Austin clean
om in the mid-1970s. In all cases,
e engineer's specifications had to
followed precisely.

Young & Pratt's work was of such
gh quality that the company was
er hired to work on clean room

YOUNG & PRATT OPERATES A 20,000-
SQUARE-FOOT FABRICATION FACILITY,
WHICH PRODUCES DUCTWORK, PIPE
ASSEMBLIES, AND SPECIALTY ITEMS
FROM SHEET METAL, RAW PIPE, STAIN-
LESS STEEL, AND PLASTIC.

DUCTWORK FITTINGS ARE READIED FOR
SHIPMENT (FAR LEFT).
PHOTOS BY REAGAN BRADSHAW

cilities at Motorola's Oak Hill
int. Today, Young & Pratt has
ongoing contract to provide
echanical contracting services
both of Motorola's Austin-area
cations.

Zern has used the company's
perience with Motorola to de-
lop a specialty in mechanical
ntracting for high-technology
ms. Data General, Abbott Labo-
tories, Advanced Micro Devices,
acor, Inc., and Dupont Photo-
ask, Inc. are among its high-
chnology clients.

"These companies have the high-
t standards imaginable for qual-
," notes Zern. "We have installed
gh-purity process piping at Mo-
rola and product piping at Abbott
boratories. At Abbott, the piping
for IV solution that goes into the
man body, so you can imagine

how pure the product has to be and
how careful and detail-oriented we
have to be."

In addition to stringent quality
standards, high-technology companies often present other special
challenges. For example, installing
plumbing and air-conditioning for
Abbott required employees to be
secured by safety harnesses as they
worked 95 feet above ground inside
the building. Young & Pratt's in-
house safety program—designed
to prevent accidents under such
grueling conditions—has been recognized as one of the nation's most
effective by the Mechanical Contractors Association of America, Inc.

Zern says technology clients also
impose extra-tight construction
deadlines. "We pride ourselves on
timely completion of our contracts," he says.

New Specialties
A growing specialty for Young &
Pratt is energy conservation systems, including retrofitting, replacing, and upgrading systems to make
them more efficient. The company
has retrofitted air-conditioning
equipment in numerous buildings
on the UT campus and has installed
filter systems and chlorinators in
City of Austin swimming pools to
prevent them from having to be
drained nightly.

"We are seeing a real upturn in
construction activity around
Austin," says Zern, "and that is good
news for all of us in the construction trades. I don't expect things to
get less competitive, though, so we
will keep looking for new niches
that are right for us."

Consolidated Insurance Agency

ONSOLIDATED INSURANCE AGENCY TRACES ITS BEGINNINGS TO 1924 and is one of Austin's oldest, largest, and most experienced insurance firms. With more than $20 million in annual sales, the agency provides commercial and personal insurance to over 4,00

customers, some of whom have been on board for more than 60 years. Similarly, Consolidated has maintained relationships with some of the insurance industry's premier carriers for more than half a century and today represents only top-rated carriers.

ans with Consolidated. Some have been with the firm for more than 30 years.

"There really isn't any turnover among our agents because we are all committed to serving our clients," says Pincoffs, noting that a majority of Consolidated's agents

the best companies, so we can ge customers the insurance they nee at a competitive price," Pincoffs says.

Consolidated represents a num ber of respected, financially soun carriers, including Aetna, Continental, Chubb, CNA, Kemper, ar Crum & Forster.

TOMMY HOLT

Commercial Insurance Specialists
As Austin's economy has grown ar diversified, Consolidated has deve oped specialties in numerous line of commercial insurance. Its com mercial customers include many technology firms, as well as restaurants, retail businesses, and communications, construction, manufacturing, professional services, and real estate developmen companies.

"Technology firms have some special concerns that we can help them with," says Brandt. "Propert business interruption, transit, pro uct liability, and directors and officers liability are all important coverages to our commercial clients. They understand the need f these coverages, and they know i can be hard to find. We represen companies that can underwrite these exposures."

Growing companies also have difficulty securing and maintainir adequate coverage because, in many cases, they have experience rapid growth. Consolidated provides the expertise to make sure client outgrows its coverage. "We are well equipped to deal with explosive growth," says Pincoffs. "Some of our clients started very small and, within a few years, had hundreds of millions of dollars in annual revenue. We have the resources and the know-how to wor with those companies."

FROM LEFT: CONSOLIDATED'S SHAREHOLDERS INCLUDE JOHN S. BURNS, JR., AND PETER PINCOFFS. THE FIRM'S OFFICE MANAGER IS BARBARA A. PAULISSEN.

Despite its success and longevity, Consolidated may not be a familiar name to many Austinites. "We don't advertise," says agency President Peter Pincoffs. "People learn about us because of our reputation, and customers stay with us because of our service."

Commitment to Service
Pincoffs, who joined Consolidated in 1974, is one of six partners in the agency. The others—John S. Burns, Jr., Chris Brandt, Joe George, Bess Roberts, and Alan Williams—are also seasoned veter-

are also shareholders. "When you buy a policy through us, you know you will deal with the same agent 10 or 15 years from now. You won't be shuffled off to someone else in the office who doesn't understand your needs."

Consolidated's approach is to spend as much time as necessary getting to know each customer's needs—from simple home and automobile coverage to complex business insurance—then matching those needs with the appropriate insurance company. "We know the best markets, and we work with

Night Hawk Restaurants

FOR MORE THAN 60 YEARS, NIGHT HAWK RESTAURANTS HAVE been a favorite place for Austinites to relax, visit, and enjoy choice steaks, hamburgers, pies, and other specialties. Today, the restaurants have expanded their menus to include more health-conscious

...shes, but one thing hasn't ...anged: Night Hawk Restaurants ...e still the place to go to mix good ...od with good conversation.

Founded in 1932, the original ...ght Hawk was a warm and wel- ...me gathering spot during the ...rk years of the Depression. Its ...me came from the fact that ...nder Harry Akin kept the small ...ngress Avenue eatery open ...ch later than others in town. ...in, a community leader who later ...came mayor, was the heart and ...ul of the Night Hawk, dictating ...gh quality standards for food and ...rvice. He was also a progressive ...d practical businessman, employ- ...g and serving minorities who ...re often excluded from other ...staurants.

Great Food, Great Atmosphere

...om the beginning, the Night ...awk was the spot where political ...d business leaders met for coffee

Senate dining room.

Although the original Night Hawk has closed, two of its off-spring are carrying on the tradition. They are run by Lela Jane Akin Tinstman, widow of Harry Akin, who maintains his high standards for the current generation. The Night Hawk Steakhouse, located at the intersection of Interstate 35 and U.S. 290, is a roomy, lodgelike restaurant popular for business lunches, family dinners, and special occasions ranging from birthdays to holiday parties. The restaurant recently played host to its first wedding.

The Frisco Shop, located at the corner of Burnet Road and Koenig Lane, has a more casual atmosphere and is also open for breakfast. With its longtime staff and loyal clientele, the Frisco often feels more like the site of a family get-together than a place of business. But most important is what

...d conversation, where deals were ...uck over drinks, and where for-...es were made over dinner. ...nong its faithful customers were ...esident Lyndon Johnson and his ...fe Lady Bird, who once had ...ght Hawk "Top Chop't" steaks ...aped like Texas flown to Wash-...ton, D.C., to be served in the

the restaurants have in common: a commitment to quality food and reasonable prices.

Though Night Hawk Restaurants have always been known for their steaks and hamburgers, they also offer a variety of lighter foods such as grilled chicken, salads, and fresh vegetables. Healthier oils and low-

fat milk are used in all recipes to give diners the healthiest, tastiest foods possible. Tinstman is also proud of the restaurants' experienced cooks, managers, and wait staff—some of whom have been with Night Hawk for 35 years or more.

"We have many longtime customers who have been coming to the Night Hawk since it opened," Tinstman says, "and their children and grandchildren eat here, too. They rely on us for consistent quality. That was Harry Akin's way. It's a considerable responsibility, and our staff takes it very seriously."

WITH ITS LONGTIME STAFF AND LOYAL CLIENTELE, THE FRISCO OFTEN FEELS MORE LIKE THE SITE OF A FAMILY GET-TOGETHER THAN A PLACE OF BUSINESS.

THE NIGHT HAWK STEAKHOUSE IS A ROOMY, LODGELIKE RESTAURANT POPULAR FOR BUSINESS LUNCHES, FAMILY DINNERS, AND SPECIAL OCCASIONS (LEFT).

PHOTOS BY LELA JANE AKIN TINSTMAN

Stripling-Blake Lumber Company, Inc.

For MORE THAN 55 YEARS, STRIPLING-BLAKE LUMBER COMPANY has made many friends among Central Texas builders, contractors, and home-owner do-it-yourselfers. The building and home improvement center boasts the area's most extensive selection of

lumber and millwork, expert staff to help customers make the right choice, and three convenient locations in Austin and New Braunfels. The main store at Steck Avenue and Shoal Creek Boulevard in North Austin has more than 40,000 square feet of retail space and 19 acres of lumber, making it one of the area's largest building supply centers.

Stripling-Blake got its start in more humble quarters—a small lumberyard in downtown Lockhart. Founded in 1938 by brothers-in-law A. Stripling and M.W. Blake, the store operated with just one other employee until an Austin branch was opened in 1944. The payroll jumped to four, and the company was on its way.

The post-World War II building boom ushered in a new era for Stripling-Blake. In 1948 the company moved into larger accommodations in North Austin and brought in Kerry G. Merritt, an ex-serviceman who had just completed his business degree. Stripling's only son-in-law, Merritt became a driving force behind the company and still serves as chairman of the board.

In keeping with family tradition, Merritt's son-in-law Alec Beck has served as president since 1983. During that time, Stripling-Blake has grown to more than 300 employees, expanded to a new Austin location in Oak Hill, and opened a store and truss mill in New Braunfels. The company has also won national recognition from *Building Supply Home Centers* as Retailer of the Year and from *Home Center Magazine* as Home Center of the Year.

Service and Selection

"We emphasize specific product lines, like lumber, and offer higher quality and better service to each

PRESIDENT ALEC BECK AND CHAIRMAN OF THE BOARD KERRY MERRITT (ABOVE) HAVE CONTINUED A FAMILY COMMITMENT TO QUALITY, SERVICE, AND VALUE.

CENTRAL TEXAS HAS DEPENDED ON STRIPLING-BLAKE FOR LUMBER AND BUILDING MATERIALS FOR MORE THAN 55 YEARS. THE TWO AUSTIN LOCATIONS CONTAIN OVER 25 ACRES OF LUMBER AND BUILDING MATERIALS (TOP RIGHT).

THE DESIGNERS SHOWCASE AT STRIPLING-BLAKE'S NORTH AUSTIN LOCATION OFFERS HOME OWNERS, ARCHITECTS, DESIGNERS, AND DECORATORS THE LATEST IN DECORATIVE HARDWARE FOR THE HOME (BOTTOM RIGHT).

and every customer," Beck says. "We have a larger selection of sizes and types of lumber than anyone else. We have our own mill where we manufacture doors, trim, and finish products. We even make roof trusses at our factory in New Braunfels—all because customers have come to depend on our quality."

That quality extends to the three

retail locations, with inventory tailored to the needs of the Austin customer. Everything necessary to build, remodel, or maintain a home can be found in one of 10 specialized departments.

Stripling-Blake also puts its experience to work for customers by providing material estimates based on architectural plans, as well as guidance on new construction ma

rials and techniques. The company conducts ongoing product arch and evaluation programs to sure that customers have access the latest technology and quality.

ceeding Expectations
e company's philosophy is sim-
. "Every customer is important
us," Beck says. "Whether they
nt to fix a faucet or build a house,
y will receive the same attention
m everyone in the company. Our
ssion is to exceed the expecta-
ns of everyone who walks
ough our doors, and that applies
every aspect of our business."

Beck adds, "We were founded to serve customers. We still spend just as much time with a small customer as we do with a large one. We believe in treating everyone right."

A Commitment to Austin

Beck, who has lived in Austin most of his life, has been instrumental in getting the company involved in worthy community causes, including the Center for Battered Women, Seton Medical Center, and Habitat for Humanity. He supports many arts and health organizations on a personal level and has served on the boards of such groups as the Greater Austin Chamber of Commerce and the Better Business Bureau, as well as professional organizations such as the Texas Lumberman's Association.

"We are all a part of Austin, and we believe in giving back to the community," Beck says. "We are here because the community has supported us, and we believe you have to give back what you get. We have developed a philosophy of doing business locally as much as possible, because local owners invest more in the community."

Stripling-Blake knows the Austin area, and its attachment to the community is a strong selling point for Beck. "No one else in the retail lumber business has been in this market as long as we have," he says, "and we really know our customers. With home builders, we're out at job sites all the time, so that we know what is needed, and we specialize in products that are appropriate for this market."

Beck adds, "More importantly, we have set the standard for a level of quality that customers have come to expect. They depend on us. Whatever success we achieve in the future will come as a result of the bond we have built through years of hard work."

Stripling-Blake has become such an important supplier to the home-building industry that most houses built in Austin during the past five decades probably include some materials supplied by the company. From the weekend home repairman to specialty contractors and the city's largest home builders, professionals and do-it-yourselfers continue to turn to Stripling-Blake Lumber Company for their building needs.

Graves, Dougherty, Hearon & Moody

GRAVES, DOUGHERTY, HEARON & MOODY IS AN AUSTIN LAW firm founded in 1946. Today, this general practice firm is known for the excellence of its lawyers and its adherence to the highest ethical standards. Graves, Dougherty is large enough to have

expertise in most practice areas, yet small enough to treat each client as an individual.

Helping Companies Relocate to Austin

Austin politics are polarized around environmental issues. The firm's real estate lawyers, led by Terry Bray, represent companies, land-owners, and developers. Since Austin features a sizable contingent of "no growth" voters and the city council reflects that political reality, it takes a skilled and experienced lawyer to navigate the city's zoning and permitting process. The firm has done the development work for numerous large companies relocating to Austin, including Schlumberger Well Services, Lockheed Corporation, and Advanced Micro Devices. Graves, Dougherty also has done most of the general development work on Circle C Ranch,

the fastest-growing planned community in the capital city.

Technology companies are the future of Austin, and the firm has the capability to serve all of the legal needs of such clients. Its intellectual property section handles patent and trademark prosecution and litigation.

A Reputation for Excellence

The firm's most senior and junior lawyers are emblematic of its reputation for excellence. Chrys Dougherty, born in 1915, was educated at Harvard Law School, is fluent in Spanish and French, and is board-certified in estate planning, probate law, and tax law. Chrys was a pioneer in developing the modern Texas practice of estate planning. He served as president of the State Bar of Texas and used his tenure to encourage law firms to provide pro bono legal services to

the indigent. Chrys has always believed that his firm should have the "brightest and best" lawyers, and the firm's newest lawyer fits that criterion. Charles Moody, born in 1966, was educated at Stanford University as an undergraduate and earned his law degree from the University of Texas. He graduated at the top of his class and was editor-in-chief of the *Texas Law Review*. After graduating, Charles clerked for the U.S. Court of Appeals, Fifth Circuit, as well as for the chief justice of the Texas Supreme Court. He also has deep roots in Texas; his grandfather was a state governor.

Graves, Dougherty is also known as a training ground for judges. Two former members of the firm have served on the U.S. Court of Appeals, Fifth Circuit. Another former member was the chief justice of the Texas Supreme Court.

Expertise in Many Practice Areas

At any given time, the firm is handling more than 900 lawsuits for more than 300 clients. Its lawyers handle complex litigation all over the country.

The real estate section serves developers, companies, and landowners in Austin. The firm's lawyers are expert in all forms of real estate financing and are well versed in all local ordinances affecting the development of land in Austin. Graves, Dougherty represents banks and corporate clients of all sizes. Its capabilities include providing comprehensive services in organizing, capitalizing, operating, merging, and selling business entities. Graves, Dougherty also has a distinguished history of representing publicly traded companies and leading banks in Austin.

Over the years, the firm has built an extensive practice in the area of wills, trusts, estates, wealth transfer, and individual planning and counseling. Its lawyers have developed subspecialties in the fields of trust litigation, individual wealth counseling, and retirement planning.

Graves, Dougherty has an active administrative law practice before state agencies, including utility regulation, state tax matters, and oil, gas, and water regulation. The firm represents employers in employment law matters and handles Title VII and wrongful termination litigation for employers. Its patent lawyers specialize in intellectual property litigation and procurement of patents and trademarks. The firm also represents clients located in Mexico who have business dealings or litigation in the United States, as well as U.S. clients interested in doing business in Mexico.

Texas Safety Association

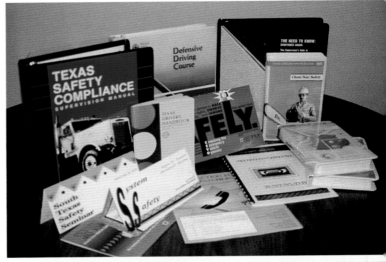

S INCE 1938 THE AUSTIN-BASED TEXAS SAFETY ASSOCIATION HAS worked with individuals, businesses, and government to make Texas a safer place to live, work, and play. With more than 3,300 dues-paying members, it is the largest chapter of the National Safety

Council and one of the nation's most active safety advocates. Its safety programs, public service campaigns, publications, and educational seminars have touched the lives of virtually everyone in the Lone Star State. Throughout its history, TSA has worked to bring together the public and private sectors to work on safety issues.

Protecting Texans

The association was originally formed to confront the growing problem of traffic accidents in the late 1930s. Working with business leaders, public officials, and con-

cerned citizens, TSA conducted an intensive statewide accident prevention campaign, and the association became the leading advocate for standardized driver's education. Over the years, TSA has continued to support driver's education training and has been an effective advocate for motorcycle safety, seat-belt use, defensive driving, and other traffic safety programs.

The association also serves the Lone Star State with a number of innovative programs. In Corpus Christi, for example, TSA implemented Operation Safe City, including a "safety town" exhibit that teaches children about personal and traffic safety. Another pilot project has been developed in several cities to help senior citizens avoid falls, accidental poisoning, and other hazards. These projects have been developed in cooperation with the Meadows Foundation and other entities in the private and

public sectors.

TSA is especially proud of its role in the implementation of administrative license revocation for drunk drivers—a tool that makes it easier to keep DWI offenders off Texas' streets and highways.

Helping Businesses Achieve Total Quality

Today, the association works to keep its corporate members informed about safety legislation and regulations. TSA teaches compliance courses for safety and health, and works with groups across the state on specific safety concerns. The association offers a variety of safety training programs for companies of all sizes and in virtually

every industry. President James P[…] Bearden says TSA's services are becoming even more valuable as companies work to make themselves more competitive. "Naviga[…]ing the 1990s is a challenge for employers and employees alike," [h]e says. "There's a real danger in losing sight of quality and in cuttin[g] corners on safety in the midst of downsizing."

Adds Bearden, "The most impo[r]tant aspect of total quality manage[…]ment is doing a job safely. Members, large and small, can count o[n] us for the technical expertise, ser[…]vices, and training to safeguard their employees at work and in th[e] community."

TSA PROVIDES SAFETY AND HEALTH TRAINING AT ITS AUSTIN HEADQUARTERS (NEAR RIGHT), AS WELL AS MANY OTHER SITES ACROSS THE STATE.

COURSE OFFERINGS AND MATERIALS INCLUDE THE NATIONAL SAFETY COUNCIL'S DEFENSIVE DRIVING COURSE (TOP RIGHT).

TSA STAFF WORK ON QUALITY ASSURANCE STRATEGIES FOR OVERALL OPERATIONS (BOTTOM RIGHT).

Stewart Title Austin, Inc.

BUYING OR SELLING A PROPERTY CAN BE A VERY STRESSFUL experience. It's easy to see why parties to a real estate transaction often walk away more frustrated than satisfied. Stewart Title Austin, Inc. strives to make both parties in a real estate transaction comfortable during the buying process and at closing.

Stewart Title traces its beginning in 1893 when Maco Lee Stewart purchased his first abstract company in Galveston. That organization became the foundation for Stewart Title Guaranty Company, which was incorporated in 1908. Stewart was instrumental in the early development of the title insurance industry, writing the first policy in Texas and helping the government develop regulations for the industry.

As title insurance became more widely purchased and eventually standard in property transactions, Stewart Title grew and opened offices statewide; it now has more than 3,000 U.S. and Canadian offices. The largest title insurance company in Texas, Stewart Title remains one of the largest and oldest companies of its kind in the nation. The publicly traded company—still run by descendants of the Stewart family—has diversified into numerous real estate information services, including mapping, surveying, and computer software.

Stewart Title Austin opened in 1946 and has grown to include three locations and 83 employees, making it the largest title company in Austin. In 1993 it wrote nearly 5,000 title policies with premiums totaling $5.4 million.

"We are known as the traditional, stable title company," says Nicki Tyler, president of Stewart Title Austin. "We bring a lot of history and experience to every transaction, and we pay attention to the details that make our customers happy."

That includes services like completing most title commitments in three days (the fastest turnaround in town), hand delivering commissions to real estate agents if funds are not available at closing, and employing full-time attorneys to provide advice on title law.

Commercial clients are treated to a Stewart trademark: the "Carlotta watercolor." Painted by Carlotta Barker, a Stewart family descendant, watercolors of historical architecture grace the covers of the firm's commercial title commitments. The documents also are arranged in the order in which they will be needed during closing to make it easier for clients to review the transaction. "You don't get that anywhere else in town," Tyler adds.

Committed to the Community

Tyler, who joined Stewart Title in 1992 after nearly 20 years as a real estate banker, is upholding the company's tradition of community involvement. In addition to supporting the Texas Capital Area Builders Association, Stewart Title is active in organizations such as the American Heart Association, United Way, Paramount Theatre, Austin Habitat for Humanity, Center for Battered Women, CASA, Big Brothers/Big Sisters of Austin, and the Greater Austin Chamber of Commerce. The company also has been a major sponsor of the Harris Branch Hot Air Balloon Festival, a popular summer event.

"We believe in professional service and quality," emphasizes Tyler, "and we believe we have an obligation to provide that for our community just as we do for our clients. Stewart Title is proud to participate in Austin's vibrant economy."

SINCE 1946 STEWART TITLE AUSTIN HAS GROWN TO INCLUDE THREE LOCATIONS AND 83 EMPLOYEES IN THE CAPITAL CITY, MAKING IT THE LARGEST TITLE COMPANY IN AUSTIN.

J.C. Evans Construction Company, Inc.

For nearly 40 years, J.C. Evans Construction Company has been building Austin. The full-service construction firm has had a hand in some of the city's most spectacular buildings and land developments and has grown into one of the area's largest employee-owned companies.

Even though it does business only in Texas, J.C. Evans is ranked among the nation's 400 largest construction companies. It provides a full range of construction services, including general commercial contracting, excavation, site preparation, subdivision development, environmental work, and utility installation.

The J.C. Evans Construction Company has made an indelible mark on the city of Austin, and its work can be seen throughout the capital city: office buildings, corporate headquarters, government facilities, schools, and even the streets in many neighborhoods. Among its repeat customers are Motorola, 3M, the University of Texas, IBM, Southwestern Bell, Austin Cablevision, and the State of Texas.

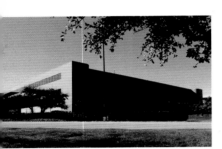

J.C. EVANS PROVIDES A FULL RANGE OF CONSTRUCTION SERVICES, INCLUDING GENERAL COMMERCIAL CONTRACTING, EXCAVATION, SITE PREPARATION, SUBDIVISION DEVELOPMENT, UTILITY INSTALLATION, AND ENVIRONMENTAL WORK.

THE FIRM'S MANAGEMENT (BOTTOM RIGHT) AND ALL OF ITS EMPLOYEE-OWNERS TAKE PRIDE IN THEIR WORK AND ARE COMMITTED TO KEEPING THE COMPANY COMPETITIVE.

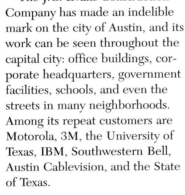

Building on an Austin Family Tradition

Founder J.C. Evans had a solid background in Austin construction when he opened his own excavation and general contracting business in 1955. The experience he had gained working on such major construction projects as Mansfield Dam on Lake Travis, coupled with his own determination, helped ensure success for the fledgling company. As the firm grew, his sons and son-in-law also got involved in the business.

In 1989 Blake Kuhlman, who had served as chief financial officer since 1982, took over management of the company and supervised its transition from family ownership to an employee-owned business.

As president and chief executive officer, Kuhlman also has overseen the modernization and expansion of J.C. Evans Construction. Today, the firm has more than 580 employ-ees in Austin and Dallas, and maintains a modern, $10 million equipment fleet. A 16-acre, in-house repair facility in North Austin helps ensure that all equipment stays in top working order. A sophisticated computerized management information system allows J.C. Evans to manage its projects to produce quality work in a timely manner.

Technology and expertise not-withstanding, Kuhlman believes the success of J.C. Evans Construction Company will remain linked to its team of dedicated employees. The employee-owners take pride in their work and are committed to keeping the company competitive. With this winning combination, J.C. Evans is poised to play an integral role in the future growth of Austin.

IEC CORPORATION

IN TODAY'S COMPETITIVE BUSINESS WORLD, AUSTIN-BASED IEC IS a rarity—a successful family-owned business that has grown and prospered for nearly 40 years. Founded in 1955 by master machinist Joe McQueen, the slip ring assembly manufacturer has been run by

his wife Beatrice since 1978, when Joe retired to devote his time to ranching.

As IEC president, Beatrice McQueen continues the company's commitment to quality materials, design, and workmanship combined with outstanding customer service.

Serving Customers Around the World

Slip ring assemblies are electromechanical devices used to transfer electrical energy from a stationary object to a rotating object. Joe McQueen designed the devices for use in oil well logging, but they are now also used in aeronautics, food processing, packaging, offshore oil drilling, and other industries.

Today, the company serves government and corporate clients in North and South America, Europe, Korea, and Australia. It also has a representative based in Scotland. IEC's standard and custom slip ring assemblies have gone to the moon, to the bottom of many oceans, and even to Monaco's Marine Museum as part of a Jacques Cousteau exhibit. They are commonly used on support ships, allowing the transmission of signals to submersible vehicles.

IEC is one of the few companies that manufactures slip ring assemblies as its main line of business. As part of its longtime commitment to service, the company maintains records on all orders, allowing customers to rebuild or replace components of every assembly ever sold. "We make good products, and we support them," says Beatrice McQueen. "We find out what the customer wants, when they want it, and how they want it. The way I see it, all you have to your name is a good product and happy customers."

Occasionally that means going out of the way. Several years ago, for example, a custom-built assembly was shipped to Canada with the wrong wires attached. Less than an hour after receiving a call from the customer, McQueen had two employees on a plane to Canada to make repairs.

"You'd be amazed how many people heard that story and called us because of it. They decided we're the kind of company they want to do business with," she says. "Of course, we'd prefer not to make mistakes, but when we do, we make things right."

A Family Organization

IEC's success has been built on quality, careful management, and good employees. The McQueens' daughter, Diana McQueen Hudson, and son-in-law, John Paul Hudson, serve as vice presidents. Their grandchildren, Heather and Casey Hudson, have also grown up in the company. About one-third of IEC's 25 employees have served the company for more than 20 years.

"This really is a family organization," says McQueen, who is known as "Mama" to most of her employees, as well as to hundreds of area

teenagers she works with through the Austin-Travis County Livestock Show and Rodeo. A longtime supporter of the event, McQueen bought the 1992 Grand Champion steer for $20,000—ensuring its owner a college education. She also hired the teenager to work part-time at IEC.

FOUNDED IN 1955 BY MASTER MACHINIST JOE McQUEEN, IEC REMAINS HEADQUARTERED IN AUSTIN (ABOVE).

"THIS REALLY IS A FAMILY ORGANIZATION," SAYS COMPANY PRESIDENT BEATRICE McQUEEN, WHO IS KNOWN AS "MAMA" TO MOST OF HER EMPLOYEES (ABOVE LEFT).

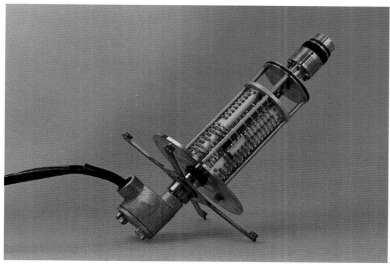

"I can't say enough about these kids and the work they put into raising their animals," she says. "To watch those little angels with their animals is one of the most satisfying things I do."

IEC MANUFACTURES SLIP RING ASSEMBLIES FOR CLIENTS IN NORTH AND SOUTH AMERICA, EUROPE, KOREA, AND AUSTRALIA (ABOVE).

Ernst & Young

ERNST & YOUNG, THE FIRST MAJOR PROFESSIONAL SERVICES FIRM to open an office in Austin, maintains the city's largest accounting practice and provides specialized services to meet the needs of existing and emerging companies. ◆ Widely recognized as the

world's leading integrated professional services firm, Ernst & Young has more than 600 offices worldwide, including 100 in the United States. The company represents more firms among the Fortune 500 and Business Week Best 100 Small Companies than any of its competitors and is the national leader in

◀ GUERRERO PHOTOGRAPHIC GROUP

RON GARRICK, AUSTIN OFFICE MANAGING PARTNER, HOSTS ERNST & YOUNG'S ENTREPRENEUR OF THE YEAR™ BANQUET, THE "EVENT OF THE YEAR" FOR LOCAL ENTREPRENEURS (ABOVE).

SCOTT YORE AND KAY MATTHEWS OF THE FIRM'S HIGH-TECH GROUP PLAN AN UPCOMING SEMINAR (TOP RIGHT).

revenues from accounting, auditing, and tax services. Nationwide, Ernst & Young is known for the quality of service it provides to the consumer products, financial services, health care, insurance, manufacturing/high-technology, media and entertainment, and real estate industries.

A Team Approach

Because so many business issues are industry specific, Ernst & Young adheres to a team approach that integrates industry knowledge with expertise in various disciplines. Teams provide seamless service for all aspects of a client's business concerns, including audit and accounting services, tax services, insurance actuarial services, management consulting, and a variety of special services.

Ernst & Young's Entrepreneurial Services Group, for example, is the U.S. leader in providing a broad range of integrated services to owner-managed companies. From developing business plans and locating financing to preparing capital development strategies, the group caters its services to help start-up companies grow and prosper.

In Austin, Ernst & Young has a history of working with companies throughout their growth process. The firm opened its local office in 1962 to provide better service to Tracor, Inc., one of the capital city's landmark high-tech firms—and a client for more than 30 years.

Ernst & Young has since developed Austin's largest professional service practice for high-tech companies. With an outstanding staff experienced in computers and peripherals, software, semiconductors, telecommunications, and biotechnology, the firm provides unmatched high-technology expertise. Its client list includes the majority of the city's top 10 publicly traded technology employers, and the firm has helped countless smaller businesses become more competitive. The Austin office also offers a variety of seminars and public forums, including newsletters, executive roundtables, and financing forums.

Personalized and Professional Service

With six partners and a staff of approximately 70, Ernst & Young delivers the personalized service and expertise necessary to handle its clients' diverse needs. And as Austin's business landscape has changed, the firm has extended its practice to accommodate new industries. For example, Ernst & Young serves virtually every privately owned hospital in Austin, as well as most of the city's major health care businesses. The company also handles a number of local consumer products clients.

The Austin office further encourages business development in the city by hosting Ernst & Young' respected Entrepreneur of the Year™ program; the local awards ceremony has become an annual highlight for entrepreneurs and business leaders. In 1988 Austinite Michael Dell, founder of Dell Computer Corp., received the national Entrepreneur of the Year™ award.

As it has for more than 30 years Ernst & Young looks forward to providing diverse professional services for a variety of local clients and remains committed to the aggressive role it has chosen to pla in Austin's growth.

Westminster Manor

A WEST AUSTIN LANDMARK, WESTMINSTER MANOR HAS PRO-
vided hassle-free living for retired Central Texans for over 25
years. Constructed in 1967 by the First Presbyterian Church
and now managed by LifeCare Services,™ it continues to be

Austin's only "life care" facility.

"A life care community is one where the needs of people are met on an ongoing basis," explains Executive Director Jim Triplett. The residents of Westminster Manor have access to a health center 24 hours a day, seven days a week, but Triplett insists quality of life is as important as health care. "We want to add life to years," he says, "not years to life."

The Manor offers more than a dozen apartment floor plans tailored to the needs of singles or married couples. Meals are served in an elegant dining room, or residents can cook for themselves.

Typical planned activities include shopping trips, out-of-town excursions, religious services, club meetings, and movie screenings. Live musical and theatrical performances are scheduled in the 150-seat auditorium named for the late Harris Bell, a member of the First Presbyterian Church that was instrumental in founding the Manor.

"My husband and I love Westminster Manor," says 67-year-old resident Sue Wallace, president of the Resident's Association. "No maintenance, no yard work, no cooking. I tell our friends that I feel as if I'm on vacation every day of the year."

Adding Life to Years

Like most Westminster Manor residents, the Wallaces are successful retired professionals who wanted to give up the daily grind of housework, home maintenance, and security concerns without sacrificing stimulating companionship and interesting activities. They were drawn by the other residents—including retired physicians, lawyers, professors, judges, engineers, and others—as well as by the active retirement lifestyle.

When they purchase their apartments, Manor residents know that their lifetime health needs will be met. Residents must not require bed care when they move in, but if their health needs change, skilled nursing care is available for as long as necessary. All services are provided on site, at virtually no additional charge, under the direction of the resident's personal physician.

"My mother was at Westminster for almost nine years, and she got excellent care," recalls Sue Wallace. "She was in a good atmosphere, and she was happy. It was the kind of care I wanted for myself, and it's the kind of care I want for my husband Reuben if I am not here to give it to him."

Many residents are attracted by a unique purchase plan that allows up to 90 percent of the entrance fee to be returned to them or to their estates. "I call it the have-your-cake-and-eat-it-too plan," says resident Irene Bowlin. "I have a beautifully decorated apartment.

It's convenient, and they offer transportation and plenty of activities. But best of all, my son will receive 90 percent of my investment through my estate."

Westminster Manor prides itself on its ability to offer complete care for its residents. The first-rate "life care" plan is only the tip of the iceberg. "Our distinctive difference," Triplett maintains, "is the quality of life afforded to our people."

WESTMINSTER MANOR OFFERS HASSLE-FREE LIVING IN AN ATTRACTIVE AND RELAXING ENVIRONMENT.

THE MANOR HAS BEEN A PART OF THE DYNAMIC AUSTIN COMMUNITY SINCE 1967.

PHOTOS COURTESY TEXAS DEPARTMENT OF COMMERCE

Texas Instruments

AUSTIN'S HERITAGE AS A COMMERCIAL TECHNOLOGY CENTER has always been linked with activities at Texas Instruments. Since 1958, when a young TI scientist named Jack Kilby invented the integrated circuit, the corporation has been a leader in

developing and manufacturing products that revolutionize the electronics industry and impact global markets. Kilby's invention and the semiconductor-based technologies that followed continue to support the growth of myriad technology firms that drive Austin's vibrant economy today.

Headquartered in Dallas, TI was founded as Geophysical Services in 1930. The company originally performed seismography for oil exploration. In 1951 Geophysical

1 million square feet under one roof, the Northwest Austin facility ranks among the city's largest structures. The site also serves as the world headquarters for Texas Instruments Custom Manufacturing Services, a business unit that provides original equipment manufacturers the flexibility to leverage TI's expertise in state-of-the-art design, engineering, manufacturing, and assembly processes. Through the utilization of these TI capabilities, customers take

9002 registration. This places TI in the best position in the industry to offer customers consistent quality standards regardless of where the products are manufactured. TI's Custom Manufacturing Services business is ranked by analysts as one of the world's top five contract manufacturers of electronics.

Texas Instruments Defense Systems and Electronics Group (DSEG), one of three groups with operations in Austin, is proudly flying the flag of the Malcolm

TEXAS INSTRUMENTS OCCUPIES A 250-ACRE SITE IN NORTHWEST AUSTIN WITH NEARLY 1 MILLION SQUARE FEET OF OPERATIONS UNDER ONE ROOF. DEER AND OTHER WILDLIFE SHARE THE GROUNDS SURROUNDING THE CAMPUS.

Services renamed itself Texas Instruments and has since evolved into a high-technology leader with 60,000 employees operating in 30 countries and 1993 worldwide revenue in excess of $8 billion. TI's many products and services include semiconductor components; defense electronic systems; software productivity tools; printers, notebook computers, and consumer electronic products; custom engineering and manufacturing services; electrical controls; and metallurgical materials.

The TI Austin facility began operations in 1967 and is one of the company's largest manufacturing sites outside Dallas. With nearly

advantage of many strategic business opportunities by shortening their time to market and delivering products in a manner that is both cost-effective and expedient.

Dedication to Total Quality
Emphasizing the company's commitment to "Customer Satisfaction Through Total Quality," all major TI sites involved in Custom Manufacturing Services—Austin, Lubbock, and Temple, Texas; Kuala Lumpur, Malaysia; Rieti and Aversa, Italy—have received ISO

Baldrige National Quality Award. The Austin group, which produces printed wiring boards for military electronics, shares this award with employees from other DSEG sites who qualified for the prestigious award in 1992. In the future, the Austin site will serve the needs of other military customers and will apply defense-oriented technologies and solutions for commercial customers.

Telecom Systems, TI's third business unit in Austin, is one of its most entrepreneurial. A growing

rategic business unit, Telecom
ystems is developing voice-
ctivated telephone services,
cluding voice dialing and caller
thorization, which make it easier
r telephone companies to deliver
array of information services.
his enterprise merges TI's 25
ears of speech recognition re-
arch and development with its
tensive semiconductor expertise
create advanced voice and multi-
edia solutions.

n Advocate for the Environment
ne of the guiding principles at
xas Instruments is to make posi-
e contributions to the commu-
ty. In Austin, the company strives
achieve this goal in many ways.
owever, no effort is more signifi-
nt than TI's commitment to
otecting the environment. This
deavor is exemplified by an
gressive waste reduction and en-
gy management program that has
abled the company to eliminate
e use of chlorofluorocarbons
FCs) from its manufacturing
ocesses. In addition, TI Austin
cycles more than 30 percent of all
ater used in manufacturing—
out 36 million gallons per year—
d has progressive recycling
ograms for paper, cardboard,
od, and aluminum. TI has been
cognized for its environmental

protection programs with a series of
awards from the Greater Austin
Chamber of Commerce as well as
other local organizations, and the
company's environmental initiatives have been held as a model for
other corporations. Ongoing management reviews and dedicated environmental staff audits ensure that
the site complies with the CLEAN
TEXAS 2000 initiative sponsored
by the Texas National Resources
Conservation Commission.

To many Austinites, however,
Texas Instruments' most visible
environmental program is the establishment and maintenance of
a 250-acre wildlife preserve surrounding the TI campus. Deer and
other wildlife occupy the preserve
in abundance, with herd manage-

ment assistance provided by the
Texas Parks and Wildlife Department. The TI Austin campus also
practices Xeriscaping, a form of
landscaping that creates an attractive environment by using hardy,
low-maintenance plants which are
native to the area.

Texas Instruments is committed
to the development of new technologies and to continuously making
improvements through total quality
processes, all in congruence with
protection of its natural surroundings. In keeping with the company
culture of striving for excellence
and being the benchmark, Texas
Instruments is proudly leading the
way in making Austin and the world
a better place to live.

Trammell Crow Central Texas, Inc.

BEST KNOWN AS A TRAILBLAZING REAL ESTATE DEVELOPER, TH Trammell Crow Company has evolved into a full-service real estate firm offering construction, leasing, management, and othe professional services to a diverse group of clients. The company'

Austin-based subsidiary, Trammell Crow Central Texas, Inc., owns and/or manages more than 20 million square feet of commercial space, making it the area's largest commercial property manager.

Dallas-based Trammell Crow pioneered such concepts as speculative building, atrium architecture, and the use of public art in office buildings. The company today continues this tradition of innovation as it expands the role of real estate services to meet a changing market. One thing that isn't changing, however, is the company's focus on the needs of the communities it serves. Trammell Crow still relies on the employees in its 70 U.S. markets to know what works best in their own cities.

An Invaluable Business Partner

Trammell Crow Central Texas, one of the corporation's eight regional divisions, handles operations in Austin, San Antonio, Corpus

▲ JAMES M. INNES

Christi, and South Texas. The division manages about 250 office, retail, and industrial buildings for more than 50 owners with more than 2,000 tenants.

In addition to building and leasing space, the company is constantly developing new services. For example, Trammell Crow Central Texas now offers its expertise in every phase of development—from land planning and permitting to property management—for companies that are building and/or occupying their own buildings. By outsourcing these time-consuming tasks to an experienced and proven expert, client companies can concentrate on their own businesses and often reduce costs.

This new service is just one example of the extra advantage the company gives clients in Texas and across the nation. For more than two decades, Trammell Crow Central Texas has been an invaluable partner that combines extensive international development experience with stability, knowledge of the local market, and a commitment to quality.

Since coming to the capital city in 1968, the company has change the Austin skyline and has raised the standards for commercial buil ing with its unique brand of stylis

high-quality development. Trammell Crow's attention to detail ca be found throughout Austin. You can see it in the modern, streamlined design of its downtown offic at 301 Congress. You can see it in the use of amenities such as underground utilities, landscaping, and jogging track at Braker Center, a industrial park in North Austin. And you can see it in the careful integration of hotel, office, and industrial uses at Southpark, located on I-35 at Ben White Boulevard.

The crown jewel of the Austin division's properties may well be the Arboretum, a bustling multiuse development at Highway 183 and Loop 360 that combines offic and retail space with a luxury hote In addition to attracting shoppers diners, moviegoers, office worker and hotel guests, the Arboretum a magnet for families and couples who stop by to relax by the fountain, enjoy the spectacular Hill Country views, trek down the nature trail to the duck pond, or pla on the nearly life-sized marble co statues.

THE ARBORETUM, A BUSTLING MULTI-USE DEVELOPMENT AT HIGHWAY 183 AND LOOP 360, COMBINES OFFICE AND RETAIL SPACE WITH A LUXURY HOTEL (RIGHT).

TRAMMELL CROW'S ATTENTION TO DETAIL IS EVIDENT IN THE MODERN, STREAMLINED DESIGN OF ITS DOWNTOWN OFFICES AT 301 CONGRESS (BELOW).

PMG Peat Marwick

A T KPMG PEAT MARWICK, SUCCESS BREEDS BOLDNESS. THE world's largest accounting firm has taken dramatic steps to strengthen its position as the global leader in business financial services by completely reorganizing itself. ◆ In a striking depar-

re from tradition, KPMG is now ructured along seven business ies: energy; manufacturing, retail- g, and distribution; information d communications; financial ser- ces; health care and life sciences; vernment services; and higher ucation, research, and other not- r-profit business. As a result, the m offers financial services that e tailored to the client's needs d based upon extensive knowl- ge of the client's industry.

For customers in the Austin area, e new alignment adds value to PMG's existing services by pro- ling unparalleled global access to ancial experts in targeted busi- ss areas. It also opens the door r new services to help local com- nies become more competitive in e international marketplace.

PARTNERS AT KPMG PEAT MARWICK IN AUSTIN ASSEMBLE A TEAM OF PROFESSIONALS TAILORED TO EACH CLIENT'S NEEDS.

cused on Austin

ome people consider our re- ganization to be radical, but it is oted in our commitment to cus- mer service," says Stan Sewell, anaging partner of the Austin fice. "The world is too complex d business moves too fast for one rson to keep track of all the nds in one industry. We recog- ze that in order to be the best, we o have to be the most focused." KPMG has been focused on ustin since 1968, when it became e first Big Six accounting firm to en a local office. Its staff of 70, cluding about 60 professionals, is tively involved in the financial rvices, insurance, government rvices, and health care industries. e firm's information and com- inications practice, which serves extensive roster of Austin-based chnology customers, is one of fastest growing business lines. 'e have a diversified practice in ustin, including public and private mpanies of all sizes in all of our

primary focus markets," explains Sewell.

With services ranging from ad- vice on start-ups and business plans to complex tax issues, KPMG can help companies at virtually every stage of their development. Under the firm's new structure, partners assemble a team of professionals tailored to each client's needs. "Our strong global and national practices are tremendous assets because we can garner resources in a hurry to help our local clients solve prob- lems," Sewell adds. For example, KPMG's international liaison desk helps Austin clients resolve issues overseas by finding the right pro- fessionals anywhere in the world.

An Eye to the Future

KPMG's structure emphasizes its international nature. With more than 830 offices in 125 countries, the firm employs more than 74,000 professionals and serves more than 40,000 clients—including 35 per- cent of the world's top 1,000 com-

panies. "The economy and business in general are becoming more in- ternational," says Sewell. "We an- ticipate larger organizations doing broader but similar things, like the recent mergers of cable and tele- phone companies. Our new struc- ture aligns our practice groups along the ways we see business restructuring now and for the fore- seeable future."

The realignment also has pointed out opportunities for new services derived from KPMG's traditional strengths. For example, the firm has created a capital desk to match capital supply and demand. Other new services include consulting on regulatory issues, benchmarking, and profit enhancement.

"We are more than just accoun- tants," stresses Sewell. "We know our clients' business better than ever before, and we can provide value-added services by leveraging our global resources for their benefit."

Amelia Bullock Realtors, Inc.

WHEN AMELIA BULLOCK AND BARBARA WALLACE MET IN 1969, neither dreamed they were embarking on an association that would grow into a major Austin company. Now, more than 20 years later, they are co-owners of Amelia Bullock

Realtors, Inc., one of the largest locally owned real estate companies in Austin history.

"Amelia and I became friends when she helped my family find a house after we relocated from Houston," recalls Wallace. "By the time we closed on the house, Amelia had opened her own business. I soon went to work with her as an agent." The company has been growing ever since.

The associates of Amelia Bullock Realtors specialize in residential real estate and relocation services. Bullock and Wallace pride them-

MORE THAN 20 YEARS AFTER FOUNDING THE FIRM, BARBARA WALLACE AND AMELIA BULLOCK ARE CO-OWNERS OF ONE OF THE LARGEST LOCALLY OWNED REAL ESTATE COMPANIES IN AUSTIN HISTORY.

selves on their team of experienced, service-oriented professionals—almost half of whom have been with the company longer than 10 years.

"This firm has a definite personality," says Bullock. "You can recognize our associates by their dedication to providing good service and their respect for customers. We like to let our customers know that we appreciate their business."

A Service Orientation

The associates at Amelia Bullock Realtors deliver a variety of services that make buying or selling a home easier.

One of the firm's most popular offerings is *Greater Austin Homes*

Magazine, a monthly publication with a circulation of nearly 20,000 that features photographs and descriptions of homes the agency lists for sale. The company also researches lending options and provides computerized assessment of home values. In addition, Amelia Bullock Realtors is the exclusive Austin affiliate for the renowned Sotheby's International Realty.

Dedication to service has made Amelia Bullock Realtors the real estate firm of choice for residents and newcomers alike. In fact, the company has led the city in residential listing sales volume every year since tracking began in 1982. The figures reflect, most of all, a high level of customer satisfaction. "It is especially rewarding to know that much of our business comes from repeat customers and referrals," says Wallace, "and that many of our agents and customers become good friends."

Dedication to Newcomers

Amelia Bullock Realtors has been working with companies for more than 20 years to help employees find the right house and feel at home when they move to Austin. The agency has provided newcomers with the popular *Overnight Austinite* handbook. This copy-

righted 200-page notebook is an indispensable tool that helps new residents find their way around their adopted home city.

The agency recently produced the award-winning "Austin Alive!"—a popular video used by numerous organizations as both an educational tool and a recruiting aid to promote Austin to prospective employees and employers. In 1993 the video received a Telly Award in the Public Service category at the 14th Annual Telly Awards in Cincinnati, Ohio.

Amelia Bullock Realtors also works with local organizations to help make Austin a better place. In addition to supporting numerous community and arts organizations, the agency's annual food drive is a primary provider to the Caritas food pantry.

Amelia Bullock and Barbara Wallace want to make living in and relocating to Austin as pleasant as possible. The company's dedicated associates and the extra services they offer have made a big difference for many families. The owners also want to "get the word out" about Austin. "It's a place that we truly believe is one of the best places on earth," says Bullock.

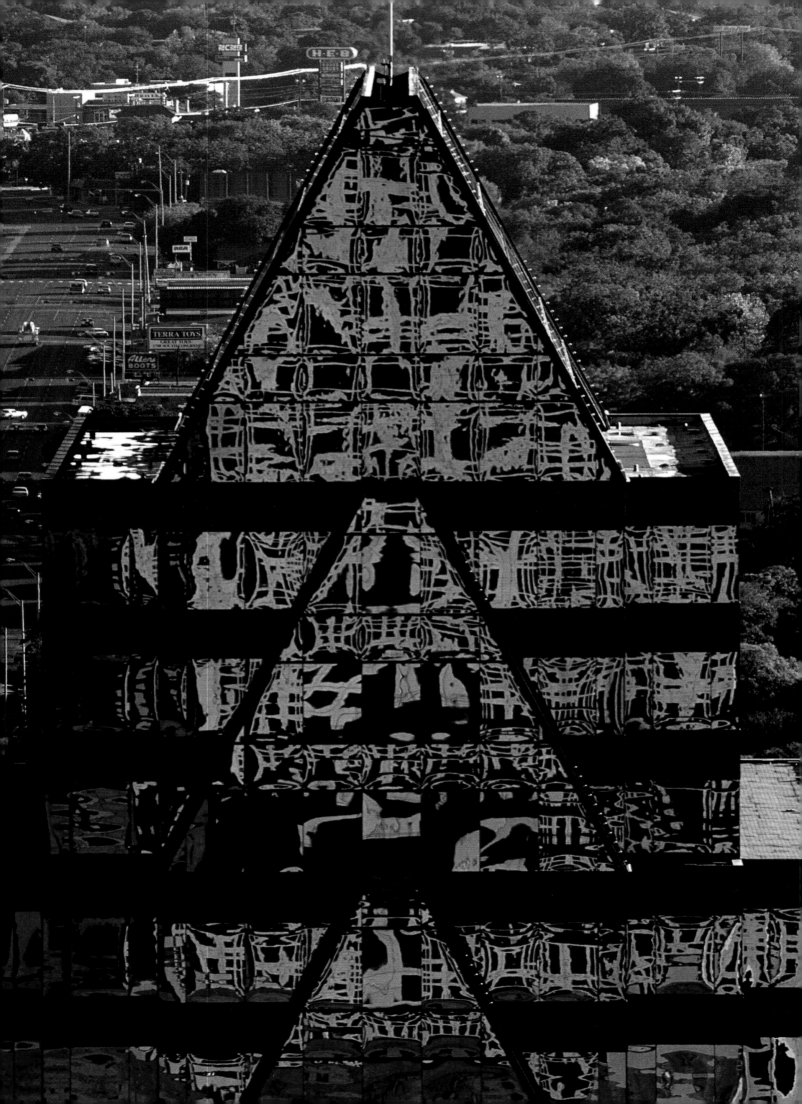

1971-1994

Year	Company	Year	Company
1971	State Farm Insurance Companies	1986	Barton Creek Properties
1972	Austin Community College	1986	Eden Box & Company Real Estate
1972	Espey, Huston & Associates, Inc.	1986	PCA Health Plans of Texas, Inc.
1973	Austin Career Consultants, Inc./Career Consultants Temporaries	1986	Technology Works, Inc.
1973	Hancock & Piedfort, P.C.	1986	VTEL Corporation
1974	Motorola, Inc.	1987	Austin Trust Company
1976	Harris Branch/Provident Development Company	1987	Buffington Homes, Inc.
1976	National Instruments	1987	Doubletree Hotel Austin
1979	Advanced Micro Devices	1987	EMC Automation
1979	Delta Air Lines, Inc.	1987	Guest Quarters Suite Hotel
1979	Prime Cable	1987	Horizon Savings Association
1981	American Airlines	1987	SEMATECH
1981	Fisher-Rosemount Systems, Inc.	1988	Franklin Federal Bancorp
1981	ROLM, A Siemens Company	1989	Conquest Airlines
1981	Tandem Computers Incorporated	1989	GLG Energy Inc.
1982	Frost National Bank-Austin	1989	MaxServ
1982	Lockheed Missiles & Space Co., Inc.-Austin Division	1989	National Market Share, Inc.
1982	Minco Technology Labs, Inc.	1989	Reedie-York & Associates, Inc.
1982	South Austin Medical Center	1989	Tivoli Systems, Inc.
1983	Austin Convention and Visitors Bureau	1990	International Biomedical, Inc.
1983	ITT Sheraton Reservations Center	1990	Strasburger & Price, L.L.P.
1983	Pharmaco LSR Inc.	1990	Summagraphics Corporation
1984	Littlefield Real Estate Company	1991	ATS Travel
1984	Price Waterhouse	1991	Ions Incorporated-Austin
1984	XeTel Corporation	1991	Oppenheimer Environmental Company, Inc.
1985	Geraghty & Miller, Inc.	1992	Apple Computer, Inc., U.S. Customer Support Center
1985	Liberty National Bank	1992	Guaranty Federal Bank, F.S.B.
1985	SAS Institute Inc.	1992	Hawthorn Suites Hotel
1985	SicolaMartin	1993	Worthen National Bank of Texas
1986	Amaturo Group Ltd.	1993	Loye W. Young, P.C.

The evolution of Austin's changing downtown might best be personified by the Gold Bank One Tower located at 221 West Sixth Street. Built in the early 1970s, it was one of the first skyscrapers in the city. And during the 1980s, it was occupied by a succession of banks during the merger/name-changing era. Remember the address, though, because the appearance won't ever be the same. During 1994 the gold-colored glass was replaced by more trendy, smoke-colored panes (page 233).
Park Street

From its founding in 1839 through the 1970s, Austin had a definite laid-back feel to it. Then, in the 1980s, the secret got out, and suddenly everyone wanted to be here. The population mushroomed, land values skyrocketed, and the face of downtown transformed into a metropolis (opposite).
Park Street

State Farm Insurance Companies

MILLIONS OF TEXANS TURN TO STATE FARM INSURANCE Companies to protect their most precious possessions—their homes, their automobiles, and most importantly, their families. It's a duty the state's largest insurer takes seriously.

"When we say that State Farm is a 'Good Neighbor,' it's not just a slogan but the underpinning of everything we do," says Bruce Romig, South Texas regional vice president in Austin. "We strive for friendly, quality service for our policyholders and top-notch training for our agents and employees. We also work to enhance people's lives in the community. That's part of being a good neighbor."

Although it has rural roots—the company was founded in 1922 to

major employer through community programs that emphasize education and safety. The Good Neigh Bear was created to teach school children about topics such as 911, poison safety, traffic lights, and pedestrian safety. Smoke Detectives, a fire safety program, is available to schools for students in kindergarten through sixth grade. These programs, which are provided at no charge, are used by dozens of local schools each year.

In 1993 State Farm was recog-

ages its employees to become involved by volunteering, voting, and getting to know their elected officials. "It sounds a little corny, but we care about our employees and our community," says Romig. "The community supports our business, and it's important for us to support the community."

At a time when many insurance companies are reconsidering their involvement in Texas markets, State Farm is renewing its commitment to Lone Star communities. A new 470,000-square-foot office complex on 71 acres near the intersection of Highway 620 and Parmer Lane was completed in mid-1994. The entire campus is designed using Xeriscaping, a new idea in landscaping that involves minimal alteration and relies on hardy native plants accustomed to the local climate. Maintaining a natural Texas look, the new facility combines classic architecture with state-of-the-art electronics to cre-

IN MID-1994 STATE FARM COMPLETED A 470,000-SQUARE-FOOT OFFICE COMPLEX ON 71 ACRES NEAR THE INTERSECTION OF HIGHWAY 620 AND PARMER LANE.

STATE FARM'S GOOD NEIGH BEAR WAS CREATED TO TEACH SCHOOL CHILDREN ABOUT TOPICS SUCH AS 911, POISON SAFETY, TRAFFIC LIGHTS, AND PEDESTRIAN SAFETY (RIGHT).

insure Illinois farmers—State Farm is big business. It is the nation's largest insurer of automobiles and family homes, and its life insurance operation is one of the 10 largest. A mutual company owned by its policyholders, State Farm is considered one of the country's best-managed companies, with a history of stability and profitability far above the industry average.

In Texas, State Farm insures more than 2.7 million automobiles and nearly 1 million homes. It also has more than $13 billion of life insurance in force. Headquartered in Austin since 1971, the South Texas regional office employs about 1,000 people who serve 2.5 million policyholders and assist agents in the southern half of the state.

Committed to the Capital City

State Farm's impact reaches far beyond its role as an insurer and

nized as Adopt-A-School's Adopter of the Year for its volunteer and financial support of area schools. The company also supports United Way, Crimestoppers, the American Red Cross, Special Olympics, and a variety of other organizations.

Internally, State Farm encour-

ate a more productive workplace.

"We believe in the value of our insurance products to our customers," Romig says. "Our new building is a symbol of the commitment we have in continuing to provide excellent service to the people of Texas."

Espey, Huston & Associates, Inc.

ALTHOUGH ESPEY, HUSTON & ASSOCIATES, INC. HAS BEEN active in Austin for over 20 years, its local contributions have most often been in supporting roles without high visibility. This contrasts the firm's statewide reputation as a high-profile leader

in environmental and engineering consulting for major industries such as electric utilities and energy developers. Locally, the company's broad identity reflects a home-grown approach to problem solving based on a wide range of capabilities and experience.

Charles Jasper, president of Espey, Huston & Associates, describes the company as a highly diversified, full-service engineering and environmental consulting firm doing business across the nation

into a world-class firm with a solid reputation for expertise and diversity. The firm's corporate headquarters are in Austin, with offices located throughout the United States.

Today, Espey, Huston & Associates continues its emphasis on diversity with professionals in over 30 disciplines. Among the firm's 400 employees are engineers in the fields of civil, chemical, mechanical, structural, electrical, environmental, and geotechnical

quality, surface mining reclamation, hazardous waste management, and habitat conservation. In response to future environmental regulations, the company will continue to expand its capabilities and services.

Locally, the firm has long been involved in safeguarding Austin's environment while ensuring orderly development. The company has helped develop the city's plan to manage storm water runoff, written ordinances that protect

THE FIRM CONTINUES A LONGTIME COMMITMENT TO SAFEGUARDING THE ENVIRONMENT IN AUSTIN AND BEYOND.

FOUNDED IN 1972, ESPEY, HUSTON & ASSOCIATES REMAINS HEADQUARTERD IN AUSTIN (LEFT).

and the world. "Few of our clients know the full extent of the services we offer," Jasper explains. "They are often amazed when they learn of the breadth and depth of our capabilities."

The firm was founded in 1972 when two former Tracor employees, hydrologist William H. Espey, Jr., Ph.D., and mathematician and computer scientist Robert J. Huston began their own company. Their initial focus was to perform water quality studies for commercial clients in response to new environmental regulations. As they learned more about their clients' other needs, Espey and Huston began to assemble a specialized team of professionals with diverse expertise. This approach has contributed to the company's growth

engineering, as well as professional surveyors. In addition, the firm employs scientists in air quality, meteorology and climatology, surface and ground water hydrology, water quality, geology, terrestrial and marine ecology, socioeconomics, and cultural resources. Supported by skilled technicians and state-of-the-art computer facilities, the staff provides clients with technically sound and cost-effective solutions to today's complex engineering and environmental problems.

Continuing a Commitment to the Environment

Espey, Huston & Associates has responded to environmental legislation and regulations by developing expertise in areas such as air

Austin's water quality, reduced environmental impacts of the high-technology industry, and designed environmentally acceptable residential and commercial development projects. Among its high-profile consulting projects was the Balcones Canyonland Conservation Plan (BCCP), a program to protect endangered species in Travis County while allowing land development to continue. As part of a project team, the firm provided biological expertise for preserve design and management, and assisted with land use and fiscal issues.

"We believe in development, but we also believe in good stewardship of the environment," says Jasper. "We have a long-term commitment to our city, both as a company and as individuals who live here. It is important to us to protect what makes Austin a special place, while enhancing the ability of the city to grow."

Austin Community College

AUSTIN COMMUNITY COLLEGE PROVES THAT COLLEGE IS more than just a place; it's a way of thinking about education. With campuses conveniently located throughout the area, the publicly supported institution has flexible class schedules,

specialized credit and noncredit courses, and innovative programs that give high school students a head start on their futures.

Thanks to its open-door policy, affordable tuition, and diverse course offerings, ACC makes college education a reality for thousands of Austinites who might not otherwise have the resources to continue their training. From basic literacy to computer skills, arts and sciences, and continuing education, ACC provides opportunities that benefit the entire community.

"Our prime function is to serve the community," says President Bill

reaches more than 30,000 individuals through 61 degree plans and 22 certificate programs. Complementing its six full-time campuses, ACC offers specialized instruction at more than 40 locations in the capital area. The college also provides resources such as televised classes, libraries, and computer, math, and writing labs. To accommodate working students, ACC offers day and evening classes in full- and part-time formats.

Founded in 1972 and opened for classes in 1973, ACC has grown to become the fifth-largest community college in Texas and ranks

Top-Notch Employees–Guaranteed

ACC is the only local institution of higher education that guarantees its graduates. "Our students will perform and do what we say they can do, or they can come back for more training at no cost to them or their employers," says Segura. "That's how convinced we are of the quality of our faculty and our instruction."

Many ACC students are nontraditional—adults seeking basic skills or technical training. The college offers credit and noncredit courses supporting their goals. Certificate programs are available in building construction, diesel technology,

ART STUDENTS FIND INSPIRATION FOR THEIR PAINTINGS IN ACC'S ONLY "VERTICAL" CAMPUS, THE PINNACLE, HOUSED IN A 10-STORY BUILDING OVERLOOKING THE TEXAS HILL COUNTRY (ABOVE).

ACC OFFERS TECHNOLOGY TRAINING IN MANY FIELDS LEADING DIRECTLY TO EMPLOYMENT IN THE AUSTIN AREA (RIGHT).

PHOTOS BY JIM LINCOLN

Segura, who joined ACC in 1993. "We support economic development in its most basic sense by helping students acquire the skills they need to succeed and, in turn, help businesses grow."

The Key to Success

ACC actively recruits students who might benefit from a community college education and provides the necessary support structure to help them succeed.

Each semester, the college

second in number of students transferring to four-year institutions. ACC has been recognized by the Texas Higher Education Coordinating Board for the ease and success of its students transfering to the University of Texas, Southwest Texas State University, and other senior institutions. As a result, more students are taking advantage of ACC's convenience, smaller classes, and excellent faculty for their prerequisite and preprofessional courses.

electronics, horticulture and landscaping, office systems technology, and many other fields. Noncredit courses cover such topics as workplace literacy, blueprint reading, and computer software and hardware.

"We work closely with local industry to gauge both current and future needs," says Segura. "Each of our technical programs is backed by an advisory committee of industry representatives who make recommendations that keep our

..ining accurate and up-to-date."

The Business and Technology ..enter, located in ACC's District ...ministrative Office, is a focal ...int for cooperative projects with ...e business community. The ...nter works with employers to ...velop and teach specialized ...ncredit courses to meet their ...ining needs.

Because fewer and fewer jobs ...e open to people without college-...el skills, ACC is also reaching out ..local high school students, giving ...em a head start on college. The ...2 Program, part of the Capital ...ea Tech Prep Consortium, offers ...gh school juniors and seniors a ...ance to learn technical skills ...ding to jobs and educational ...dit at ACC.

For example, a Tech Prep pro-...am in electronics was developed ..teach skills that local employers ...quired for their entry-level posi-...ns. "Companies were looking for ...ployees with a nucleus of elec-...nics knowledge and skills that ...ey can expand on," notes Segura. ..he Tech Prep electronics cur-...ulum is one pathway that we ...ve created for students into the

local high-tech industry."

While making pathways into high-tech fields, ACC is also assisting service industries in their training. For example, ACC's child development faculty helped the Continuing Education Department design courses in child development. "We are always pushing the envelope to find ways to better serve our customers," adds Segura. "Offering training through continuing education makes sense because child care workers put in long hours and earn modest salaries. Their work is so important, and they need the training; but they are not likely to enroll in a semester-long, college-credit program."

Segura also emphasizes ACC's commitment to keeping up with the community: "Austin places a very high value on education. The community is always pushing us to get better, and we are always pushing ourselves. It's one of the things that makes Austin so special."

Education for All Austinites

In 1986 Austin-area residents approved a local tax to support ACC

and its programs. Residents also elect the college's nine-member board of trustees—three trustees are up for election every two years—assuring that ACC stays in touch with its constituents.

Responsiveness and innovation are evident in ACC's approach to all its students, regardless of age, gender, race, ethnicity, or educational background. "We value diversity," says Segura. "That has been a constant throughout our history, and it will continue to be an important part of our mission. Education doesn't belong to one segment of the population; it belongs to all of us."

Looking to the future, Segura sees Austin Community College as a place of lifelong education for a growing number of Austinites. "Education isn't a one-time experience anymore," he says. "I foresee that students will be trained at ACC, go to work, then come back for retraining and upgrading—maybe several times over the course of a career. That's the direction I believe our economy is taking."

Austin Career Consultants, Inc./Career Consultants Temporaries

R ECRUITING PERSONNEL IS ONE OF THE MOST EXPENSIVE AND time-consuming aspects of doing business. That's why many Austin companies turn to the experts at Career Consultants. A professional search and placement firm, Career Consultants

specializes in matching the needs of employers with the talents of prospective employees. With separate divisions to handle permanent and temporary placements, Career Consultants can meet a variety of hiring needs.

The firm offers a blend of staffing services including professional search, administrative support placement services, temporary staffing, and professional and managerial contract staffing. All of Career Consultants' services are tailored to clients' needs.

Professional Searches. Professional Results

Founded in 1973 as a professional search firm, Career Consultants has developed specialties that reflect the hiring needs of its clients, which range from small local businesses to Fortune 100 firms. Because of this diversity, Career Consultants conducts searches locally, regionally, and nationally.

The company's professional recruitment division specializes in identifying, screening, and recruiting professionals in fields such as sales and marketing, finance, accounting, mortgage banking, data processing, and engineering. It also uses state-of-the-art screening and evaluation to refer qualified candidates for clerical and administrative support positions.

Recruiters at Career Consultants have extensive experience and are well respected in the industry. Clients view Career Consultants' recruiters as an extension of their personnel departments, and they know that when they discuss a search, the company will listen to their needs and follow through. In addition, many of the associates have significant tenure within the firm, which is important because clients count on experience and the continuity of relationships. Both

are reasons why many clients turn to Career Consultants for all their staffing needs.

The Work Force of the Future

"Temp" services were initiated in 1988 after the firm surveyed its clients and found that virtually all of

them could use temporary placements. Today, the company views temporary employment as an important part of the work force of the future.

Career Consultants now provides temps for clerical and administrative support, accounting and bookkeeping, word processing, data entry, and general clerical jobs.

Protecting the quality and integ-

rity of the local work force and business environment are prime concerns for Austin Career Consultants/Career Consultants Temporaries. The firm is a member of the Greater Austin Chamber of Commerce, Better Business Bureau, and local, state, and national

professional associations.

While the pace of change may have increased over the years, one thing remains constant: the dedication to providing the highest standard of service—the very principl upon which the firm was founded Career Consultants has a vested interest in the future of Austin, an will continue to make sure that future will be bright.

AUSTIN CAREER CONSULTANTS HAS BEEN GROWING WITH THE CAPITAL CITY SINCE 1973.

Hancock & Piedfort, P.C.

H ANCOCK & PIEDFORT BEGAN IN 1973 AS A PARTNERSHIP between Don Hancock and Pascual Piedfort, two entrepreneurial young lawyers who had recently graduated from the University of Texas School of Law. The firm has grown to

include seven attorneys and a highly trained staff of paralegals and administrative assistants serving clients throughout Texas and the nation.

Embracing Change

The practice of law has changed dramatically during the past 20 years, and like most successful law firms, Hancock & Piedfort has embraced change. The firm uses the latest technology to increase productivity and ensure its ability to deliver value to its clients. Hancock & Piedfort also invests heavily in training to enhance the ability of its attorneys and staff to meet the challenges of the future. While the

firm has been willing, even eager, to change the way it serves clients, its core values have remained constant.

Clients were the firm's most important asset in 1973, just as they are today. Hancock & Piedfort strives to know its clients' businesses, to discuss legal issues in language clients understand, and to be direct and realistic about objectives and fees.

Now, more than ever, clients want a trusting, professional relationship with their attorney. They want a lawyer who will take the time to earn their trust—a lawyer who will keep them informed and who is accessible. Clients expect

not only quality legal services, but also quality client services.

Experienced Professionals

Hancock & Piedfort is a mature firm. Its seven attorneys have a combined 113 years of legal experience in the areas of real estate law,

representation of commercial creditors, litigation, bankruptcy, estate planning, and small-business services. The majority of its lawyers have been certified by the State Bar of Texas as having special competence in one or more specific areas of law. Likewise, the staff of Hancock & Piedfort receives regular technical skills training, as well as training in quality management and personal skills development.

A commitment to the latest technology, from cutting-edge document assembly software to electronic legal research and communication facilities, enables the firm to deliver legal services on time, efficiently, and at competitive prices. "When you need a lawyer, we hope you will consider Hancock & Piedfort," says Don Hancock, founding attorney. "Serving you will be our pleasure."

OVER THE YEARS, HANCOCK & PIEDFORT HAS GROWN TO INCLUDE SEVEN ATTORNEYS AND A HIGHLY TRAINED STAFF OF PARALEGALS AND ADMINISTRATIVE ASSISTANTS SERVING CLIENTS THROUGHOUT TEXAS AND THE NATION.

DON HANCOCK (FAR LEFT) AND PASCUAL PIEDFORT FOUNDED THE FIRM IN 1973.

Motorola, Inc.

THE CAPITAL CITY'S LARGEST PRIVATE EMPLOYER IS ALSO ONE OF its most exciting. Named Austin's best employer in a recent Gallup survey, Motorola, Inc. has staked out an enviable position on the frontier of new technology. ◆ At the company's Austin campuses—

Ed Bluestein and Oak Hill—employees are creating, designing, producing, and marketing semiconductors found in countless everyday products. Apple computers, Canon cameras, Hewlett-Packard printers, Motorola cellular phones, Sega video games, and Sony video cameras are all powered by Motorola semiconductors produced in Austin.

Motorola was drawn to the city in 1974 by its quality of life, its pool of talented employees, and the presence of a major university. Opening its doors with just six employees, the company now employs more than 8,500 Austinites and has long been a magnet for other technology companies.

Headquartered in Schaumburg, Illinois, Motorola is one of the world's leading providers of wireless communications, semiconductor technology, and advanced electronics equipment and services for commercial, industrial, and

governmental customers. Worldwide, the company has more than 120,000 employees and is ranked among the 40 largest U.S. industrial firms according to total sales.

Motorola's fundamental objective is total customer satisfaction. Reflecting that commitment, the company received the first Malcolm Baldrige National Quality Award in 1988 for its superior companywide management of quality processes.

A Leader in Semiconductor Technology

The two Austin groups are part of Motorola's Phoenix, Arizona-based Semiconductor Products Sector. Accounting for nearly one-third of annual sales, semiconductors are the company's largest business segment.

As Motorola's leading semiconductor manufacturing site, Austin is home to the Microprocessor and Memory Technologies Group

(MMTG) and the Microcontroller Technologies Group (MCTG). Each of these groups has manufacturing operations and four divisions reporting to it. Austin is also the home of the Advanced Products Research and Development Laboratory (APRDL), which is dedicated to supporting the development of CMOS and BiCMOS memory and microprocessor technology, as well as new designs and device packaging.

Some of Motorola's most important products were born in Austin, including the 68000 family of microprocessors, which paved the way for the company's subsequent microprocessors and microcontrollers. The Austin operation also pioneered breakthroughs in RISC and Digital Signal Processor technologies that have made Motorola a leader in these fast-changing areas.

The Fast Static RAM division is one of the most reliable U.S. providers of advanced technology for

MOTOROLA DEVELOPS MICRO-CONTROLLERS, MICROPROCESSORS, AND OTHER DEVICES AT ITS OAK HILL FACILITY. OPENED IN 1984, THE SITE ALSO HOUSES PRODUCT ENGINEERING, PRODUCTION CONTROL, AND MARKETING OPERATIONS.

design, product and test engineering, marketing, and management of Fast Static Random Access Memory (FSRAM) components and modules. Working with its PRDL engineers, Motorola has developed proprietary design and manufacturing processes that have resulted in some of the world's most competitive memory devices. Scientists, engineers, and researchers come from around the world to work at the Austin facilities. In addition to drawing from the University of Texas, Motorola attracts some of the brightest minds from Japan, Taiwan, China, India, Canada, and Europe.

State-of-the-Art Austin Facilities

The original Austin facility, Ed Bluestein, includes some of the world's most advanced fab lines— where the latest technology is used to manufacture microprocessors and memory products. One of its lines, MOS 8, pioneered the use of submicron integrated circuit technology, the most important arena in the future of the semiconductor industry. Likewise, Bluestein's state-of-the-art central plant facility, with its deionized water system, is critical to the high-quality circuits manufactured by the three MOS lines. Bluestein is also home to PRDL and its 300-plus dedicated engineers.

Located across town is the Oak Hill facility, where Motorola's microcontrollers, microprocessors, and other devices are developed.

Opened in 1984, Oak Hill also houses product engineering, production control, and marketing operations. MOS 11, the company's newest and most advanced fab line, was designed and built at Oak Hill. Capable of screening out contaminants as small as 0.1 micron, the line exceeds standards for a Class 1 facility and was the world's first eight-inch commercial wafer fab line.

Both Austin facilities have been recognized by the Occupational Safety and Health Administration's prestigious Star program for providing safe work environments. In fact, the campuses are the only semiconductor sites to receive the Star designation since the program began in 1981.

In an effort to improve on the already high levels of safety and efficiency at its local sites, Motorola requires its Austin employees to participate in personal and professional training programs, including 40 hours of annual on-the-job training. Through Motorola University, employees have ready access to a wide range of classes and educational opportunities.

Celebrating 20 Years in Austin

Throughout its local history, the company has made major contributions to Austin's quality of life. For example, Motorola supports a variety of community organizations, including the Center for Battered Women, Austin Adopt-A-School, Texas Alliance for Minority Engineers, and many others. The com-

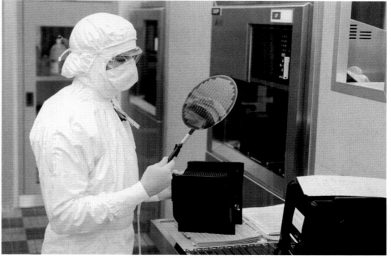

pany also underwrites the closed captioning of a local TV newscast. Complementing this corporate involvement, employees volunteer their time and talents as board members of local groups and as mentors for at-risk students, and by cleaning up local neighborhoods and advocating improved recycling programs.

In 1994 Motorola celebrated its 20th year in Austin by throwing a party for the entire city. Held in conjunction with the Motorola Marathon, an annual spring race that attracts several thousand runners, the party featured food, fireworks, and live entertainment.

"We believe in playing an active role in helping Austin become an ever-better place to live," says Barry Waite, senior vice president and general manager of MMTG. "We will continue to do so as a corporation and as individuals."

National Instruments

THE NATIONAL INSTRUMENTS CORPORATE HEADQUARTERS LOOK out over the scenic Loop 360 bridge, Lake Austin, and in the distance, the Austin skyline. The site is impressive, but not as impressive as the company it houses. ◆ National Instruments, a

BRUCE KELLERMAN, OF THE CHEMICAL AND PETROLEUM ENGINEERING DEPARTMENT AT UT AUSTIN (RIGHT), USES LabVIEW TO MONITOR AND CONTROL A VACUUM CHAMBER DURING RESEARCH ON SEMICONDUCTOR MATERIALS.

ENGINEERS AT SCHLUMBERGER LTD. IN SUGAR LAND, TEXAS, TEST THE FUNCTIONALITY OF INTEGRATED CIRCUITS USING A SYSTEM BASED ON LabWINDOWS (FAR RIGHT).

PHOTOS BY JAMES MINOR

NATIONAL INSTRUMENTS WAS FOUNDED IN 1976 BY (FROM LEFT) JEFF KODOSKY, VICE PRESIDENT OF R&D; DR. JIM TRUCHARD, PRESIDENT AND CHAIRMAN OF THE BOARD; AND BILL NOWLIN, CHIEF QUALITY OFFICER.

THE COMPANY'S CORPORATE HEADQUARTERS OVERLOOKS THE SCENIC HILL COUNTRY AS WELL AS THE DOWNTOWN SKYLINE (FAR RIGHT).

maker of automated hardware and software tools, has found great success on the cutting edge of high technology, and the company is growing fast. Employment doubled between 1991 and 1993, and sales have increased about 40 percent annually in recent years. National Instruments is also adding a new 125,000-square-foot manufacturing facility in North Austin. In addition to more than 600 local employees, the privately held company employs about 170 people at sales offices in the United States and Canada, and at direct branch offices in Europe, Japan, and Australia.

Its award-winning application software programs, LabVIEW® and LabWindows,® are widely recognized for their innovative design and programming flexibility. James J. Truchard, Ph.D., cofounder and president, has been recognized as one of the nation's leading high-tech entrepreneurs. Scientists and engineers around the world depend on the company's products to research, design, and test everything from personal computers to NASA space shuttle systems and on-board experiments.

Success in Niche Marketing

Founded in 1976, National Instruments has become a model of success in high-tech niche marketing. "We are the leading developer of products that link computers to instruments," says Truchard. "This process is revolutionizing the instrumentation industry."

With LabVIEW and LabWindows, users turn their personal computers into "virtual instruments" that mimic various scientific tools. For example, a personal computer can function as an oscilloscope, a tool for observing and measuring electrical signals. The company also manufactures plug-in boards and hardware interfaces needed to capture these signals in computers. Products are compatible with the most popular computers and operating systems from companies such as IBM, Apple, Sun, and Microsoft.

A Tradition of Ingenuity and Expertise

Like numerous other Austin-based technology companies, National Instruments traces its roots to the University of Texas. Truchard and cofounders William Nowlin and Jeffrey Kodosky were test and measurement specialists at UT's Applied Research Laboratories when they decided to put their talents and skills to work in the

▲ ALAN KRESS

private sector.

All three founders remain activ in daily management of the company, and they point with pride to the fact that many employees have spent their entire careers at National Instruments.

"This level of expertise forms t technical backbone of our company. Thanks to rapid growth, we can regularly recruit new talent," says Truchard. "National Instruments maintains a specialized, cr ative team that will continue our history of innovation and assure o position as a market leader."

Delta Air Lines, Inc.

WHAT DO THE AUSTIN BALLET AND WALT DISNEY WORLD have in common? Delta Air Lines serves as the official air carrier for both. "Serving the ballet is one way we can make a contribution to the Austin community," says Ray Fountain,

strict sales manager for Delta. We truly believe in the arts, so elta serves as the official airline of veral local arts groups. We help em bring in guest artists and ake it possible for Austin troupes perform in other cities or even erseas."

Anywhere You Want to Go

elta prides itself on its ability to ke Austinites across the state or und the world. Since beginning rvice to the capital city in 1979, e company has become the area's rd-largest commercial air car-r, with connections to more ernational destinations than any er airline serving Austin.

Delta offers daily direct flights to allas, Atlanta, and Salt Lake City, th connections to more than 0 cities in 34 countries. Global iances with Singapore Airlines d Swissair give international ssengers the added benefit of mpetitive joint fares, one-stop keting, and convenient connect-g schedules. The Delta Connec-n—a series of regional carriers luding ASA, Business Express, OMAIR, and SkyWest—connects ssengers to dozens of cities roughout the United States, nada, and the Bahamas.

Putting a Premium on Service

hile Delta has become one of the rld's largest air carriers—with a rldwide work force of 73,000— e airline prides itself on taking re of the little things that make ssengers happy. Its popular Fre-ent Flyer program, for example, ows members to accumulate leage when they fly on Delta or lta Connection. Members can ickly earn bonuses such as seat-g upgrades, rental car and hotel counts, and free domestic or ernational travel.

Perhaps the most familiar sign of

Delta's commitment to customer service is the team of red-jacketed Passenger Service Agents who greet each flight. The agents have the information necessary to direct passengers to connecting gates and can also take care of special needs.

As the Official Airline for Kids,™ Delta offers a special Fantastic Flyer program for children two through 12 years of age. In addition to activities and gifts, the program offers Fantastic Flyer Funfeast meals featuring foods like pizza and chicken nuggets. The meals are packed into take-home containers lined with an activity place mat and filled with toys.

Delta Crown Room Clubs, with locations in many North American airports, offer extra amenities to frequent travelers. Ranked in 1992 and 1993 by the *Robb Report* as the "Best of the Best," Delta's Crown Room Clubs give travelers a chance to rest, relax, and conduct business while waiting for a flight.

The airline also offers a full range of worldwide cargo services. In fact, Delta's Cargofax computerized tracking system has made the company a leader in monitoring ship-ment movement, accounting, and invoicing.

Connecting the capital city with hundreds of destinations across the globe, Delta Air Lines has opened the world to Austinites. In addition to its experience and resources, Delta brings to Austin a commit-ment to its customers unparalleled in the industry. "Customer service is important to each one of us at Delta," says Fountain. "This is a very family-oriented company, and taking care of our customers is like taking care of family."

CLOCKWISE FROM ABOVE: DELTA'S COMMITMENT TO PASSENGER SERVICE AND SATISFACTION IS UNPARALLELED IN THE INDUSTRY.

THE MD-88 IS AMONG THE NEWEST AIRCRAFT IN DELTA'S FLEET, ONE OF THE YOUNGEST FLEETS OF ITS SIZE IN THE WORLD.

PASSENGER SERVICE AGENTS IN THEIR FAMILIAR RED COATS ARE ALWAYS READY TO TAKE CARE OF CUSTOMERS' SPECIAL NEEDS.

Advanced Micro Devices

ADVANCED MICRO DEVICES OF SUNNYVALE, CALIFORNIA, IS rapidly acquiring a Texas tilt that promises to become even mor[e] pronounced when its new Austin Fab 25 facility opens in late 1994. ◆ "We expect that the investment represented by Fab 2[5]

will ensure our ability to provide leading-edge silicon products to the international marketplace for the balance of this decade and into the next century," said AMD President Rich Previte at the Fab 25 ground-breaking ceremony.

World Leadership in Integrated Circuits

Founded in 1969, AMD is the fifth-largest U.S.-based manufacturer of integrated circuits. The company produces microprocessors and related peripherals, memories, programmable logic devices, and circuits for telecommunications, office automation, and networking applications. In addition to Austin and Sunnyvale, AMD maintains manufacturing facilities in Japan, Thailand, Malaysia, Singapore, and England.

While AMD may be known best for its microprocessors—especially the Am386 and Am486 models manufactured in Austin—nearly two-thirds of the company's reve-

nue comes from other businesses. AMD's diversification has been a key to its growth and enhanced competitiveness: In 1993, on the heels of a successful five-year plan to reinvent the company, AMD earned record operating income of $305 million on sales of $1.64 billion. The new AMD is leaner, more focused, and more committed to quality than ever before.

These high standards are what will set the Fab 25 facility apart from AMD's three existing wafer fabrication areas in Austin—and from most other facilities in the world. The plant will produce advanced CMOS logic integrated circuits with features of one-half micron and smaller, and will be capable of producing about 5,000 eight-inch wafers with these tiny features each week.

In conjunction with Hewlett-Packard, AMD is developing semiconductor process technology that will allow the company to build logic devices and microprocessors

with up to 15 million transistors—about 15 times more than its prev[i]ous state-of-the-art microprocesso[r]

AMD in Austin

AMD and the capital city have grown together since 1979, when the Fortune 500 company opened [a] facility in Austin to produce 16K dynamic random access memory (DRAM) chips. Its original plant was 130,000 square feet and employed 100 people.

Today, AMD has more than 700,000 square feet of research,

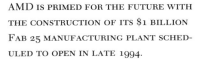

AMD IS PRIMED FOR THE FUTURE WITH THE CONSTRUCTION OF ITS $1 BILLION FAB 25 MANUFACTURING PLANT SCHEDULED TO OPEN IN LATE 1994.

TOP RIGHT: AMD CHAIRMAN AND CEO JERRY SANDERS (LEFT) WITH PRESIDENT AND COO RICH PREVITE.

velopment, and manufacturing [fa]ce in three buildings on its [5]-acre campus in Southeast [Au]stin. The company employs [mo]re than 2,800 people locally—[ab]out one-fifth of its worldwide [wo]rk force—and its local payroll [pu]mps more than $100 million into [th]e economy every year. Fab 25 will [ad]d another 700,000 square feet to [AM]D's campus and could provide [up] to 1,000 more jobs.

[F]our of the company's seven [bu]siness groups are headquartered [in] Austin: Personal Computer [Pro]ducts, Embedded Processors, [Co]mmunications Products, and [Cu]stomer Specific Products.

[T]he Personal Computer Prod[uc]ts division produces a variety of [mi]croprocessors for makers of [IB]M-compatible PCs. In fact, [AM]D is the world leader in 386-[mo]del microprocessors, with more [tha]n 16 million units—70 percent [of] those ever sold—shipped by [th]e end of 1993. The Embedded [Pro]cessor division develops and

manufactures the 29K™ family of integrated products that allow cost-effective system upgrades, while the Communications Products division focuses on providing analog line cards for digital switches, terminals for digital PBX and ISDN applications, and wireless communications. AMD's newest group, Customer Specific Products, capitalizes on the strengths of the other six divisions to develop, manufacture, and market differentiated products for customers.

The company also works hand in hand with many other Austin firms. "Over the past few years AMD has entered into several strategic partnerships to ensure our continued viability and success in the rapidly changing global electronics business," Previte says. "Our collaboration with SEMATECH has yielded advancements for the U.S. semiconductor manufacturing industry and has helped provide the road map for the equipment selection and design of Fab 25. Our membership in Austin-based MCC, a research consortium of American computer companies, has provided AMD with critical circuit-packaging technology. We work closely with our customers to provide them with enabling technologies for products ranging from shirt-pocket PCs to intelligent cellular telephones." AMD, for example, recently announced devel-

opment of a controller—made in Austin—that powers Sony Corporation's newest cordless telephone.

Connected to the Community

One AMD hallmark has been its concern for the community, especially in the areas of education and human services. In 1993 the company participated in more than 50 initiatives with local organizations, including a $100,000 corporate grant to the Capital Area Food Bank, the largest single donation ever received by the group. AMD is also a major supporter of the Austin Project, a coalition of business and civic organizations banded together to combat social problems. Kid-Tech, a program that locates used computer equipment, refurbishes it, and donates it to schools, was founded and coordinated by an AMD employee.

Additionally, AMD is the largest supporter of the Del Valle Independent School District's Adopt-A-School program, with an average of 50 employees donating their time each week as tutors and mentors. The company plans to have the same impact on Johnston High School, its recent adoption in the Austin Independent School District.

"We are committed to sharing our success with organizations that improve the quality of life in our communities," says Allyson Peerman, manager of community relations in Austin. "It's one way that we can help strengthen the local business environment and secure a strong future for the area."

CLOCKWISE FROM ABOVE: ALWAYS READY TO LEND A HELPING HAND FOR THE COMMUNITY, AMD EMPLOYEES ASSIST A SPECIAL OLYMPICS ATHLETE DURING THE ANNUAL STATE GAMES.

THIS SUBNOTEBOOK-CLASS PERSONAL COMPUTER, BASED ON AMD'S 3.3-VOLT AM386SXLV MICROPROCESSOR, ALLOWS CONSUMERS TO RUN WINDOWS APPLICATIONS VIRTUALLY ANYWHERE.

A VARIETY OF 29K™ FAMILY DEVICES POWER SUCH TOP-NAME LASER PRINTERS AS IBM, LEXMARK, COMPAQ, AND TEKTRONIX.

Prime Cable

THE INFORMATION SUPERHIGHWAY OF THE FUTURE IS ALREADY under construction, and, when completed, it will certainly run directly through the offices of Prime Cable in downtown Austin. One of the nation's most experienced multisystem cable operators

Prime Cable is leading the way in the introduction of new electronic technologies as it prepares for a fast-approaching information explosion.

television, and a full 90 percent have access to cable. While current coaxial cable technology limits the number of channels available, the combination of fiber optics and

and operating cable systems. He put together a strong management team and created the company as a vehicle for acquiring troubled cable systems, improving their operations and cash flow, and ultimately selling them. That strategy established Prime as a good manager, which led to an outstanding reputation in the financial services community.

From its headquarters in Austin, Prime Cable serves 537,000 cable customers nationwide. With about 70 employees locally and 1,100 nationally, the company operates cable systems in Las Vegas, Nevada; Chicago, Illinois; Anchorage, Alaska; Hickory, North Carolina; and several towns in suburban Houston.

As the 1990s approached, Prime Cable began to branch out into related communications businesses. The company now owns retail video franchises in several major cities, provides hotel pay-per-view service, has an interest in cellular technology, and is involved in alternative access. Prime Cable is also positioning itself to make new technology available to customers as quickly and efficiently as possible. The company has formed a partnership with BellSouth Corp. to explore a broad array of communications services, including interactive television, pay-per-view, and alternative communications for business and residential customers.

"We see the issue of the future as one of choices," Hughes says. "There have never been more or better communications products available. We have a history of making the right choices at the right times, thanks to a combination of good instincts and careful research. We believe choices will continue to proliferate, leaving our future in our hands. We couldn't ask for more."

Delivering New Technology

"Television has become our primary source of information, and it is about to become even more important," says cable entrepreneur Robert W. Hughes, Prime Cable's founder, CEO, and chairman of the board. "Within the next few years, the home television set will essentially become a computer—combining video, voice, and data. We believe that cable will play a critical role in delivering this new technology to consumers."

More than 60 percent of American households now have cable

digital compression will open up as many as 500 channels, with virtually limitless programming options.

Prime was early to enter the "alternative access" business, utilizing fiber optics to deliver long distance telephone calls for commercial customers from their offices to their long distance carriers.

Expanding Service Through Smart Business Moves

When Hughes founded Prime Cable in 1979, he had more than a decade of experience in building

American Airlines

WITH A LONG HISTORY OF INNOVATION, AMERICAN AIRLINES continues to be a leader in bringing new services to Austin: daily nonstop flights to San Jose, Los Angeles, and Nashville, as well as long-standing service to Dallas/Fort Worth.

ustin travelers can now reach he West Coast without layovers, pending more time on business or ecreation and less time in airports. he addition of service to Nashville ot only brings the nation's music enters closer together but also ves travelers the option of additional connections to destinations the eastern United States or urope.

With 17 daily departures, including 10 to Dallas and four to Chicago, American offers connections more destinations than any other r carrier serving Austin. When mbined with its American Eagle

gional airline associate, American rves 361 cities, including 94 international destinations.

In addition to conveniently ned flights and an extensive route stem, Austin passengers appreciate American's extra touches. The dmirals Club, the only executive b at Austin's Robert Mueller unicipal Airport, gives members lace to relax and conduct business while waiting for a flight.

novation and Leadership

unded in 1929, American has mained a leader in the airline lustry. Among its many innova-

tions over the years are the introduction of coast-to-coast service, discounted "super saver" fares, one-stop check-in, air travel cards for credit purchases, and the first frequent flyer plan. Introduced in 1981, AAdvantage is the industry's largest and most innovative frequent flyer program, offering various travel awards to valued customers.

American was the first to form alliances with regional carriers to provide service to smaller markets. The airline also developed SABRE, the industry's most extensive travel agency automation network and the world's largest privately owned real-time computer network. FlyAAway Vacations, which offers comprehensive, competitively priced tour packages, has become the world's largest airline-owned tour business.

"It's hard to imagine what air service would be like today if American hadn't been a pioneer," says Josephine DeOro-Cooper, manager of passenger sales in Austin. "Our emphasis has always been on introducing services of value to the flying public. That's why we created new nonstop flights from Austin—and travelers have responded by making the routes successful."

Travelers have also made American one of the most honored airlines in the world. In 1993, for example, American was named the best U.S. carrier by several independent rating groups and industry experts. Readers of London-based *Executive Travel* magazine chose American in 1993 as the best U.S.-based carrier for a record 11th consecutive year.

The commitment of American and its parent company, AMR Corporation, goes even deeper than providing outstanding service. AMR is a major local employer,

with about 500 employees working at the airport, ticket locations, and the AMR Cargo Quality Information Center. Opened in 1992, the center handles reservations for domestic and international cargo shipments for AA Cargo, a division of American Airlines.

AA Cargo provides a range of shipping alternatives for domestic cargo, including deliveries that arrive the same day, next day, or second day. A fleet of more than 3,000 vans and trucks extends American's door-to-door service to more than 27,000 communities. Internationally, the division provides millions of pounds of airlift each week to major cities in Europe, Canada, Mexico, the Caribbean, and South and Central America. Through cooperative agreements, AA Cargo can transport shipments to virtually any country in the world.

AMERICAN'S PEOPLE MAKE THE DIFFERENCE. WHETHER SERVING CUSTOMERS FACE-TO-FACE OR BEHIND THE SCENES, THE AIRLINE'S WORK FORCE IS COMMITTED TO QUALITY.

FAR LEFT: AMERICAN FLIES STATE-OF-THE-ART JETS INTO AND OUT OF AUSTIN, INCLUDING THE MCDONNELL DOUGLAS SUPER 80 (TOP) AND THE BOEING 757 (BOTTOM).

Fisher-Rosemount Systems, Inc.

WHAT DO DISPOSABLE DIAPERS, BEER, PLASTICS, GASOLINE, and pharmaceuticals have in common? They, like a variety of other manufactured goods, require pinpoint accuracy during the manufacturing process. Fisher-Rosemount Systems, Inc.

since its beginnings in 1880, has helped industry improve product quality, save energy, reduce waste, and meet environmental, safety, and health requirements.

Part of the Austin community since 1981, the company has become a world leader in providing quality process management systems—the "brains" of a factory—to help manufacturers streamline their processes. Today, Fisher-Rosemount Systems is part of the Fisher-Rosemount family of companies owned by Emerson Electric.

plant's manufacturing equipment—such as a control valve—what to do and when."

He adds, "Fisher-Rosemount products are so widely used that if our measurement devices, valves, regulators, and process management systems suddenly vanished, many of the world's process plants would have to shut down."

A Tradition of Ingenuity

Fisher-Rosemount Systems traces its roots back to an evening in 1880, when a fire raged through the Iowa

developed numerous control valve and grew into an industry leader. 1969 Fisher Controls became an independent subsidiary of Monsanto and began manufacturing a line of electronic instrumentation The division responsible for the electronic control systems moved to Austin in 1981. In 1992 the company was acquired by Emerso Electric, owner of Minnesota-based Rosemount Inc., another leader in process controls. The control-system businesses of these two companies were then consoli

MANY OF THE COMPANY'S SYSTEMS ARE ASSEMBLED AND TESTED IN AUSTIN (ABOVE).

PROCESS MANAGEMENT SYSTEMS FROM FISHER-ROSEMOUNT SYSTEMS PROVIDE AN EASY-TO-USE TOOL FOR MONITORING AND CONTROLLING MANUFACTURING OPERATIONS (RIGHT).

"In essence, Fisher-Rosemount Systems provides advanced solutions that help customers control 'wet' processes," explains John Berra, president. "By that, we mean any material that flows through a pipe—whether it's steam, baby formula, gasoline, or chemicals used to make carpet fiber. Fisher-Rosemount Systems' products are used to monitor and adjust the flow, temperature, pressure, and other properties of materials being processed in a plant. Our digital instrumentation actually tells the

farm community of Marshalltown. Exhausted from a long night of hand throttling the steam-driven water pumps, a young engineer, William Fisher, figured there had to be a better way to maintain constant water pressure. Several months later, the 24-year-old inventor developed a constant-pressure pump governor. By 1888 sales were so strong that Fisher left his bicycle and camera business to concentrate solely on the new product.

Over the years, the company

dated to form Fisher-Rosemount Systems, Inc., headquartered in Austin.

The company's 32-acre campu in Northeast Austin has about 250,000 square feet of manufactu ing, research, and administrative space. The company also maintai key manufacturing and technolog centers in Minnesota, California, Canada, England, and Singapore. With a local work force of over 60 a global staff of 1,800, more than 7,500 installed systems, and annu revenues of over $300 million,

AN EDUCATION CENTER PROVIDES
SPECIALIZED TRAINING TO HELP
CUSTOMERS MAKE THE MOST OF THEIR
FISHER-ROSEMOUNT SYSTEMS PROD-
UCTS (LEFT).

THE COMPANY'S HEADQUARTERS IS
HOME TO MORE THAN 600 ENGINEERS,
TECHNICIANS, MARKETING SPECIALISTS,
AND OTHERS (BELOW).

[Fis]her-Rosemount Systems is one [of] the world's largest process man[ag]ement suppliers.

[Int]egrated Solutions

[Fis]her and Rosemount brought [com]plementary strengths to their [uni]on. Fisher Controls specialized [in v]alves and control systems, while [Ro]semount excelled in measure[me]nt and control systems. By pool[ing] these resources, the team [dev]eloped integrated solutions [tha]t combine products, systems, [and] services from the Fisher-[Ro]semount family of companies to [giv]e manufacturers up-to-the-[sec]ond real-time information about [pla]nt and business operations. [T]hese solutions allow Fisher-[Ro]semount Systems' customers to [int]egrate information about their [ma]nufacturing process into other [pla]nt computer systems. This easy [acc]ess to data helps managers, [eng]ineers, and others make deci[sio]ns based on current, accurate [inf]ormation. To better serve a [wid]e range of industries, Fisher-[Ro]semount provides customization [to m]eet the individual customer's [nee]ds.

[ ] The introduction of these major [new] solutions illustrates our com[mit]ment to the future of advanced [pro]cess control technology," Berra [say]s. "We are aggressively involved [in r]esearch and development here [in A]ustin and at several other [loc]ations."

As a result, Fisher-Rosemount Systems is already developing the next generation of process management solutions, including "intelligent sensors" that can predict process conditions and outcomes that are difficult to measure. For example, using neural networks, these sensors will be able to learn from experience to determine when a problem is about to occur so preventive steps can be taken.

Pioneers in Total Quality

Fisher-Rosemount's commitment to total quality dates back to the 1950s, long before the concept gained popularity among corporations. Bill Fisher, grandson of founder William Fisher and company president from 1954 to 1969, was known to say: "Quality people plus quality products equals quality profits." The philosophy remains in force today, and the Austin site recently received ISO 9001 certification for meeting international quality standards.

"We not only empower our teams to achieve continuous improvement," says Berra, "but we also want customers around the world to know that we try to do things right the first time, which is why we sought ISO 9001 certification. At the same time, we are committed to taking responsible care of the environment and the workplace. Our worldwide pledge is to conduct our operations safely,

to protect the environment, and to help our customers do the same."

Proving its commitment to the environment, Fisher-Rosemount

Systems has installed packing machines that use compressed, recycled paper rather than foam. The company also encourages employees to become active in local causes such as the United Way, Austin Adopt-A-School, Texas Alliance for Minorities in Engineering, Junior Achievement, and others. "We take pride in supporting the needs of the local community," says Berra, "because Austin provides a solid home base for our global activities."

Harris Branch

JUST 12 MINUTES FROM DOWNTOWN IS ONE OF AUSTIN'S BEST REA estate values, Harris Branch. This spacious, 2,200-acre, master-planne community features a popular residential neighborhood filled with amenities and includes 600 acres of commercial property that is hom

to major employers from across the country.

A wide, sweeping entrance sets a proper stage for a master-planned community that offers more style and attention to detail than any other comparably priced neighborhood in Austin. A tree-lined boulevard leads into the community, winding past lakes and sails, greenbelts, gazebos, brick-sculpted fences, and jogging trails.

Austin's Partner in Economic Development

The residential section of Harris Branch is complemented by the neighboring office and commercial sites, known as The Commerce Park at Harris Branch. Top national companies such as Applied Materials have migrated to The Commerce Park, providing growth and opportunity for Austin and long-term stability for Harris Branch.

Over the years, the professional team at Harris Branch has worked closely with Austin community leaders and the Greater Austin Chamber of Commerce to attract major employers from around the country to Central Texas. The opening of the Applied Materials complex at The Commerce Park was the direct result of this partnership effort.

Close to Perfect, Close to Downtown

Harris Branch has a quiet and relaxing atmosphere, but home owners don't feel cut off from the commerce and activities of Austin. Downtown office buildings are only minutes away, and IH-35 and major shopping areas are just six minutes from the Harris Branch entrance, via Bluebonnet Parkway (Highway 290 East).

Harris Branch is known for its family atmosphere and country

TOP NATIONAL COMPANIES SUCH AS APPLIED MATERIALS HAVE MIGRATED TO THE COMMERCE PARK, PROVIDING GROWTH AND OPPORTUNITY FOR AUSTIN AND LONG-TERM STABILITY FOR HARRIS BRANCH.

▶ GREG HURSLEY

serenity. Manicured landscaping, accentuated by various water features, provides a picture-perfect backdrop for walks and outdoor recreation.

The hub of the neighborhood is an attractive and modern community center, which serves as a focal point for many neighborhood activities. The community center has a Junior Olympic-size swimming pool, tennis courts, and an exercise facility. And down the road a bit is the Harris Branch Country Store, where neighbors often congregate to chat over a cup of coffee or to pitch horseshoes.

The Family-Value Community

Harris Branch offers the kind of neighborhood value that is impor tant to individuals and families alike. For the price of a home in small subdivision, Harris Branch residents get the amenities and lifestyle of a carefully planned ar developed community.

The core of that community spirit can be found in the neighbo hood elementary school that was recently completed at Harris Branch. This glistening new facil represents a commitment to edu tional excellence that is reflected every aspect of the neighborhood

Soon, Harris Branch will have

THIS 2,200-ACRE, MASTER-PLANNED
COMMUNITY FEATURES A POPULAR
RESIDENTIAL NEIGHBORHOOD FILLED
WITH LAKES AND SAILS, GREENBELTS,
GAZEBOS, BRICK-SCULPTED FENCES,
AND JOGGING TRAILS.

ʌn child care facility, providing a ʌarm and inviting environment for ɾeschoolers in a location that is ɔnvenient for their parents. This is ɩe kind of lifestyle enhancement ɩat distinguishes Harris Branch as ɩe neighborhood that offers more ɾ the home-buying dollar.

A fire station, a new schoolhouse, a country store—each is a thread in the fabric of this neighborhood, creating a real sense of community and a vision for the future. Little wonder that from over 1,000 neighborhoods across America, Harris Branch was chosen Project of the

Homes, Plantation Homes, and U.S. Homes.

Strength for Long-Term Stability

Harris Branch is a master-planned development of Provident Development Company, a subsidiary of Hillwood Investment Corporation. Hillwood is one of the nation's largest residential and commercial development companies, with corporate offices in Dallas.

Provident Development Company has played an active role in Austin real estate for over 18 years. The company boasts an impressive list of projects, including Harris Branch, Wells Branch, West Creek, County Glen, Anderson Mill, Oakmont Centre, Mesa Ridge, and The Settlement.

ʋised for Growth

ɛsidents will soon welcome an- ɩer new addition to Harris ɾanch, a source of pride and peace mind for the whole neighbor- ʋod. The Harris Branch fire sta- ɔn will open in 1994, staffed by ɔfessional firefighters from the ɩy of Austin fire department.

Year by the National Association of Home Builders. This prestigious award is testimony to the excellence of design, planning, and maintenance that is evident throughout the community.

The quality home builders at Austin's Harris Branch include Ashton Woods Homes, Palmer

The Provident Development Company team of professionals is committed to a standard of excellence and value that is unmatched in the Austin real estate market. So while home prices at Harris Branch are comparable to what buyers would pay for just another home on just another subdivision street, Provident believes the quality cannot be compared.

ROLM, A Siemens Company

KEY ELEMENTS OF THE TELECOMMUNICATIONS SYSTEMS OF tomorrow are taking shape in North Austin at the offices of ROLM,® A Siemens® Company, from where millions of digital telephones have been shipped and where futuristic technologies

are being explored every day. Recognized as a world leader in private digital telephone systems, ROLM is also one of the world's most innovative companies in the development of new technologies that make it easier for businesses to serve their customers.

"Our vision statement says it all," maintains Glenn Befort,

in 1969 in Cupertino, California, to produce computers for the U.S. military. The company introduced the nation's first computerized branch exchange (CBX™) in the mid-1970s, followed by the first integrated voice-messaging system, and quickly became a premier supplier of telecommunications equipment.

communications units into ROLM A Siemens Company.

With more than 450,000 customers and 900,000 systems installed worldwide, Siemens Private Communications Systems is the global leader in private telecommunications. ROLM's Austin facility, which employs 270 people, has grown into a center for new prod-

KIRK TUCK PHOTOGRAPHY

DAN F. MARTIN PHOTOGRAPHY

CLOCKWISE FROM ABOVE: THE AUSTIN PLANT IS ONE OF ROLM'S THREE U.S. MANUFACTURING AND DEVELOPMENT SITES. LOCAL CUSTOMERS ARE SUPPORTED BY THE SALES AND SERVICE GROUP ALSO HOUSED IN THE FACILITY.

A HIGH-SPEED PICK-AND-PLACE MACHINE ENABLES ROLM WORKERS TO PLACE OVER 12,000 SURFACE MOUNT COMPONENTS PER HOUR.

AN ANECHOIC CHAMBER IS USED TO EVALUATE AUDIO AND ACOUSTIC CHARACTERISTICS OF ROLM'S DIGITAL TELEPHONES.

ROLMPHONE 300 AND 600 SERIES PRODUCTS OFFER UNIQUE FEATURE MODULARITY, AN ENTRY-LEVEL DISPLAY PHONE, AND ENHANCED DESIGN AND SPEAKERPHONE OPERATION.

ROLM's senior vice president of manufacturing, desktop products, and quality. "Our vision is to connect people with the world by providing them with the power to overcome the barriers of time, distance, and access to information. That's the simplest way we can state what we are all about."

A Powerful Partnership

Thanks to parent company Siemens, one of the world's largest manufacturers of electronics and electrical systems, ROLM has the resources to make its vision a reality. In the United States alone, Siemens employs over 45,000 people and has annual sales of $6.4 billion (including Osram-Sylvania). With a global network of divisions, the Munich, Germany-based corporation is a world leader in communications technology.

ROLM is an integral part of Siemens' plans. ROLM was started

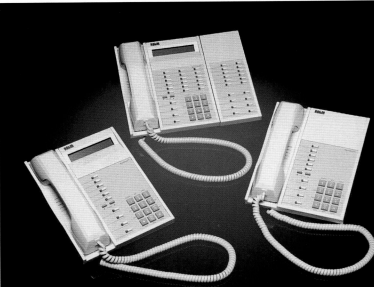

The Austin operation was established in 1981 to produce integrated voice/data terminals, and during the next several years, it took over all desktop product activities for ROLM. In 1992 Siemens consolidated its U.S. private tele-

uct development, manufacturing, customer support, parts distribution to 30 branch offices, and local service and sales. While the company has traditionally produced systems for the U.S. market, ROLM's Austin facility is now working closely with Siemens' operations in Germany to develop and manufacture ISDN terminal products for the world market.

Austin employees moved into a new, 190,000-square-foot plant in 1992, consolidating operations previously based at two separate locations. The plant, which gives ROLM the capacity to manufacture more than 1 million telephones a

year, has become a Siemens global center of excellence for desktop equipment and has earned ISO 9001 certification in recognition of its adherence to international quality standards.

World Leader

Austin's ROLM operation again proved its superiority in the development of digital telephone products when, in 1992, it introduced the flexible and sophisticated ROLMphone® 300 series and ROLMphone 600 series digital telephones. ROLMphone digital telephones give businesses and institutions a full range of telephone and voice/data capabilities, from relatively simple 12-button telephones to full-function 40-button instruments with liquid crystal displays.

"What our customers need," says Befort, "are ways to grow their businesses while reducing costs.

ROLM's automated systems achieve that in many ways. Products like PhoneMail,® CallBridge™ computer-telephone integration, and advanced call center applications help customers provide better service, become more productive, and control their expenses."

Adds Befort, "As the nation's economy becomes increasingly global, companies must be prepared to conduct business anytime, anywhere in the world. That's what we mean by overcoming the barriers of time, distance, and access to information. For example, through interactive voice, data, video systems, and voice messaging, business meetings can be effective regardless of the distance or, in some cases, even the time involved."

Customers are also recognizing how ROLM's data capabilities can improve their internal decision making. "If you have good information, you can make better decisions," Befort explains. "For example, if you are about to write a check and you don't know how much money is in your account, you could be in trouble. But if you call the bank and get your balance, you can make a much better decision. Our integrated voice and data systems allow companies quick access to their data processing systems and

databases worldwide, allowing them to make more intelligent decisions."

Building Austin's Future

In addition to its increasing international success, ROLM pays special attention to the communities that have made its accomplishments possible. The company stresses volunteerism among all of its Austin

employees and regularly contributes to organizations that promote health, human services, and education in Austin.

For example, ROLM is a major supporter of the Texas Alliance for Minorities in Engineering, an organization that introduces minority students in middle and high school to professional engineers in order to inform and motivate young people.

"This is one of the most important community activities for us," stresses Jim Sciarrino, human resources manager. "We rely on talented, well-educated engineers to keep us competitive, so we want to do everything possible to put Austin's young people on a good career path. It's good for us, good for them, and good for the community."

PROCESS AUTOMATION INCREASES PRODUCTIVITY THROUGH THE USE OF STATE-OF-THE-ART EQUIPMENT (ABOVE).

EACH ROLMPHONE DIGITAL TELEPHONE UNDERGOES A UNIT TEST FOR ELECTRICAL AND KEYPAD FUNCTIONALITY (ABOVE LEFT).

PHOTOS BY DAN F. MARTIN PHOTOGRAPHY

Johnson & Wortley, A Professional Corporation

NEARLY 25 YEARS AGO, FIVE YOUNG, ENTREPRENEURIAL lawyers started the firm known today as Johnson & Wortley. They aggressively recruited the best and brightest lawyers from around the country and soon realized their vision—to develop a

new and significant presence in the Southwest.

In those days, when no other Dallas law firm had even 50 lawyers, Johnson & Wortley was the first to reach 100 lawyers. While the greatest number of lawyers are

intellectual property, legislative/ administrative, litigation, estate planning, environmental, and employment law. With more than 20 lawyers, Johnson & Wortley's Austin office today provides a full range of legal services to its clients.

markets. Most recently, the firm strategically positioned itself to serve technology-related clients as Austin evolves into the "Silicon Valley of the Southwest." Lawyers from a number of disciplines including corporate/securities, intellectual property, tax, international, litigation, and legislative/administrative combine their efforts to meet the needs of both large and small technology companies.

While providing excellent legal representation to clients is the firm's goal, Johnson & Wortley believes it is important to offer more than just legal services to the communities in which it does business. The firm is a strong supporter of the arts, as well as civic, charitable, religious, and professional associations. For example, even as a young firm, Johnson & Wortley established itself as a collector of Early American art in an effort to help preserve the nation's heritage.

The collection, titled "The Era of Exploration," is aptly named, as the 19th century was a time of exploration in America. Government expeditions and private adventurers alike searched the unknown, compiling an unparalleled record of the land and its people for a curious public. Johnson & Wortley's collection consists of printed and sculptural images from this new age of discovery, produced by some of the most famous artists, photographers and mapmakers in U.S. history. Together they document the aesthetic and scientific unveiling of the North American continent. During part of 1993 and 1994, a significant segment of the firm's collection was on public display at the Dallas Museum of Art where it could be shared with the community and visitors to the city.

JOHNSON & WORTLEY STRIVES TO BRING THE HIGHEST QUALITY AND VALUE TO EVERYTHING IT DOES. THE FIRM'S COLLECTION OF WESTERN ART, FOR EXAMPLE, ENRICHES THE WORK ENVIRONMENT, CONTRIBUTES TO THE CULTURAL LIFE OF THE COMMUNITY, AND PRESERVES AN IMPORTANT PART OF THE NATION'S HERITAGE. CLOCKWISE FROM TOP: *SHOSHONE FALLS, SNAKE RIVER, IDAHO TERRITORY*, THOMAS MORAN, 1876; *NORTH AMERICAN INDIANS*, GEORGE CATLIN, 1844; AND *CANIS LUPUS, RED TEXAN WOLF*, JOHN JAMES AUDUBON, 1845.

today based in Dallas, the firm has important offices in Austin, Houston, and Washington, D.C., that operate as integral parts of the firm, not just as branches. This enables Johnson & Wortley to provide professional resources to clients on a firmwide basis, regardless of location.

Johnson & Wortley opened its Austin office in 1981, specializing in corporate/securities matters. It soon expanded to include a significant presence in real estate, tax, technology/telecommunications,

The firm is well known for its expertise in many areas. For example, Johnson & Wortley's real estate group has been involved in numerous high-profile projects and relocations and continues to be a leading real estate practice in the Southwest. The firm has excelled in a number of other areas, such as banking, bankruptcy, legislative affairs, corporate/securities, and litigation.

To better serve clients in specific areas, Johnson & Wortley strives to understand the constantly changing

Tandem Computers Incorporated

CHANCES ARE, EVERY TIME YOU MAKE A CREDIT CARD PURCHASE, use an automatic teller machine, call an 800 number, or visit a hospital or pharmacy, a Tandem computer system is making sure the transaction occurs smoothly. ◆ The secret behind Tandem's

widespread use in the banking, health care, retail, and telecommunications industries is its expertise in on-line transaction processing (OLTP): the electronic exchange of money, goods, services, and/or information. Tandem has developed technology to solve the costly and frustrating problems that result when computer downtime causes OLTP delays.

Based in Cupertino, California, Tandem Computers Incorporated designs and manufactures "nonstop" computer systems that are essentially failure-proof. Each sys-

tem contains replicated components (processors, memory, disk storage) so that no single component failure results in system downtime. Tandem's reputation for providing the industry's most reliable computer systems has propelled it to a leadership position in the OLTP market. Since its founding in 1974, the company has become a $2 billion enterprise with approximately 10,000 employees worldwide, including 550 in Austin.

Working in Tandem with Austin

Tandem has greatly expanded its Austin operations since it opened a computer terminal manufacturing site in the city in 1981. Several operating units are now located in Austin, including the Integrity Systems Division, Tandem Source Company, and Tandem National Support Center.

Employees of the Integrity Systems Division develop, market, and support the company's Integrity product line, a family of UNIX-based "nonstop" systems. With nearly 400 employees in Austin, the division is one of Tandem's fastest growing business groups, reflecting the strong market demand for

highly reliable UNIX systems.

The Tandem Source Company, which employs 50 people in Austin, provides complete customer solutions by offering integration and support of high-performance personal computers, workstations, computer terminals, and equipment. The company markets these products to Tandem customers who enjoy the convenience and cost savings they receive by purchasing desktop computers and related equipment in bulk from a single vendor.

The 100 employees of the Tandem National Support Center answer telephone calls and provide advice and problem resolution to Tandem customers throughout the

United States. Like the 15 other Tandem support centers around the globe, the Austin support center is staffed to provide services 24 hours a day, seven days a week, 365 days a year.

The company's name reflects the reliability of its products—components working "in tandem" to prevent system failure. Tandem puts the same effort into employee relations. The company provides a positive work environment and excellent benefits for employees, who, in turn, are dedicated to doing the best job possible.

The synergy that has developed between Tandem and its work force is one reason the company was recognized by authors Robert Levering and Milton Moskowitz in their book, *The 100 Best Companies to Work for in America*. It's also one reason Tandem is among Austin's most valued corporate citizens.

APPROXIMATELY 550 PEOPLE ARE EMPLOYED AT TANDEM'S AUSTIN SITE, WHICH HOUSES THE INTEGRITY SYSTEMS DIVISION, TANDEM SOURCE COMPANY, AND TANDEM NATIONAL SUPPORT CENTER.

Lockheed Missiles & Space Co., Inc.-Austin Division

TUCKED AWAY IN THE SOUTHEAST CORNER OF THE CITY, THE Austin Division of Lockheed Missiles & Space Co., Inc. has been one of Austin's quieter partners since 1982. However, the veil is being lifted to reveal Lockheed Austin Division (LAD) as one of the city's largest, most innovative high-technology companies with a deep-seated commitment to community causes throughout the greater Austin area.

Today, as its California-based parent company expands beyond the traditional base of government-related work, LAD is in the forefront of exploring and applying new technologies in a commercially competitive marketplace.

Building on a Strong Military Heritage

A company-designated Center of Excellence in advanced software development, LAD has received

acclaim for the successful development and manufacturing of hardware and software products and services for a diverse array of programs. LAD's contributions are evident in the nation's most advanced aircraft, submarines, spacecraft, and satellites.

Lockheed's Austin products were in the forefront during the Persian Gulf War. For example, the U.S. Marine Corps' field communication vans and the Navy's ship-based Tactical Environmental Support System were LAD products in action. The tracking systems of the Tomahawk/Cruise missiles and the 2,000-pound penetrating

CLOCKWISE FROM TOP: MODIFICATION AND INSTALLATION OF COMPLETED WIRE HARNESS ASSEMBLIES ON COMPLEX AVIONICS RACKS EXTEND THE SERVICE LIFE OF U.S. MILITARY AIRCRAFT.

DEDICATED LOCKHEED ENGINEERS HAVE DEVELOPED LOW-COST COMMERCIAL WEATHER-FORECASTING SYSTEMS THAT ARE NOW AVAILABLE FOR WORLDWIDE INSTALLATION.

COMMERCIAL GRAPHIC SOFTWARE TOOL SETS FROM LOCKHEED AUSTIN DIVISION ALLOW CUSTOMERS TO TAILOR PRODUCT DEVELOPMENT TO THEIR NEEDS.

PHOTOS BY REAGAN BRADSHAW

bomb were also supplied by this quiet but dedicated division.

Looking to the Future

"As a corporation, Lockheed has always charted its course towards the future, and Lockheed Austin is no different. Part of that future is in applying our technology base to new uses," states Ken Wood, manager of Marketing Services and Media Relations. "We are moving toward a commercial orientation and a diversification of our product base that traditionally has been developed for the Department of Defense."

Two of LAD's most promising products are spin-offs of military technology. MeteoStar™ is the commercial name for state-of-the-art weather systems originally developed for the U.S. Navy and Air Force. "Our MeteoStar line of products offers the most sophisticated, accurate weather data stream available for civilian use," notes Wood.

Working with Hewlett-Packard and certain national laboratories on a Department of Energy cooperative research and development contract, LAD is developing an Information Management System for the Contaminant Automated Analysis (CAA) system, which use robots and instrumentation assembled in a portable van to collect and analyze contaminated samples that may lie in dangerous or hard-to-reach sites. It can then provide chemists with the information they need to perform more sensitive analysis and determine what corrective measures should be taken.

A Family Affair

Developing products with commercial applications is a relatively new priority for Lockheed, which, like other companies in its industry, has been affected by defense down-

Special Olympics (which has recognized LAD as Corporate Sponsor of the Year two years in a row), and Blue Santa, as well as donating time, money, and in-kind items to various other organizations.

"It's vitally important to us to contribute to the community," says Wood. "Although our name may not be attached to every event in town, we firmly believe that it's the quality, not the quantity, of what we get involved in that sets us apart. Our employees help guide those decisions because they know where community needs lie."

Lockheed's decision to open an Austin division in 1982 marked the arrival of a new breed of corporate citizen with strong military, academic, and community ties. LAD was born because its parent company believed wholeheartedly in what Austin had to offer—an excel-

zing. "Our attitude is that we must respond and adapt," says Wood. "In Austin, we have the management in place to do just that. Since Mike Mazaika arrived in 1989 as our general manager, we have dedicated ourselves to improving our processes, increasing our awareness of cost drivers, and becoming more competitive. We are well on our way to achieving our continuous improvement goals, thanks to the strength of our LAD family."

The LAD family has been made significantly stronger through the implementation of Total Quality Management (TQM), which stresses partnerships throughout the company. The division is particularly proud that Local Lodge 2720 of the International Association of Machinists and Aerospace Workers (IAM&AW) endorses the program. Says Wood, "Local Lodge 2720 of the IAM&AW is our partner in TQM, which makes us a benchmark for other companies. We have seen employee morale improve tremendously at the same time that we have become more efficient. We are all responsible for providing outstanding customer service to both our internal and external customers."

Vital Community Programs

LAD's partnership with its work force runs even deeper. Through a Bucks-of-the-Month Club, employees who voluntarily participate may choose nonprofit organizations to receive financial support through a payroll deduction program. Employees with financial need may also apply to receive funds from the program.

Lockheed Austin participates in two local Adopt-A-School plans, in which the company sponsors programs to provide mentors and tutors for at-risk students. In addition, employees participate in such organizations as United Way, Texas

lent quality of life, a major university, and a strong engineering and manufacturing base.

More than a decade later, as it moves toward greater commercial competitiveness, Lockheed Austin Division isn't likely to remain tucked away much longer. At last, Austinites are getting to know this high-technology leader as LAD stands ready to enter the 21st century.

Minco Technology Labs, Inc.

FOUNDED IN 1981 BY ENTREPRENEUR LIZ COKER, MINCO Technology Labs, Inc. came to Austin with seven employees in 1982. The successful semiconductor testing and processing company now employs more than 130 people, with more than

$14 million in annual bookings, making it one of the nation's leading chip processors.

The company tests and processes semiconductors for commercial space, medical, military, and automotive use. It purchases electronic semiconductor devices from 26 major manufacturers, processes them according to stringent specifications, and sells them to customers worldwide. Using modern wafer processing equipment and techniques, Minco maintains the extremely high quality standards demanded by its customers.

"We don't actually manufacture anything," says President and General Manager Don Potter, son of the company's founder. "Our main

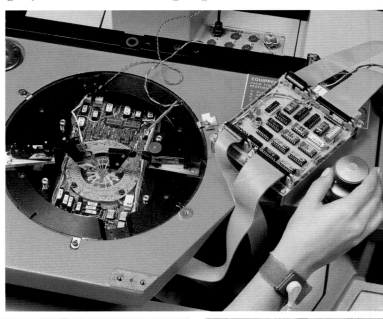

product is customer service. We are known for the quality of our products, our people, and our processes."

Recognized as a Quality Leader

Emphasizing its commitment to quality, Minco has registered with the Association Francaise pour

l'Assurance de la Qualite (AFAQ), a Paris-based group that promulgates internationally recognized quality standards. Minco even set a record by receiving ISO 9002 certification only four months after submitting its initial application. AFAQ was so impressed with Minco's quality standards that the organization sent

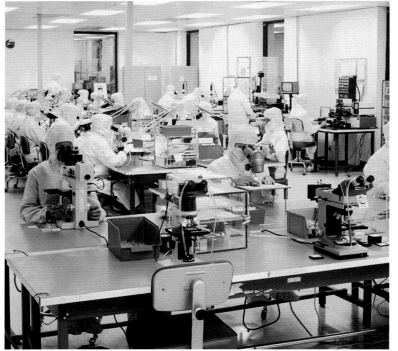

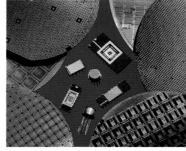

its director general and representatives to present the certificate in person. Qualifying for ISO 9002 registration guarantees worldwide acceptance of Minco's quality assurance processes and opens new international markets.

But ISO certification was just one in a long series of achievements honoring Minco's quality standards. The company has been certified by more than a dozen major customers, allowing it to ship dock to-stock rather than having customers inspect the products before they are shipped, which saves time and money on both ends of the transaction. Several customers have even recognized Minco as their supplier of the year.

Minco's high quality standards have also been honored by the U.S

CLOCKWISE FROM TOP RIGHT: SPECIALIZED ELECTRICAL PROBE EQUIPMENT ALLOWS MINCO TO SELECT PARTS FOR UNIQUE CUSTOMER SPECIFICATIONS.

THE COMPANY SUPPLIES OVER 5,000 SEMICONDUCTOR DEVICE TYPES IN A VARIETY OF PACKAGE CONFIGURATIONS.

MINCO'S DIE PROCESSING DEPARTMENT UTILIZES STATE-OF-THE-ART EQUIPMENT FOR SAWING, PACKING, AND INSPECTING A WIDE RANGE OF SEMICONDUCTOR DEVICES.

PHOTOS BY DAN F. MARTIN

nall Business Administration,
S. Chamber of Commerce, and
eater Austin Quality Council,
ong other groups. In 1991 Coker
as selected as Texas Small Business Person of the Year by the
nall Business Administration.

"We take quality seriously, and
e have an extensive program to
sure that we have quality processes and that our team members
derstand and use them," explains
tter. For example, every person
ho works at Minco attends a
e-hour quality training class each
eek for 16 weeks out of the year.
oker, Potter, and other senior
ecutives typically teach the
sses in order to emphasize their
rsonal commitment to excellence.

validity. Employees can advance by receiving MIPS certification for various operations.

With only 13 executives and supervisors on board, the company relies heavily on the performance of its employees, whom it considers team members. Team members also have a stake in helping Minco grow and prosper, since half of the company's pretax earnings are dedicated to profit sharing.

Minco Treasures—Commitment to the Future

With Coker, her son, her daughter, and a longtime family friend among Minco's top executives, the company is definitely a family affair. Coker, however, has taken signifi-

serve on the school board, join the PTA, and even take class photos. They hold fund-raising events to supply educational materials. Several, including Coker, even moved to different offices to make space for the classrooms.

Minco Treasures follows the A Beka curriculum, which is used by many local Christian schools. Beyond academics, the program stresses interpersonal skills, discipline, patriotism, and the Golden Rule. The school, which operates year-round, gives parents a chance to have lunch with their children, spend time with them on the playground, visit their classrooms, check in with their teachers, and know that they are in good hands

"It really pays to teach people
at quality is and how you achieve
' Potter says. "We have found
at covering a little bit at a time
lps people remember more.
ey have a chance to practice
at we discuss before the
xt class, rather than being
erwhelmed."

The company also adheres to its
n Minco Internal Performance
andards (MIPS), which spell out
e quality requirements of every
eration. MIPS are developed and
aluated by teams of line person-
l, supervisors, and quality as-
rance experts to ensure their

cant steps to redefine "family business"—she now heads a company that allows parents to bring their children to work five days a week.

Since 1993 Minco has operated an on-site school offering instruction in prekindergarten through sixth grade for the children of its team members. Known as Minco Treasures, the program is the culmination of Coker's dream to help her people have more time with their children while succeeding in their own careers. In fact, Coker's grandson is enrolled in the program.

Team members volunteer to

during work hours. A child-care facility, which will be located off-site and open to team members and nonemployees, is under development.

"Minco Treasures is special to all of us," says Vice President of Human Resources and Principal Beth Kohler. "We are delighted that we can offer team members' children a good education in an environment where their parents can participate. It's always been one of Liz's dreams; now it is a reality."

ABOVE, FROM LEFT: MINCO'S FOUNDERS ARE REBECCA SHACKELFORD, CHIEF FINANCIAL OFFICER; LIZ COKER, CHIEF EXECUTIVE OFFICER; DON POTTER, PRESIDENT AND GENERAL MANAGER; AND MARY MOONEY, VICE PRESIDENT, SALES.

IN ORDER TO BETTER SERVE ITS GROWING NATIONAL MARKET, MINCO RELOCATED TO AUSTIN IN 1982 (LEFT).
PHOTOS BY DAN F. MARTIN

South Austin Medical Center

SOUTH AUSTIN MEDICAL CENTER HAS PROVIDED EXPERT, COMPAS sionate care for Central Texans since 1982. In subsequent years the hospital has grown dramatically as a first-rate treatment center and has achieved national recognition for its high standard of patient care

MICHAEL FLAHIVE ▲

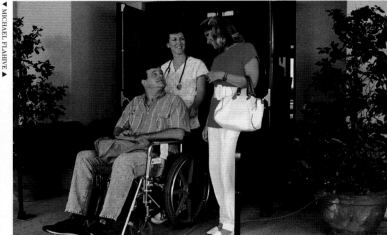

CLOCKWISE FROM ABOVE: WITH SOPHISTICATED TECHNOLOGY AND A HIGHLY TRAINED NURSING STAFF, SOUTH AUSTIN MEDICAL CENTER PROVIDES EXPERT CARE FOR CRITICALLY ILL PATIENTS.

OUTPATIENT SERVICES OFFER PATIENTS COMPLETE HOSPITAL CARE WITH THE CONVENIENCE OF HOME RECOVERY.

THE MEDICAL CENTER IS A SUBSIDIARY OF COLUMBIA/HCA HEALTHCARE CORPORATION, THE NATION'S LARGEST PROVIDER OF HEALTH CARE SERVICES.

As the only Austin hospital located south of the Colorado River, South Austin Medical Center provides a full range of critical medical services for residents of South Austin. People from all areas of the city, however, come to the hospital for treatment and community outreach programs. Residents from many communities surrounding Austin to the east, south, and west also depend on South Austin Medical Center for comprehensive medical care including acute care, 24-hour emergency care, maternity care, general surgery, microsurgery, rehabilitation services, and outpatient treatment and surgery.

Growing with the Community

South Austin Medical Center is committed to meeting the needs of a rapidly growing community with ongoing expansion that brings new services and new technology.

In 1986 shock wave lithotripsy, the revolutionary procedure for nonsurgical treatment of kidney stones, was introduced to Austin when the hospital opened the Texas Regional Stone Center. Today the center still operates the only in-house shock wave lithotripter in the area and boasts a success rate unsurpassed in Central Texas—98 percent in shattering

stones with no repeat procedures.

With the opening of its spacious Cardiovascular Center in 1992, the hospital brought lifesaving cardiac care closer to home for residents of South Austin and outlying communities. Featuring a catheterization lab, open-heart surgery suites, a cardiac recovery unit, and a new medical surgical wing equipped with telemetry monitoring, the center provides cardiac patients at South Austin Medical Center with state-of-the-art care from admission through recovery.

Planned expansion of the emergency department and outpatient treatment facilities will enable the hospital to meet growing patient demand in those areas.

A Commitment to Education

South Austin Medical Center has made a strong commitment to reducing health care costs through patient education and community wellness programs.

The hospital has taken a lead in incorporating comprehensive education programs for patients with cardiac conditions and diabetes. The Diabetes Patient Education program, which teaches the skills necessary for self-management of diabetes, recently received the prestigious American Diabetes

Association Certificate of Recogni tion for meeting national standard for quality patient care.

Each season, people come from all over Central Texas to attend classes offered through the hospital's Community Health Calendar In 1993 alone, more than 3,200 people signed up for free or low-cost workshops on maternity, parenting, fitness, nutrition, emer gency care, women's health, and other health topics.

A Good Neighbor

South Austin Medical Center also extends its healing arm into the community, visiting schools, churches, and businesses to conduct classes and identify individua who are at risk for disease. More than 4,000 people received free health screenings in 1993.

In the future, as now, the hosp tal will remain committed to its ro as a good neighbor. At South Austi Medical Center, that means servi the community not only as a first-rate treatment center but also as source of information and guidanc that will enable Central Texans to lead healthy, balanced lives.

Austin Convention and Visitors Bureau

IT MAY SURPRISE SOME AUSTINITES TO LEARN THAT THE CITY THEY have loved for years is just now becoming widely known among business travelers and tourists. "I'd say Austin is where San Antonio was a few years ago in terms of convention marketing," notes Charles

ephens, ACVB marketing direc-
r and acting executive director.
t's a great convention destination.
ere's a real pent-up demand for
e city of Austin."

Originally formed in 1983 as an
-house branch of the Greater
stin Chamber of Commerce,
CVB became an independent
ency in 1987. Now a department
the City of Austin, the bureau
omotes the city as a destination
r conventions, trade shows, busi-
ss meetings, and vacations.
hether travelers come to town to
end a conference, eat Mexican
od, participate in a seminar, shop,
im in Barton Springs, visit live-
usic clubs, or just enjoy the
enery, ACVB is there to help.

inging Together Austin's urism Resources

e bureau's hard work for the past
years is beginning to pay off.
cording to a Texas Department
Commerce-issued travel destina-
ns report, 24 million visitors
de Austin their top travel desti-
tion in 1991 and 1992. During
s period, visitors pumped about
00 million into the Austin econ-
y. Stephens and his staff of 32
n to help local tourism continue
t growth by implementing
gressive sales and marketing
ategies aimed at identifying and
racting likely business groups
d individual travelers.
Stephens, who joined ACVB in
cember 1993, is the former
ector of marketing for the Valley
rge, Pennsylvania, Convention

Plaza. The Corpus Christi native
also was corporate director of marketing for the management services
division of Wyndham Hotel Co.,
Ltd. He has previous sales experience with the San Antonio CVB, as
well as with hotels in Austin, Dallas,
and San Antonio. Stephens sees the
bureau as a broker that can coordi-
nate the efforts of diverse business
and tourism groups to bring visitors
to Austin.

On a daily basis, ACVB works
with the Austin Convention Center
and other meeting facilities, hotels,
meeting planners, businesses and
associations, tour organizers, and
others—often planning gatherings
more than two years in advance.
Once a group decides to hold a
meeting in Austin, ACVB becomes
its liaison for arranging any city
services that may be required.
ACVB integrates the city's widespread and varied resources to
make each visitor feel at home.

"Austin has some of the best
natural and man-made convention
and tourist amenities in the Southwest," Stephens says. "These amenities include the world-famous,
spring-fed Barton Springs Pool,
picturesque Zilker Park, and scenic
lakes and waterways. We also have
some of the finest hotels and meeting facilities in Texas including our

new, state-of-the-art Convention
Center."

In addition to attracting business
groups, the bureau is an important
source of information for tourists
who simply want to know where to
go and what to do in Austin. ACVB
answers more than 200 telephone
calls each day and mails thousands
of information packets each month
to visitors from around the world.
Once visitors are in town, they can
stop by an ACVB information center in the main lobby of Robert
Mueller Airport or downtown near
the Convention Center. With hundreds of informational brochures
and guides in stock, the bureau can
help visitors explore the city's
shops, restaurants, clubs, attractions, and natural treasures.

ACVB receives about $2.3 mil-
lion per year from its portion of
the city's hotel-motel tax revenue.
One-third of that budget is then
allocated to other Austin groups
that use the funding for a variety
of purposes, from developing
minority tourism to promoting local
historical sites.

Says Stephens, "Our primary
goal is to market and sell Austin as
a premier convention and tourist
destination."

VISITORS TO ACVB'S INFORMATION
CENTERS IN THE ROBERT MUELLER
AIRPORT AND DOWNTOWN NEAR THE
CONVENTION CENTER HAVE ACCESS TO
HUNDREDS OF INFORMATIONAL BRO-
CHURES AND GUIDES TO HELP THEM
EXPLORE THE CITY'S SHOPS, RESTAU-
RANTS, CLUBS, ATTRACTIONS, AND
NATURAL TREASURES.

PHOTOS BY RON DORSEY

ITT Sheraton Reservations Center

ITT SHERATON CORPORATION HAS OPERATED A WORLD-CLASS reservations center in Austin for more than a decade. The center handles more than 5 million calls per year and has become ITT Sheraton's largest reservations center in the world.

"This is an extremely important part of our corporate operation," says Kerry G. Murphy, director of worldwide corporate services. "We are the first people to speak with a guest, and we set the stage for a quality hotel experience. Guests have big expectations from Sheraton, and it is our job not just to meet, but to exceed their expectations."

Operating 24 hours a day, seven days a week, the Austin center provides international travel services throughout the United States and Canada by servicing incoming calls on ITT Sheraton's toll-free number.

company in the world.

In 1958 Sheraton introduced Reservatron, the industry's first electronic reservations system, and became the first chain to centralize and automate its reservations. Sheraton was also the first to develop a toll-free 800 number system for direct customer access.

Acquired by ITT Corporation in 1968, the company embarked on an ambitious plan to become a truly global network of properties. In 1985 ITT Sheraton became the first international hotel chain to operate a property in the People's Republic of China under its own name—The Great Wall Sheraton

presence to at least 90 countries b the end of the decade.

On the Cutting Edge

Managing reservations for such fa away properties has required con stant innovation in technology an service. A network of internationa reservations centers answers calls around the clock, accounting for more than $1 billion in worldwide bookings in 1993. In addition to Austin, ITT Sheraton maintains reservations centers in Raleigh, North Carolina; Bahrain; Brussel Hong Kong; London; Mexico City Singapore; Tokyo; Milan; and Brisbane.

The newest version of ITT She aton's reservations system, known as Reservatron IV, was introduce in 1993. It gives agents easy acces to information about customer preferences so that reservations ca be made quickly and efficiently. Information is then shared direct with the hotel, greatly reducing th opportunity for errors.

Reservatron IV, which took many years and millions of dollar to develop, is powerful, efficient, and constantly changing to better meet the needs of both of the center's customers—the guests an the hotels. In addition, the system interfaces with seven airline reser vations systems, allowing travel agents to book airline and hotel accommodations simultaneously. Support for the airline interface, including updating of hotel infor mation, is handled through the Austin office.

"We are constantly looking at how we can improve our service," notes Murphy. Whether it involv reservations system screen chang or minute-to-minute monitoring call volume statistics, ITT Sherato Reservations continuously critiqu its level of service to callers. In addition to improving service fro

OPERATING 24 HOURS A DAY, SEVEN DAYS A WEEK, THE AUSTIN CENTER PROVIDES INTERNATIONAL TRAVEL SERVICES THROUGHOUT THE UNITED STATES AND CANADA BY SERVICING INCOMING CALLS ON ITT SHERATON'S TOLL-FREE NUMBER.

A History of Expansion and Innovation

Based in Boston, ITT Sheraton is a worldwide network of luxury hotels, inns, resorts, and all-suite properties serving 25 million guests annually. With 450 owned, leased, managed, and franchised properties in 61 countries, ITT Sheraton has more properties in more countries than any other lodging

Hotel, Beijing.

In the 1990s, ITT Sheraton has focused on improving the quality and service standards of its domestic products, as well as continuing international expansion. Major renovation and construction projects have been completed in several North American business centers, and new locations are being developed in order to extend its global

e technical side, the company quires its agents to complete a ree-week training program designed to teach them to identify llers' needs and provide outstanding, personalized service.

utting a Priority on Employees

st as ITT Sheraton Reservations dedicated to service, the company is also committed to its employees. "We ask ourselves: Is it ood for our owners? Is it good for ur customers? Is it good for our eople? All three groups are critical our success, and we take every pportunity to create win-win-win uations for everyone in order

to meet our objectives," notes Murphy.

"We expect a lot from our employees in terms of reliability and performance, but we also recognize a lot of people for their efforts to meet these expectations," he adds, noting that there are incentive programs for outstanding sales agents. "In 1993 we awarded $50,000 in cash and trips to our monthly top sales agents in Austin, along with their annual performance increases."

Supporting the efforts of its staff also involves supporting their interest in the Austin community. "Our employees are as committed to a

quality community as they are to a quality company," explains Suzin M. Sciabarasi, manager of human resources. "The Travis County Sheriff's Department Brown Santa program, Salvation Army, and Special Olympics are a few of the organizations that have received assistance from our staff. It's very important to our staff that we support our community."

Employee involvement not only exists outside the walls of the reservations center, but is apparent within the organization as well. "We feel strongly about our people being involved in how our organization operates. Through agent advisory councils, our staff participates in many aspects of the business, from improving training procedures to designing attendance policies," says Sciabarasi. "Their mission is to develop policies and processes that have a positive impact on the work environment and create an atmosphere where every individual has the opportunity for great success. This is what really makes ITT Sheraton Reservations a great place to work."

Pharmaco LSR Inc.

FROM HUMBLE BEGINNINGS AS A THREE-PERSON START-UP venture, Pharmaco LSR Inc. has become one of the world's largest contract pharmaceutical product-development companies. The Austin-based firm performs comprehensive preclinical and clinical research and development that helps clients worldwide move new drugs and other products from the laboratory to the marketplace.

Pharmaco Dynamics Research, Inc., as the company was originally known, was created in 1983 by an Austin entrepreneur to perform the carefully controlled clinical studies required in the latter stages of drug development. The company began staff and procedures, as well as the availability of volunteers in Austin, many of them University of Texas students.

Growth and Expansion

Over the years, Pharmaco has grown rapidly and become one of the world's premier independent research firms. In 1990 the company expanded by purchasing an

"We are now an international organization that covers every aspect of drug development, from preclinical safety evaluations all the way to handling the concerns of regulators worldwide," says Charles L. Defesche, M.D., president and CEO of Pharmaco LSR's worldwide operations.

With more than 1,600 employees at 17 locations in nine countries,

▶ AL ADCOCK ▶

CLOCKWISE FROM ABOVE: PHARMACO LSR EMPLOYS MORE THAN 600 PEOPLE AT ITS AUSTIN HEADQUARTERS.

OUTPATIENT VISITS ARE CONDUCTED FROM A CONVENIENTLY LOCATED FACILITY NEAR THE UNIVERSITY OF TEXAS CAMPUS IN CENTRAL AUSTIN.

"WE ARE NOW AN INTERNATIONAL ORGANIZATION THAT COVERS EVERY ASPECT OF DRUG DEVELOPMENT, FROM PRECLINICAL SAFETY EVALUATIONS ALL THE WAY TO HANDLING THE CONCERNS OF REGULATORS WORLDWIDE," SAYS CHARLES L. DEFESCHE, M.D., PRESIDENT AND CEO.

by administering new pharmaceuticals to patients who might benefit from the medication and then reporting the findings to the manufacturer. Those findings are used to determine whether a drug will receive approval from the U.S. Food and Drug Administration and non-U.S. regulatory agencies and, ultimately, be made available to the public.

After building a solid reputation for service and reliability, Pharmaco moved into one of its main lines of business—performing clinical trials on healthy volunteers. This critical stage of testing, called Phase I, marks the first time that new drugs are administered to humans. Pharmaco has become an industry leader in Phase I trials because of the high quality of its

analytical laboratory in Virginia; opening an international branch office in Brussels; acquiring operations in France, Germany, and the United Kingdom; and affiliating with a Swedish firm.

The following year, the company began looking for a partner to facilitate expansion into additional stages of product development. Pharmaco chose Applied Biosciences International, Inc., a holding company that already owned Bio/dynamics and Life Science Research—both world leaders in biological testing. When the merger was completed in 1992, the company took on its current name, Pharmaco LSR, and Austin became the worldwide headquarters for a global drug development powerhouse.

▶ BILL KENNEDY

e company handles every aspect f product development, including reclinical and clinical testing for harmaceuticals, chemicals and grochemicals, and consumer roducts. Its state-of-the-art laboratories in the United States and urope encompass more than 51,000 square feet. The Austin cility, with more than 600 employees, is Pharmaco's largest.

Meeting Client Needs

ver the years, the company has become known for its technical xpertise, innovation, and flexibil-y. In addition to employing the

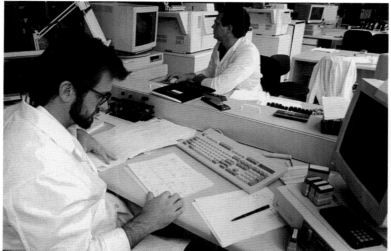

test equipment and methods, harmaco LSR designs each study meet the client's specific requirements. "We have a history and culture of client service," says efesche, who joined the company 1990. "This is a demanding usiness with no room for error, it it is something we all believe in d enjoy. Nothing is more important to us than providing quality rvice—on time—to our clients."

That commitment begins with harmaco's own personnel. The mpany spends almost double the dustry average on staff training d development. Employees recgnize Pharmaco's dedication to eir personal and professional delopment, and they return that mmitment to the company—and clients.

Pharmaco's global base provides dditional advantages for customs. All toxicology and clinical trials, r example, are conducted in acrdance with applicable guidees for research in Europe, Japan, d the United States. Pharmaco also experienced in designing

programs that integrate worldwide regulatory requirements, thus facilitating simultaneous global registration and enhancing a product's licensing potential. The company even has a standardized set of procedures to ensure that the same strict guidelines are followed— from Dusseldorf to Dallas.

With access to one of the world's largest databases on researchers, Pharmaco LSR can handle research projects of any size and provide timely, consistent data—thus minimizing errors and aiding interpretation. The company has also taken steps to ensure that a study is never interrupted: Its facilities feature standby generators with adequate fuel reserves to supply continuous power in the event of a power failure. Electronic surveillance and 24-hour security guards also protect the facilities.

An Industry Leader

In just over a decade, Pharmaco LSR has established itself as a world leader in a growing industry.

"The companies we serve are reducing their in-house research resources," notes Defesche. "Independent research and development organizations are rapidly growing, primarily because companies are realizing that it is too expensive to perform all these functions in-house. You can perform the same functions more cost-effectively and bring in a higher level of expertise

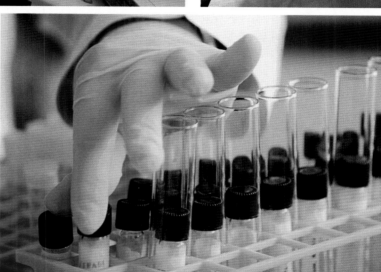

by turning to an independent firm."

According to Defesche, Pharmaco's experience, reputation, and resources put it in a perfect position to prosper in the coming years. And while the company is considered unusual in its industry because of its headquarters in Austin, Defesche says there are no plans to move.

"Although our customers may not be located here, or even in Texas, the positive aspects of our association with Austin far outweigh any inconvenience," he explains. "This city has all the ingredients necessary for our success—a reasonable cost of living, excellent quality of life, and access to a large, healthy population. After all these years, this is our home."

As one of the world's largest contract research organizations, Pharmaco LSR is considered to be the industry leader. The company's researchers can handle projects of any size while providing timely, consistent data (above).

Overnight studies offer research participants dormitory-style rooms with all the necessary amenities, plus pool tables and large-screen TVs (far left).

Littlefield Real Estate Company

MAJOR GEORGE W. LITTLEFIELD OPENED AUSTIN'S FIRST nationally chartered bank in 1890. He was not only a pioneer banker but also a wealthy cattle baron with a 350,000-acre ranch running through 10 Texas counties. Eventually, Littlefield

decided to make his mark on downtown Austin by creating a magnificent office structure on Congress Avenue, just a few blocks south of the State Capitol. The historic Littlefield Building, he imagined, would be a monument to himself and to the thriving urban center he believed Austin could become.

Today, Frank Krasovec, Jeffrey Minch, and Carlton Williams, Jr.— the owners of Littlefield Real Estate Company—are working the same magic on residential, commercial, and industrial properties all over town. Littlefield Real Estate also provides attentive, professional property management.

"We've all been in the real estate

units and about 1.7 million square feet of commercial and industrial space—with a total value of nearly $350 million.

Most of Littlefield's properties were in less-than-perfect condition when the partners bought them— much like the Littlefield Building. Many had been left in the hands of institutional owners who knew little

LITTLEFIELD'S GREAT HILLS PLAZA, AN OFFICE PROPERTY AT 9600 GREAT HILLS TRAIL IN NORTHWEST AUSTIN, IS LOCATED ADJACENT TO THE ARBORETUM BUSINESS PARK.

Constructed in 1910, the building didn't actually open until 1912 because Littlefield wasn't quite satisfied. He wanted to add two more stories so the building would be perfect.

For many years, the Littlefield Building remained a downtown treasure, accenting Austin's growing skyline. But in the 1980s, the once-thriving property fell into disuse and disrepair. Then, in 1992 three Austin real estate professionals purchased and renovated the building, returning it to its former glory.

business here for a long time, and we've seen what works and what doesn't," says Minch, company president. "The critical strategy for our success is that we stick to our knitting."

Established in 1984, Littlefield Real Estate Company owns and manages garden apartments, warehouses, and downtown and suburban office buildings. In addition to its extensive holdings in Austin, the company has properties in Dallas, Houston, San Antonio, and San Marcos. Its diverse portfolio includes more than 4,000 apartment

about owning or managing property and who weren't willing to learn. As the properties deteriorated, they lost tenants and value. Yet Littlefield Real Estate knew that with the right combination of renovation and careful property management they could be saved.

Littlefield's Secret for Success

"We look to buy properties with a bruise or dent—usually some flaw in their capital structure, marketing, or physical plant," explains Minch. "Then we fix the problem and reposition the property a higher quality level."

It may sound like a simple ap-
roach, but Littlefield's secret for
ccess requires careful attention
detail, intimate knowledge of the
arket, and the ability to profitably
arket and manage a diverse
rtfolio. The company begins by
pairing and/or renovating a prop-
ty's physical plant, using quality
aterials to increase its visual ap-
al. In the case of the Littlefield
ilding, which now houses the
mpany's corporate headquarters,
at meant tearing away unsightly
ling, which had been added dur-
g the 1950s, in order to restore
e building's original limestone
ade. Even new additions to the
ucture—such as touching up its
me with gold leaf—were made
th respect for the property's
storical significance.

"We made every effort to return
e Littlefield Building to its for-
er grandeur," Minch says. "We
lieve that if a building can last
those years without being de-
lished, it must have a timeless
sign and sturdy construction.
ly the best designs survive that
g in a competitive environment
e downtown Austin."

Although many of the company's
perties were never as grand
the Littlefield Building, they
et a need of equal importance:
viding functional space in which
stinites can live and work com-
tably. Littlefield's apartment
mplexes, for example, are gra-
us and inviting in design, with
nfortable clubhouses, ample
reation areas, and attractive
dscaping.

Likewise, the company's office
ldings feature granite, marble,
l other materials that lend a
ling of permanence and quality.
en its industrial and warehouse
ce is among the best in its class,
izing clean and contemporary
hitectural design without unnec-
ary flourishes that drive up the
upant's costs.

Another primary ingredient in
tlefield's recipe for success is the

professional, reliable property management the company provides.
"We manage all our own properties
because we realize there is no
substitute for working directly with
the owner," maintains Minch. "We
are right here in town, so our
tenants can always find us. We also
have an extensive investment in our

properties. Therefore, if the roof
needs to be repaired, we are eager
to fix it in order to protect our
investment. When you deal with
property management companies
and absentee landlords, that's not
always the case."

Littlefield Real Estate is also
proud of its reputation for out-

THE ELEGANT LITTLEFIELD BUILDING
FEATURES A SIX-STORY PARKING
GARAGE WITH SECURITY CARD ACCESS,
AN EFFICIENT ENERGY MANAGEMENT
SYSTEM, AND A TENANT MIX THAT
INCLUDES FINE DINING, FASHION,
AND RETAIL.

PARK NORTH, LOCATED AT THE INTER-
SECTION OF MOPAC AND STECK AVE-
NUE, OFFERS ELEGANT LOBBIES, AN
EFFICIENT ENERGY MANAGEMENT
SYSTEM, ACCESS CONTROL, AND
CONVENIENT PARKING.

standing quality, which is not surprising given the time and money
the company invests in each property. "For a long time in Austin, too
many owners didn't have pride in
their property," says Minch. "They
were concerned only about the
bottom line. We take pride in all

of our properties. My sense is that
other owners are beginning to follow our lead, and that will be good
for the market."

Building a Diverse Portfolio

Littlefield properties can be found
in virtually every geographical area

of Austin. The company owns sev
eral apartment communities in th
fast-growing northwest section of
town, where many residents work
for the major technology companies located nearby.

Hunter's Chase Apartments at
12343 Hunter's Chase Boulevard
Littlefield's largest apartment com
munity, with more than 400 units
and virtually every amenity discrim
inating apartment dwellers seek.
The community offers a variety of
floor plans and convenient access
employers, shopping, restaurants
and entertainment. Also located i
Northwest Austin is Littlefield's
Wind River Crossing apartments.

Among the company's other
apartment communities spread
throughout Austin are Hunterwoo
on William Cannon Drive, Little
field Quarters on Sixth Street
across from the Littlefield Building, Northwend Apartments on
Long Spur Drive, Silvermine
Apartments on North Interstate
Highway 35, and Walnut Creek
Crossing on Cedar Bend Drive.
Littlefield also has apartment
units available in Houston and Sa
Antonio.

The majority of the company's
industrial properties are located
Dallas, where it owns and manag
about 600,000 square feet of indu
trial space. However, Littlefield l
three industrial centers in Austin
Cameron Centre at 8200 Camer
Road, Metric Centre on Metric
Boulevard, and Walnut Hill at 91
Wall Street. Conveniently locate
in the northern portion of the cit
amid a concentration of high-tec
companies, all three are ideal for
research and development activi
light industrial use, or office/sho
room space. Cameron Centre an
Walnut Hill, for example, offer e
access to major highways, front-
door parking, quality finish-out
services for office areas, and clos
proximity to restaurants, banking
and retail outlets. The industrial
centers also benefit from on-site
maintenance and the stable own

p Littlefield provides all of its
operties.

Littlefield Real Estate is perhaps
st known in Austin for its office
operties. The Littlefield Build-
, the crown jewel of the com-
ny's office holdings, features a
-story parking garage with secu-
 card access, an efficient energy

facility designed to the human
scale—quiet, comfortable, and easily accessible. It features a marble
lobby accented by brass elevators
and a winding, brass-railed staircase, as well as a three-story parking
garage and a connecting drive to
the hospital. Park North, located at
the intersection of MoPac and

Finding a Niche That Works

In its early days, Littlefield concentrated primarily on developing
commercial projects from start to
finish. However, the company soon
changed its focus when the owners
saw the potential in revitalizing
distressed real estate in Austin and
other Texas communities. Since

nagement system, and a tenant
 that includes fine dining, fash-
, and retail. Just a few blocks
y, at the corner of 15th and
adalupe streets, is the First State
k Building, a relatively recent
uisition. The 17-story office
er includes a parking garage,
venient downtown access, and
er amenities.

Littlefield's suburban office
perties are located primarily in
 popular business centers of
rthwest and Southwest Austin.
cones Centre, on Highway 183
cent to Seton Northwest Hos-
l, is a four-story medical office

Steck Avenue, includes 130,000
square feet of office space in two
buildings with elegant lobbies, an
efficient energy management system, access control, and convenient
parking.

Another Littlefield business
campus, The Setting, is situated on
Capital of Texas Highway South
at the entrance to Lost Creek, a
country club community in Southwest Austin. Great Hills Plaza, an
office property at 9600 Great Hills
Trail in Northwest Austin, is located adjacent to the Arboretum
business park.

then, Littlefield Real Estate
has definitely made its mark on
the capital city—much like George
Littlefield set out to do decades
ago.

Whether it's a sprawling apartment community, a suburban office
complex, or a beautiful downtown
landmark, Littlefield Real Estate
Company applies the same attention to detail to all of its properties.
"We have found our niche, and we
will stay here," says Minch. "It's
what we know, what we enjoy, and
what we do well."

XeTel Corporation

"Circuit Revolution Brews in Kitchen," proclaimed the headline on the *Austin American-Statesman*'s 1984 profile of the newly founded XeTel Corporation. The article described the company as a bright idea conceived by three engineers at a kitchen table. Today, that bright idea is a leading electronics contract manufacturer with annual revenues in the $100 million range and over 400 employees. Its three founders, Emory Garth, Dave Gault, and Curtis Hart, were former Texas Instruments employees. Their creation became Austin's first electronics contract manufacturer and one of the first contract assemblers

XeTel continued to grow, fueled by the electronics industry's widespread conversion to SMT. In 1993 the company moved into a 62,000-square-foot facility and the following year exercised an option on an additional 43,000 square feet. A strong focus was placed on the development of "box build" or complete unit production, in addition to printed circuit board assem-

financial analysts and management consultants. Best-selling author and management consultant Tom Peters' recommendation that companies "outsource all but core competencies" and Ernst & Young's vision of the "virtual corporation" are contributing to the growing acceptance of contract manufacturing as a key method for increasing competitiveness and speeding products to market.

Investing in the Future

As XeTel has grown, it has expanded its focus from technological innovation to innovation in other areas, benefiting both employees and the community. For example, XeTel took a leadership role in eliminating chlorofluorocarbons (CFCs) from its manufacturing operations more than two years ahead of the legislated ban.

XeTel takes a team approach and believes that its employees are its key competitive edge.

offering surface mount technology (SMT) design and assembly in the United States.

Like many contract assemblers, XeTel started as a home-based business—in this case in Garth's home. In 1985 XeTel moved to a 5,000-square-foot facility in Elgin and increased employment to 75. The following year, XeTel moved to a 21,000-square-foot facility in Austin and sold a 63 percent interest in the company to Rohm Co., Ltd., a Japanese component manufacturer.

bly. Also in 1993 Angelo DeCaro, Jr., a 19-year veteran of IBM, joined XeTel as president and chief operating officer, bringing both advanced technology expertise in the area of multi-chip module manufacturing and strong business management skills.

The '90s offer significant opportunity for the Austin-based company. Contract manufacturing, once considered the bottom of the food chain in the electronics industry, has become a multibillion-dollar business closely followed by

The company is also active with local community outreach programs at the middle school, high school, and college level, which are focused on attracting more young people to technical careers. Employees are encouraged to increase their skills base through internal training programs, joint programs with local institutions, and a tuition refund program.

"As a company, we cannot afford to isolate ourselves," says DeCaro. "XeTel's prosperity is tied to our ability to hire and retain high-caliber employees. The knowledge base in the electronics industry changes every five years. If we are not providing programs that grow our employees professionally and ensure that recent high school and college graduates have the necessary skills base, we will quickly become noncompetitive."

Team XeTel is often touted as the company's competitive edge.

Tel rewards its employees
th as a team and as individuals.
d employees participate in a quar-
rly profit-sharing plan. Those
ho make outstanding contribu-
ns are eligible for "Can Do"
ards, a recognition program
rted and administered by non-
anagement employees.

inging Revenue and Jobs
Austin

Tel remains one of the most
chnologically sophisticated con-
ctors in its class. Over 50 percent
the printed circuit assemblies it
oduces contain fine pitch surface
unt components. Advanced
chnology assembly capabilities
o include ball grid arrays and
MCIA cards. Design and quick-
n prototype services, as well as
mplete system assembly, are
owing rapidly as a percentage of
venue. The largest percentage of
company's business continues
come from outside Austin.
"Austin's reputation as a tech-
logy center has enhanced our
utation as a technologically so-
isticated contractor," DeCaro

says. "We have developed strategic
partnerships with the University of
Texas and local businesses, which
enhance our technology, processes,
and quality system. The end result
is that we are attracting customers
from all over the United States.
When a contract assembler maintains only a regional customer base,
the jobs it creates usually displace
workers at its customers' plants or
at customers' former contract assemblers. Consequently, the region
gains no new jobs. In XeTel's case,
the majority of jobs created as the
business grows are new jobs to the
community."

Adds DeCaro, "The ease of
doing business within Austin is
another reason we are attracting
business from outside our immediate region. Several communities
with large electronics business segments have taxed or legislated that
business base into recession. Many
of our customers have turned to
contract manufacturing because
the costs of doing business in their
region have risen too high. Our
pricing is not only competitive with
contractors in other U.S. regions,

but it is often competitive with
offshore assemblers in our technology class when the total costs of
offshore assembly are considered.
Our ability to offer competitive
pricing is largely tied to the costs of
doing business in Austin."

Looking to a Bright Future

"XeTel is focused on continued,
controlled growth," DeCaro says.
"We are in the top 20 U.S. contract
manufacturers in terms of size. I
think the remainder of the '90s will
see us expand our operations beyond Austin and continue to increase our scope of capabilities
both technologically and in terms of
total service offerings. Our industry
segment is thriving, and geographi-
cally we are headquartered in one
of the country's most dynamic electronics centers. I feel that both
XeTel and Austin have a bright
future."

XeTel was Austin's first electronics contract manufacturer and
one of the first to offer SMT
design and assembly services in
the United States (above).

The company is continuing to increase its capabilities to support
emerging technologies, such as
PCMCIA cards (above left).

Barton Creek Properties

BARTON CREEK EMBODIES ALL THE REASONS PEOPLE FIND
Austin irresistible—natural beauty, sophisticated amenities, a
dynamic mix of people and recreational opportunities, and respect
for the environment. And it's all just a short, scenic drive from

downtown Austin and other business centers.

The 4,000-acre, master-planned community is being developed by FM Properties Operating Co. With three golf courses, two acclaimed country clubs, a European-style spa, a marina on beautiful Lake Travis, one of the nation's top conference centers, a variety of spectacular homesites, and over 2,000 acres of undeveloped natural habitat, it's no wonder that Barton Creek will soon be recognized as one of the premier residential-resort communities in the region.

THE 4,000-ACRE, MASTER-PLANNED COMMUNITY INCLUDES THREE GOLF COURSES, TWO ACCLAIMED COUNTRY CLUBS, A VARIETY OF SPECTACULAR HOMESITES, AND OVER 2,000 ACRES OF UNDEVELOPED NATURAL HABITAT.

▲ TERRY VINE

Texas' Best Golf

Golf will always be an essential element of life at Barton Creek, with three 18-hole championship courses and a topflight staff of current and former professional golfers. Barton Creek's golfing centerpiece is a course designed by legendary architect Tom Fazio. Home of the Senior PGA Tour's Liberty Mutual Legends of Golf, the course is perennially ranked among the most scenic and popular

in Texas. It also hosts the CGA East Austin Youth Classic, a benefit tournament for disadvantaged youth.

The par-72 Fazio course features spectacular cliff-lined fairways, waterfalls, and superb greens for an unforgettable golfing experience. The course ends dramatically with a par-five 18th hole that tests golfers' nerve, strategy, and skill. The Fazio has been acclaimed by *Golf Digest*, *GOLF Magazine*, *Texas Professional Golfer*, and other publications.

Barton Creek's second golf course was designed by Austin native Ben Crenshaw, winner of the Master's and other tournaments, and his partner, Bill Coore. Emphasizing the natural beauty of the Hill Country, this par-71 course offers a rare taste of traditional golf course design featuring broad, rolling fairways and widely varied green sizes. It is both forgiving for the novice and a pleasurable challenge for the seasoned golfer who appreciates the distinctive heritage of Scottish links design.

The Palmer-Lakeside course, located west of Barton Creek, rewards golfers with breathtaking panoramic views of Lake Travis. Designed by Arnold Palmer, the

par-71 course has open, rolling fairways and excellent bent-grass greens geared to the skill level of most active club golfers.

Serving Business and Leisure Guests

There is much more to the development than golf. Two country clubs—Barton Creek and Barton Creek-Lakeside—reflect the lifestyle, tastes, and interests of their international membership. The Barton Creek Spa, patterned after famous European spa hotels, is an exceptional amenity for residents, resort guests, and country club members, offering a state-of-the-art fitness facility, specialized personal services, and luxurious accommodations.

The Barton Creek Conference Center, ranked as one of the nation's top 10 conference centers, makes available the amenities of the spa, country club, and resort. Designed to host corporate business meetings, conferences, and seminars, the resort boasts 147 tastefully appointed guest rooms and suites, 16 conference rooms, a 156-seat amphitheater, and a comprehensive multimedia center. Six on-site restaurants offer a full range of dining, from casual to Continental.

The executive conference center
Barton Creek is designed and
staffed to provide complete program support for a wide range of
meeting formats, from high-impact
multimedia presentations to informal discussion groups in smaller
meeting rooms. The media center
allows centralized control of the
audiovisual system, which is designed to provide "touch-button"
control throughout the resort.
Although Barton Creek specializes in corporate and executive
conferences for groups of 30 to 50
individuals, the Governor's Ballroom can accommodate more than
500 people. Operated by Club
Resorts Inc., which has more than
50 years of experience in private
club management, the conference
resort is renowned for its excellent
facilities and service.

Wonderful Place to Live

Now that private residences and
homesites are available at Barton
Creek, the development is taking
on a new level of appeal. "Barton
Creek is both a wonderful place to
play and a wonderful place to live,"
says Vice President of Marketing
and Sales J.J. Collins.

This new development activity,
however, has been carefully
planned to maintain the area's
beautiful natural surroundings.
"We believe that man and nature
can coexist to preserve the environment," Collins says. "That's why
we are using the most sophisticated
and scientifically sound ecological
approach to land planning and
development. Three-quarters of
this property will be left in its
natural state. Barton Creek has won
numerous awards for its environmental planning and safeguards."

Plans stipulate that approxi-

mately 2,000 residences will be
built at Barton Creek, including
only 100 along the golf courses.
Austin's best home builders offer a
variety of architectural styles and
home sizes on sites ranging from
one-quarter acre to two acres.
Many lots offer spectacular views of
the Hill Country, Barton Creek, or
the golf courses.

"The low density of development
allows us a high level of detail for
the land plan," says Collins. "That
makes Barton Creek a superb place
for young families, retired families,
and, of course, golfers of all ages."

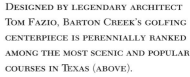

DESIGNED BY LEGENDARY ARCHITECT
TOM FAZIO, BARTON CREEK'S GOLFING
CENTERPIECE IS PERENNIALLY RANKED
AMONG THE MOST SCENIC AND POPULAR
COURSES IN TEXAS (ABOVE).

THE PAR-71 PALMER-LAKESIDE COURSE,
DESIGNED BY ARNOLD PALMER, HAS
OPEN, ROLLING FAIRWAYS AND EXCEL-
LENT BENT-GRASS GREENS GEARED TO
THE SKILL LEVEL OF MOST ACTIVE CLUB
GOLFERS (LEFT).

Price Waterhouse

MANY COMPANIES VIEW THEIR ANNUAL AUDIT AS AN ORDEAL that must be endured. However, clients of Price Waterhouse consider it one of many professional services that can help them grow and prosper. ◆ "While we are proud of our reputation for

excellence in accounting, we are far more than accountants or auditors," says Ryan Burdeno, managing partner of Price Waterhouse's Austin office. "We are business advisers who are available year-round to help our clients with a wide range of problems and opportunities. We develop ongoing business relationships so we can always provide the assistance our clients need."

FROM LEFT: BOB SMITH, AUDIT PARTNER; RYAN BURDENO, MANAGING PARTNER; AND BILL WILLIS, TAX PARTNER.

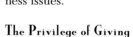

BRENDA LADD PHOTOGRAPHY

Austin's Blue-Chip Firm

One of the Big Six accounting giants, Price Waterhouse is recognized as the "blue-chip" firm because of its international reputation and the quality of its clients. The firm is perhaps best known for tallying the Oscar ballots for the Academy Awards and for representing such prominent companies as Anheuser-Busch, IBM, DuPont, and Walt Disney, to name a few.

Founded in 1890, Price Waterhouse has 13,000 employees, nearly 1,000 partners, and 100 offices throughout the United States. Internationally, the firm employs 33,000 people at 450 offices in more than 100 countries. Its annual revenue is nearly $3 billion, including about $1.2 billion generated in the United States.

Price Waterhouse established its Austin office in 1984 and has grown to a staff of more than 50. The local office has developed specialties in financial services, health care, and high technology. Among its local clients are public and private businesses of all sizes, including numerous high-technology companies that have worked with Price Waterhouse since their early days.

Burdeno, formerly of the firm's Chicago and London offices, arrived in Austin in 1987 with a strong specialty in high technology. Tax partner Bill Willis, who helped establish the Austin office, also has a background in high technology. Audit partner Bob Smith brought his expertise in technology, real estate, and financial services to the office in 1988.

"We bring together people from many specialties, with many ways of looking at the world," says Jennifer Sullivan-Whitney, audit manager. "Our clients benefit from our diverse expertise."

As part of an international corporation, Price Waterhouse offers its Austin clients extensive global resources. "If we don't have the right specialist on our staff, we won't hesitate to fly one in from another office," stresses Sullivan-Whitney. "The right people are never more than a phone call away."

Consequently, the firm provides a wide range of consulting services from strategic planning to initial public offerings, from developing venture capital funding to international expansions. Clients have the added advantage of membership in a CFO roundtable, a regular networking session that provides a forum for discussion of key business issues.

The Privilege of Giving

Price Waterhouse also has earned a reputation in Austin as a concerned corporate citizen. The firm makes regular contributions to such groups as United Way, Big Brothers and Big Sisters, American Heart Association, American Diabetes Association, and a variety of local cultural organizations.

"As a business, we get a lot out of the community," says Burdeno. "It is not only a responsibility but a pleasure to be able to give something back."

Geraghty & Miller, Inc.

FOR NEARLY 40 YEARS, GERAGHTY & MILLER, INC. HAS HELPED companies across the nation meet a variety of environmental challenges. A pioneer in the assessment and protection of ground-water resources, the firm has expanded its services to help clients comply with increasingly complex and extensive environmental regulations.

"Our engineers, geologists, and regulatory specialists have extensive experience in soil, ground-water, waste management, and regulatory compliance projects," says Jeffrey R. Henke, operations manager in Geraghty & Miller's Austin office. "That's why we are able to provide innovative, cost-effective solutions to environmental problems."

Establishing New Areas of Expertise

There have been many changes at Geraghty & Miller since it was established in 1957. Founded on Long Island, New York, with a handful of employees, the company is now headquartered in Denver and employs 1,250 people in almost national and international offices. The full-service firm can provide engineering design, hydrocarbon recovery, computer modeling, geophysics, risk assessment, regulatory support, air-quality, and soil and groundwater remediation services from offices nationwide.

Changes in the laws governing industry prompted Geraghty & Miller to focus on helping clients comply with the seemingly endless set of environmental regulations.

The company can also perform multimedia compliance audits that give clients a complete picture of how well they are meeting the requirements of applicable environmental regulations. "We are one of the oldest, largest, and most experienced full-service environmental consulting and engineering firms in the nation," says Henke.

Geraghty & Miller has been ranked by *Forbes* as one of "the best 200 small companies" and is recognized by *Engineering News-Record* as one of the top design firms, both in pure design and in hazardous waste management. The firm has also been ranked among the leading air-quality services companies since its 1993 acquisition of Acurex Environment Corporation.

Serving the Needs of Texas

Geraghty & Miller opened an Austin office in 1985 in order to expand its Texas services and provide regulatory assistance to new and existing clients in the central and eastern portions of the state. The firm now has a total of four Texas offices.

Client needs can be met by Geraghty & Miller's local professional staff with assistance from the firm's international network. The Austin office houses experts in regulatory compliance, soil and groundwater remediation, waste management and permitting, litigation support, environmental site assessment, air quality, and engineering design. The company has also been recognized for its expertise in determining the level at which contaminants pose a public health risk. This process of risk assessment is vital to clients who want to operate in a clean and safe manner. Geraghty & Miller's expertise in this field was recognized

in 1992 by the State of Texas, which requested the firm's input on the development of new risk assessment rules.

"Austin is one of the most environmentally aware cities in the country," notes Henke. "Our approach is to help clients be proactive in the treatment of environmental issues instead of waiting for a problem to erupt. We believe that is the right way to do business in this community, both for us and for our clients."

A FULL-SERVICE FIRM, GERAGHTY & MILLER CAN PROVIDE ENGINEERING DESIGN, HYDROCARBON RECOVERY, COMPUTER MODELING, GEOPHYSICS, RISK ASSESSMENT, REGULATORY SUPPORT, AIR-QUALITY, AND SOIL AND GROUNDWATER REMEDIATION SERVICES FROM OFFICES NATIONWIDE.

Liberty National Bank

AUSTIN-BASED LIBERTY NATIONAL BANK KNOWS ABOUT defying odds. Established in 1985, the bank has made a habit of achieving what was thought impossible. Of the 40 banks chartered in Austin during the 1980s, Liberty is one of only

three still in existence—and the bank is stronger than ever. It has grown from a single location with $17 million to a six-branch banking system with $140 million in assets.

The experts were skeptical when, in 1988, Liberty National named 30-year-old Edward Z. Safady president and chief executive officer. Safady, a former bank examiner and regulatory consultant, became one of the youngest bank CEOs in Texas. Despite early skepticism about his level of experience, Safady has led Liberty National toward great success and is today

Safady remembers. "We believed there was still a need for a good commercial bank that allowed customers to talk to a real person on the phone. Individual and business customers were also looking for a bank that could give them one-week turnaround on loan requests." Liberty jumped in to fill those needs and has met with much success.

In addition to the downtown branch at 900 Congress Avenue and its main office at 5555 North Lamar Boulevard, Liberty National now has branches at 501 South

financial services, automatic teller machines, mortgage lending, Small Business Administration (SBA) lending, and a new credit card program.

Originally founded by a group of local investors, Liberty still retains a hometown feel. Five of the six directors live in Austin, and the bank promises a quick decision on loan requests. "We are locally based and operated," Safady says, "so lending decisions are made right here."

He also touts the bank's progressive attitude toward its employees.

E. POWELL THOMPSON (LEFT), SENIOR VICE PRESIDENT AND BRANCH MANAGER OF THE DOWNTOWN LOCATION, AND EDWARD Z. SAFADY, PRESIDENT AND CEO.

known throughout the bank and the community for his vision and expertise.

Liberty defied the odds again when it opened a downtown branch in October 1990, making it one of the few Austin-based banks with a downtown presence. Within the first two years, that branch alone brought in $40 million in new deposits.

"It surprised everyone that a little independent bank could come downtown and do well, especially with the much larger banks failing,"

Congress Avenue, 7101 Highway 71 West in Oak Hill, and 11212 Interstate 35 North in North Austin, as well as a downtown motor bank at 206 East Ninth. A new branch near the Arboretum will open in late 1994, bringing Liberty's employment to over 100.

A Progressive Hometown Bank

Liberty National has entered the world of big banking by offering a full range of services, including a variety of checking and savings accounts, personal and commercial

"We go a little against the grain," says Safady. On Fridays, for example, staff members abandon formal business attire in favor of bank T-shirts and jeans. They also receive several personal days off each year, enjoy periodic socials, still earn Christmas bonuses, and rest easy knowing that 100 percent of their health insurance premiums are paid by Liberty.

"Our employees are our best asset," emphasizes Safady. "There are far too many banks in this country where the employees com-

THE BANK'S DOWNTOWN BRANCH AT 900 CONGRESS AVENUE (LEFT; OPPOSITE, RIGHT) IS LOCATED JUST A BLOCK FROM THE STATE CAPITOL.

plain about the management and ownership. How happy do you think their customers can be?"

Support for Small Business

While Safady describes Liberty National's customer base as diverse, the bank has become especially popular among small businesses. Within 18 months of being certified by the SBA, the bank became the largest SBA lender in the San Antonio-Austin district. Liberty consistently ranks among the city's top lenders in loan-deposit ratio, with many of its loans going to small businesses.

The bank prides itself in helping small businesses grow and prosper. Proof of its success came in early 1993 when the Greater Austin Chamber of Commerce recognized a select handful of local businesses. Three of the honorees—Chez Zee restaurants, Guiltless Gourmet, and Conner & Tate—are small business customers of Liberty National.

At the same time, Safady was honored as Professional of the Year for his contributions to banking, civic, and community organizations. Liberty also has been recog-

nized for its support of local arts organizations and is one of the few local banks rated as outstanding in its compliance with the Community Reinvestment Act.

Safady, though, warns against categorizing the bank. "We are always ready to make a $3,000 used car loan or to lend our legal limit on a real estate transaction," he says. "Some customers may be too big for us, but no customer is too small. We have brought some of our business customers to the point where we can no longer be their only bank, and we are delighted that we have played a role in their success."

Making a Difference

The bank encourages its staff to get involved in local organizations ranging from Ballet Austin to AIDS Services of Austin to Austin Adopt-A-School.

"As far as advertising dollars go, we believe our money is better spent getting involved with community organizations, supporting those organizations, and getting to know people," Safady asserts. "I personally sit on nine boards. That's representative of the level of

THIS NEON SIGN SHINES OUTSIDE LIBERTY'S DOWNTOWN MOTOR BANK AT 206 EAST NINTH STREET.

involvement we encourage. Many of our employees are longtime Austinites, and they like the idea of being able to make a difference. Basically, we want to be known as a strong Austin-based commercial bank that is an integral part of the community, both as a human resource and as a financial resource."

So far, the strategy appears to be working: Liberty National Bank is growing and continuing to make a difference throughout the Austin community.

SicolaMartin

WHEN YOU WALK INTO TOM SICOLA'S OFFICE, THE FIRST thing you notice is the organized collection of three-ring binders filled with marketing and strategy plans for his well-known clients. Nearby there's a wall and credenza

covered with leadership and business awards, along with articles that have featured his growing company. And on the windowsill, not far from the pictures of his family, there is a well-worn copy of the classic children's book, *The Little Engine That Could.*

These are just the sort of things you would expect to find in the

advertising agency that's built a reputation on the impact and performance of its unique creativity, based on a philosophy that states, "Don't be afraid to be different, but be terrified of being invisible."

For most observers, and even for clients, that's where the predictability ends.

In 1985 nobody would have pre-

ment of reflection. "Even though we didn't coin the phrase, we were all determined to consistently 'Exceed Expectations.' That starts with honesty and integrity, and goes to superior thinking, a genuine client success focus, and a company environment that feels inviting from the minute you walk in the door."

Indeed, the company goals have

CLOCKWISE FROM ABOVE: SINCE 1985 TOM SICOLA (LEFT) AND STEVE MARTIN HAVE HELPED THE AGENCY BECOME ONE OF THE SOUTHWEST'S MOST PROMISING ADVERTISING AND MARKETING FIRMS.

MAJOR NATIONAL COMPANIES LIKE IBM AND VERYFINE JUICES HAVE TURNED TO SICOLAMARTIN IN AUSTIN.

IN 1988 THE AGENCY DONATED $250,000 OF IN-KIND SERVICES TO THE GREATER AUSTIN CHAMBER OF COMMERCE WITH THE CREATION OF THE BUY GREATER AUSTIN CAMPAIGN.

office of the president and CEO of what many consider the Southwest's most promising young advertising and marketing agency.

Right next door, in Steve Martin's office, the scene is a bit different. There, you'll notice the wild surfboard leaning against the couch. Or maybe the life-size inflatable elk head, the horned Jackalope wearing the captain's hat, or more traditionally, the row of bronze broadcast awards that line the window. And in a frame, next to it all, you can't miss the vintage photo of a Depression-era newspaper boy with the headline, "By diligence, a quick-witted young fellow can rise from rags to riches."

Once again, just what you might expect to find in the office of the executive creative director of an

dicted that a little agency called Sicola Martin Koons Frank could open its doors and survive during one of the worst economic periods in Texas history. Well, nobody except the founding partners whose names were on the door.

"From the very first day we all shared the same goals for the company," Sicola says, after a mo-

never changed, but the original group has. In 1989 Marianne Koons retired from the agency to be a professional mom. Then in 1993 George Frank died after a hard-fought, nine-month battle with cancer.

Even when faced with major setbacks, the agency has always taken on challenges with renewed

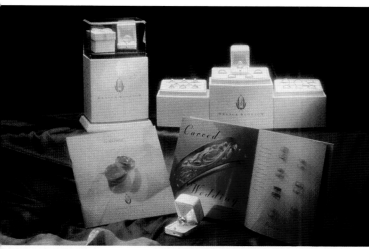

And the impressive numbers go on for clients and projects on the consumer front, including the *Austin American-Statesman*, McLane Company, M&M/MARS, Mobil, Stop n Go Convenience Stores, I Can't Believe It's Yogurt, Mr. Gatti's Pizza, and Orange Blossom Rings.

The agency's considerable technology experience and portfolio includes Motorola, IBM, Dell Computer, 3M, TechWorks, VTEL, Tadpole Technologies, Tivoli, and many others.

Throughout its growth, Sicola-Martin has never forgotten the value of home and community. Over the years, through pro bono campaigns for the United Way, Buy Greater Austin, KLRU, Partners in Literacy, and the Austin Steam Train Association, the agency has donated in-kind services totaling more than $725,000.

In 1993 *Adweek* magazine named SicolaMartin one of the "Top 5 Hottest Southwest Agencies." In a feature article, they wrote, "SicolaMartin has been working quietly for more than eight years to turn themselves into an

ON THE CONSUMER FRONT, THE AGENCY DOES WORK FOR ORANGE BLOSSOM RINGS (TOP LEFT).

SICOLAMARTIN'S CLIENT LIST ALSO INCLUDES SEVEN DIVISIONS OF MOTOROLA (BOTTOM LEFT AND BELOW).

termination. In 1988, for example, the agency lost 80 percent [of] its billings in a three-month [pe]riod. Few companies can survive [tha]t kind of hurdle, but again [ex]pectations were exceeded. In the [ye]ar that followed, the lost business [wa]s not only replaced, but it was [inc]reased by 20 percent.

That degree of determination [an]d extra effort hasn't gone unno[tic]ed. Perhaps that's why compa[nie]s like IBM have come all the way [fro]m White Plains and Atlanta to [tur]n critical business over to Sicola-[M]artin. And perhaps that's why [Ver]yfine Juices came from Boston [to] Austin to award its national [con]venience store promotions to [the] agency.

[W]hen you look beneath the sur[fac]e at the agency's performance [rec]ord for its clients, it's easy to [un]derstand why companies from [aro]und the country are attracted to [Sic]olaMartin. For example, when

Houston-based Stop n Go chose SicolaMartin to handle the marketing and advertising for its national chain of 1,100 convenience stores, the first year's efforts alone increased sales by 22 percent over the prior year.

When a division of Motorola hired the agency to develop a national sales force incentive program, their effort played a role in producing results that were 300 percent higher than original projections. That success led to internal referrals, and six new Motorola divisions were eventually added to the agency's client list.

For the McLane Company, a $7 billion subsidiary of Wal-Mart, the agency reintroduced a national retailer program that boosted store participation by 430 percent in just six months. This no doubt influenced the selection of SicolaMartin as the company's primary marketing resource.

We finally found a board the 68302 multiprotocol processor can't radically improve.

overnight success." And with a staff of 60 professionals, a billings increase of 52 percent in 1993, and projected billings of $25 million for 1994, that seems right on target.

So what expectations will Sicola-Martin exceed next? It's hard to predict. But if this Austin agency's past offers any clues for the future, you should set your expectations high and just sit back and watch.

SAS Institute Inc.

WITH MORE THAN 3 MILLION PRODUCT USERS WORLDWIDE, SAS Institute Inc. is an international leader in information delivery systems and one of the 10 largest independent software companies in the world. Its flagship product, the

SAS® System, serves virtually every segment of business, industry, education, and government and operates in almost every computing environment—from personal computers to giant data processing centers.

THE AUSTIN OFFICE IS LOCATED IN ONE OF THE CITY'S MOST BEAUTIFUL CORPORATE SETTINGS—A WOODED 96-ACRE CAMPUS NEAR HIGHWAY 620 THAT FEATURES SPECTACULAR VIEWS OF THE HILL COUNTRY.

AN INFORMATION DELIVERY SYSTEM INTEGRATES DATA, TRANSFORMS IT INTO USEFUL INFORMATION, AND DELIVERS IT TO DECISION MAKERS (NEAR RIGHT).

WITH MULTIVENDOR ARCHITECTURE™, SAS® SYSTEM APPLICATIONS ARE COMPLETELY PORTABLE ACROSS HARDWARES (FAR RIGHT).

into more useful information and allows them to transmit that information quickly to facilitate effective decision making. The SAS® System's capabilities include Executive Information Systems (EIS), spreadsheets, graphics, data analysis, report writing, quality improvement, project management, computer performance evaluation, client/server computing, database access, decision support, and applications development. Because of its versatile MultiVendor Architecture™ (MVA™) design, the applications are portable across many computer platforms and can be used with a variety of computer systems manufactured by different companies.

Perhaps the most important component in the Institute's investment in the future is a commitment to its employees and their quality of life. For example, SAS Institute offers employer-funded child care

The Austin Regional Office

SAS Institute employs more than 100 people in the capital city. In addition to being the oldest and largest regional office—providing sales, marketing, and training for Texas, Oklahoma, New Mexico, and Louisiana—the Austin operation is the company's only research and development center outside its North Carolina headquarters. Local software engineers conduct research and development related to the SAS® System and SYSTEM 2000,® a popular data management system that was developed in Austin. The staff also produces corporate publications and provides quality assurance services for SAS products.

The Austin office is located in one of the city's most beautiful corporate settings—a wooded 96 acre campus near Highway 620 that features spectacular views of the

Investing in the Future

SAS Institute is the industry leader in terms of revenue percentage devoted to research and development; in 1992 the company invested about 35 percent of its total revenue into new product research. This commitment has enabled SAS Institute to provide its customers with products that continually push the limits of technology.

Cutting-edge technology, backed by worldwide service and support, helps customers transform data

and fitness club memberships, as well as a free on-site health care center for employees and their families. As a result, the Institute's turnover rate is less than one-fifth the industry average. National publications continually praise the organization for its progressive approach. For five consecutive years, *Working Mother* has recognized SAS Institute as one of the top U.S. companies for working women.

Hill Country. Employees can get closer to nature on hiking trails in nearby canyon.

Leading the way in international computer software development, SAS Institute has proved itself to one of the most progressive companies in the nation. As it looks to the future, SAS Institute will continue to invest in the employees and the city that helped it achieve success.

Amaturo Group Ltd.

NO OTHER RADIO STATIONS HAVE BROUGHT BACK MORE MEMOries to more Austinites than the three owned by the legendary Joe Amaturo. In 1986 Amaturo created the "magic" format that has spurred thousands of adults to turn on the radios in their homes,

rs, and offices.

Austin's "magic" station is KMJ-FM 95.5—MAJIC 95.5—hose soft, contemporary favorites yesterday and today have made it favorite among adult listeners for early a decade. Sister station FGI-FM 94.7—FROGGY 94.7—ays rock-and-roll oldies from the 0s, '60s, and '70s. The newest ddition to the Amaturo family is JCE-AM 1370—The JUICE—hich debuted in 1993 with ustin's only "solid gold" soul rmat.

While each station has its own rsonality, all three play hits that ppeal to Austin's sizable population of active, educated, and fluent adults.

Successful Format

tracting and keeping adult listens has been the goal of Amaturo roup Ltd. since the company troduced the "magic" format to ustin. MAJIC 95.5 features familir hits, more music and less talk, nited commercial breaks, and omotions that keep listeners ned in throughout the day. Lisners also appreciate the station's bility; all of its major on-air rsonalities have been on board r at least six years.

"There's very little turnover at r stations," says Lon Bason, vice esident and general manager of naturo Group Ltd. "We hire the st people, train them well, and ep them. That goes for on-air rsonalities, production and operions people, and sales staff. We love radio and take pride in what e do."

FROGGY 94.7 and The JUICE e variations on the successful nagic" theme. Each station plays lies that evoke special memories d emotions. The JUICE is

Austin's first soul station catering to adult African-Americans with a combination of Motown classics, blues, gospel, and jazz. FROGGY's "no-repeat workday" promise makes the station a favorite all day long, because listeners know they won't hear the same song twice. The station's 30-foot inflatable frog and its mascot, Mr. Froggy, are attention grabbers at store openings and special events all over town.

Meeting the Needs of Advertisers

"What we do better than anyone else in town is pay attention to the needs of our advertisers," says Bason. Thanks to the stations' common management, advertisers can reach a desirable audience easily and effectively through packages that put their messages on all three stations.

"We have the best-trained and a very retail-educated sales staff. They work for their clients, learning to understand their businesses and what kind of media mix will get them the best results. We know what makes ads effective, and we have a creative department that can produce them quickly," says Bason.

"We can respond quickly when clients need us to. That's one of the

MAJIC 95.5 FEATURES FAMILIAR HITS, MORE MUSIC AND LESS TALK, LIMITED COMMERCIAL BREAKS, AND PROMOTIONS THAT KEEP LISTENERS TUNED IN THROUGHOUT THE DAY.

things that sets radio apart," he notes, adding that radio is the only medium that goes wherever people do, is used throughout the day, and stimulates listeners to tap their imaginations.

Under Amaturo's guidance, all three stations support community affairs that are important to their listeners. "We are deeply involved in women's and children's issues and the arts because those things are important to our audience," he says. "It's not just part of our licensing requirements. We feel it is important to strengthen our ties with Austin and with our listeners."

FROGGY'S 30-FOOT INFLATABLE FROG AND ITS MASCOT, MR. FROGGY, ARE ATTENTION GRABBERS AT STORE OPENINGS AND SPECIAL EVENTS ALL OVER TOWN.

Eden Box & Company Real Estate

ONLY ONE RESIDENTIAL REAL ESTATE BROKERAGE IN AUSTIN is affiliated with Great Estates International, the prestigious organization that brings together buyers and sellers of distinctive homes. Only one has been chosen by the network of finest luxury brokers, *Who's Who in Luxury Real Estate*. Only one has a boat to deliver buyers to the door of waterfront homes. And only one is owned by its agents. That firm is Eden Box & Company Real Estate.

"We work exclusively with the existing and emerging executive market," says Eden Box, who founded the company in 1986 with 10 veteran brokers. "We deal with young executives who are on their way up and with older executives who are on their way to the golf course. In many cases, we help their children find a first home or help their parents find a retirement home. The executive market in Austin is as diverse as the city."

Box emphasizes that her firm handles properties in all price ranges. "If you want the most interesting house, call us," she says. "Whether you're looking for a little cabin or a unique house on an extraordinary lot, we're the ones who can find it. It may take a little more time, but it will be worth it when it's exactly what you're looking for."

Meeting Special Needs

The company's services have become as diverse as the market it serves. Armed with an in-depth knowledge of the Austin market, brokers assist their clients in buying and selling residential and investment properties throughout the area. The firm has extensive experience in corporate and individual relocation, maintains an aggressive advertising program, and works closely with its affiliated national networks. In addition to Great Estates, Eden Box & Company is the Austin affiliate for All Points Relocation Service, the nation's oldest and largest premier independent brokers' network.

"We provide all the services that surround the buying and selling of property, and we are willing to add new services if our clients have special needs," says Box. For example, when clients expressed the desire to view lakefront property from the water, she bought a boat. Prospective buyers now have the opportunity to view available homes by water in order to get a fuller appreciation of their appeal.

Superior Agents and Properties

Remaining firmly focused on customer needs has been one key to

THE COMPANY HANDLES PROPERTIES IN THE ESTABLISHED AREAS OF AUSTIN, FROM ECLECTIC DOWNTOWN NEIGHBORHOODS TO MORE REFINED DEVELOPMENTS WITH STUNNING VIEWS.

cess for Eden Box & Company.
other has been assembling a
soned, professional team of real
ate brokers with a personal stake
he company's success. All of
firm's two dozen agents are
reholders of the privately held
poration. All are experienced,
nmitted, and attentive to details.
"Many of our clients are CEOs or
ners of their own companies,"
s Box. "When they work with
agents, they are working with
ople who also own their own
npany. When you work owner to
ner, both parties know what to
ect from the transaction. They
w they can count on us to
iver."

Also experienced, committed,
attentive is the superior staff
embled at Eden Box & Com-
y. A nationally recognized relo-
ion director strategizes with the
oming and outbound clientele
are referred to the appropriate
nt or, when leaving Austin, to
best out-of-town company.
e five staff members work as a
erior team," says Box.

he adds, "Our agents and staff
ction in a context of mutual
ect, corporate commitment,
dedication to excellence. Some
s are fifth-generation Austin-
. Others are transplants who can
reciate the perspective of new-

comers and relocating families. But
all of us are enamored of Austin,
charmed by its natural beauty, and
invigorated by its unique culture."

As Austin has grown, it has
provided newcomers an expanding
array of housing choices—from
eclectic downtown neighborhoods
to more refined developments with
stunning views. "Many people are
overcome by the views," says Box.
"They are amazed that you can find
40-mile Hill Country views or spectacular city views just a few miles
from town. They just can't believe
they are in Texas."

Strength Through Community Activity

Box's commitment to honesty and
integrity in real estate transactions
extends beyond the company. Appointed to the Texas Real Estate
Commission by Governor Ann
Richards, she oversees licensing
and regulation of the state's real
estate agents. "Serving on the commission is demanding, but it's also
satisfying to know that consumers
and licensees are fully informed
and protected," says Box, who
currently serves as chair of the
commission.

"One of our strengths is that so
many people in the company are
community minded and have leadership roles in worthwhile causes,"

says Box. "All of us have served on
the boards of Austin Lyric Opera,
Paramount Theatre, Austin Symphony League, Ronald McDonald
House, Better Business Bureau,
Austin Junior League, KLRU-PBS,
Center for Battered Women, Meals
on Wheels, and many other organizations. It helps us stay in touch
with what's most important in life."

SEMATECH

W HEN SEMATECH GOT ITS START IN 1987, MANY WONDERE₁
whether the unprecedented consortium could succeed in
America, where fierce competition flourished and industry
cooperation was minimal. However, SEMATECH quickly

proved to the world that combining
the best minds and talents could
restore U.S. leadership in the manufacture of semiconductors—the
electronic chips that run everything
from coffeemakers to military
hardware.

When SEMATECH began
searching for a home, Austin pre-
vailed over more than 130 other
communities. As the hub of a
nationwide network, the consortium of semiconductor manufacturers, government, and academia has
drawn hundreds of highly skilled
people and at least 30 companies
to the capital city in less than a
decade.

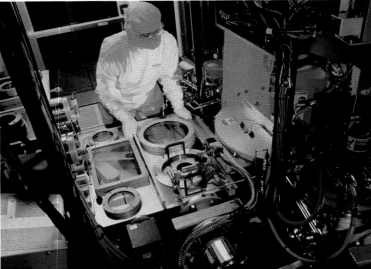

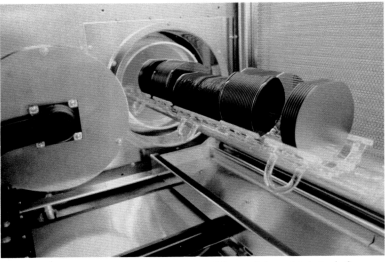

SEMATECH IS DEDICATED TO
CREATING FUNDAMENTAL CHANGE IN
MANUFACTURING TECHNOLOGY AND
THE DOMESTIC INFRASTRUCTURE IN
ORDER TO HELP U.S. SEMICONDUCTOR
COMPANIES MAINTAIN THEIR STATUS
AS WORLD-CLASS SUPPLIERS.

Many of these high-tech firms
were influenced by the unique level
of cooperation between city, state,
and federal governments; the University of Texas; and the people
of Austin. The degree to which
these groups work together for the
common good is considered by
SEMATECH to be a major factor
in attracting other businesses.

Creating Fundamental Change
SEMATECH, which stands for
Semiconductor Manufacturing
Technology, is a nonprofit research
and development consortium of

American semiconductor manufacturers working with the government and academic sectors to create
fundamental change in manufacturing technology and the domestic
infrastructure in order to help U.S.
semiconductor companies maintain
their status as world-class suppliers.
SEMATECH's mission is quite
simply to solve the technical challenges required to keep the United
States number one in semiconductor manufacturing. In Austin, the
consortium develops advanced
semiconductor manufacturing
materials and equipment, and vali-
dates its innovations in a "proofing"
facility that simulates production
lines. Results of the research are
shared with consortium members,
who use it for commercial and
military applications.

SEMATECH's funding is provided by member companies and
the federal government. For every
dollar contributed by member
companies, the federal government
matches a dollar, and more dollars
are invested by suppliers of manufacturing tools and materials. The
result is a leveraged investment
for all parties. The high-stakes
development undertaken by

SEMATECH allows member co₁
panies to spread the risk across a
large segment of the industry.

The consortium uses a majorit
of its funds to form joint develop
ment projects or equipment
improvement programs with the
suppliers, most of whom are sma
businesses. SEMATECH serves
the role of articulating equipmen
performance specifications, cost
profiles, and time windows in
which the member companies ne
the equipment.

In addition to facilitating coope
ation among chip makers and the
suppliers, SEMATECH provides
return on investment in other wa
One of these ways is the teaming
talent represented by its membe
companies' employees. The cons
tium rotates loaned "assignees"
from its member companies
through positions at SEMATECI
every two years. As a result, the
assignees comprise about one-thi
of the consortium's work force,
providing a dynamic exchange of
fresh ideas and technology transf

As a national investment, the
consortium has clearly been valu
able. In five years, SEMATECH
helped put American makers of

Bold Plans for the Future

The world has seen a steady stream of product innovations based, in part, on computer chips that are smaller, faster, and more functional, yet less expensive. That productivity march is threatened unless semiconductor manufacturing costs are reduced and the barriers to smaller circuit sizes are overcome. SEMATECH is positioned to support the cooperative efforts of industry, government, and academia toward accomplishment of this feat through execution of the semiconductor industry's national road map.

SEMATECH's mission is aligned with the critical tool and material requirements and technology gaps identified in the national road map. The consortium has developed programs that will close those gaps and help the United

...niconductor factory equipment ...ck on top of a $10 billion global ...rket, helped restore U.S. chip ...nufacturers to world leadership ...the $63 billion semiconductor ...rket, and developed plans for ...ure factory designs that will ...ng the U.S. semiconductor in-stry and domestic manufacturing ...o the 21st century.

Good Neighbor with a ...tional Mission

...addition to its national contribu-...ns, the consortium has remained ...ive in neighborhood and com-...nity projects. Each year, ...MATECH volunteers partici-...e in community outreach activi-...s, ranging from delivering meals ...area residents to serving as ...ntors for local students. ...Sharing a commitment to the ...vironment with the nation and ...Austin community, SEMA-...CH has integrated environ-...ntal, safety, and health research ...o both its projects and its daily ...erations. As a result of outstand-...performance, the consortium ...received environmental awards ...m Keep Austin Beautiful. The ...ults of SEMATECH's clean-

room research are transferred to member companies and made available to the rest of the industry through material and equipment suppliers.

The consortium also is working with member companies and leading computer chip associations to provide the U.S. semiconductor industry with a strategic national road map focusing on pollution prevention, worker health and safety, environmental preservation, and economic competitiveness.

States remain competitive. Examples of those research areas include lithography, a key technology that involves development of a circuit pattern on a chip, and semiconductor packaging, which ensures product linkage between manufacturers and their customers.

Building on its past successes, SEMATECH plans to confront the technical challenges of the future and offer the solutions required to keep the United States number one in the global semiconductor industry.

AT SEMATECH'S VAST AUSTIN FACILITY, 750 EMPLOYEES AND "ASSIGNEES" WORK TO HELP THE UNITED STATES REMAIN NUMBER ONE IN THE GLOBAL SEMICONDUCTOR INDUSTRY.

VTEL Corporation

A COMMUNICATION REVOLUTION IS TAKING PLACE. TELEphone, facsimile, and modem technologies that were adequat only five years ago could be limiting a company's competitive advantages today. Likewise, the basic voice and image feature of common videoconferencing provide a simple solution to the need for face-to-face meetings. But today's intensely competitive world requires the ability to combine the power of computers and documents with the force of human interaction.

Austin-based VTEL Corporation, the world's leading supplier of interactive videoconferencing systems, is responding with advanced systems that go beyond traditional

FROM LEFT: THE COMPANY PROVIDES A RANGE OF DESKTOP SYSTEMS, INCLUDING THE VTEL 115, THROUGH ITS RELATIONSHIP WITH INTEL CORP.

THE VTEL 227 BK ALLOWS COLLEAGUES TO MEET AND SHARE COMPUTER DOCUMENTS, INCLUDING TEXT, DATABASES, SPREADSHEETS, AND CAD FILES.

VTEL'S 227 SYSTEMS ARE THE LEADING SOLUTIONS FOR DISTANCE LEARNING APPLICATIONS.

THE COMPANY'S SYSTEMS ARE ALSO USED IN THE HEALTH CARE INDUSTRY FOR PATIENT CONSULTATIONS.

conference calling and videoconferencing to provide an experience that is as natural and productive as actually being there.

The result isn't just better meetings, it's better communication. While ordinary videoconferences let participants see one another, VTEL systems let them exchange computer files, work together on documents or slides, and share critical information to provide genuine understanding. VTEL calls it MediaConferencing™—putting the power of various communication media to work within the context of videoconferencing.

"With MediaConferencing, organizations aren't limited by conventional concepts of time and place," says Dick Moeller, chairman and chief executive officer. "Success isn't measured by miles traveled or hours spent, but by results achieved."

Communication Without Boundaries™

VTEL systems allow people to communicate without boundaries—to interact across distance with all the elements they would normally use in face-to-face meetings. From simple videoconferencing to full-featured MediaConferencing—which also allows users to fax documents and send VideoMail™—VTEL offers versatile, easy-to-use systems that make long-distance meetings as productive as personal gatherings at a fraction of the cost. With systems that range from desktop and portable models to fixed conference room systems, VTEL products can help organizations of all sizes become more productive.

What sets VTEL apart is its focus on helping customers solve their communication problems in a cost-effective manner. All VTEL products are designed around an open, PC-based architecture; are controlled by software; and conform to international videoconferencing standards set by the Telecommunications Standardization Sector of the International Telecommunications Union (ITU-T). This approach makes system enhancements and upgrades more afforda ble and convenient—and protect the initial investment.

"VTEL is the only manufactur offering a complete line of systems—from the desktop to the conference room—designed to function in the customer's applications environment," says Glenn A Pierce, Jr., president and chief operating officer. "With our ope architecture and PC platform, w adapt to the user's existing work environment. And because our sy tems are software controlled, we provide unparalleled investment protection."

Making Technology Work for People

Founded in Austin in 1986, VTE is based upon the philosophy tha technology should work for peop rather than limiting what people can achieve. The company's prod ucts have been developed from t beginning with the needs of educ tion, health care, and business in mind.

MediaConferencing has made

TEL the undisputed leader in stance learning technology, allowg educators to reach geographilly isolated students as effectively if they were in the same classom. VTEL's interactive capability s students and teachers pass leo images of documents back d forth as easily as in a real ssroom, even if they are hunds of miles apart or the teacher addressing multiple classes multaneously.

Health care providers rely on EL's telemedicine capabilities r remote diagnosis, doctortient visits, and even continuing ucation for staff. MediaConfercing can transmit still images h as X-rays or EKGs with such rity that specialists can advise al providers on what treatment initiate without time-consuming lays. By letting patients, primary re providers, and specialists eract with each other, Mediamferencing brings quality health re to areas that otherwise would ve none.

The needs of business are ually demanding and diverse,

whether a company operates locally or globally. MediaConferencing eliminates the barriers of travel costs and scheduling problems, allowing companies to disseminate information, solve problems, and make decisions in a timely, effective manner. For example, colleagues can work on a single computer document—including text, databases, spreadsheets, and CAD files—in real time. Coworkers who are not able to attend can be left a VideoMail message regarding the outcome of the meeting.

A Successful Pioneer

A pioneer in the design, manufacture, and worldwide marketing of interactive videoconferencing and multimedia conferencing systems, VTEL has achieved remarkable success. The company was ranked 21st on *Inc.* magazine's 1992 list of the 100 fastest-growing small public companies, with a 3,948 percent growth in sales revenues between 1988 and 1992.

VTEL's DeskMax,™ the platform on which its desktop videoconfer-

encing systems are based, was recognized in 1993 as Most Significant Advance in Teleconferencing Overall and Most Significant Advance in Desktop Videoconferencing Products by *Teleconference* magazine.

Also in 1993, VTEL signed a landmark partnership agreement with Santa Clara-based Intel Corp., through which the two companies will cross-license existing technology and undertake cooperative research and development efforts in the video arena. In addition, Intel purchased 10 percent of VTEL's stock and has warrants to purchase almost an additional 10 percent.

VTEL employs a staff of more than 250 at its Austin headquarters and is represented overseas by VTEL Europe, a wholly owned subsidiary located in Reading, England. The company's sales network includes 14 regional sales offices in the United States and an international sales office in London.

Technology Works, Inc.

PERHAPS THE MOST IMPORTANT THING TO KNOW ABOUT TechWorks is that each of the company's products features a shark, the company mascot. "We're an aggressive company," say: Mike Frost, founder, president, and chief executive officer of the

fast-growing computer hardware and software firm. "In this business, it's lead or get out of the way. We intend to be a leader."

A true entrepreneurial success story, TechWorks grew from just three employees in 1986 to more than 110 and $60 million in revenue in 1993. "We were the epitome of a bootstrap operation when we started," recalls Frost. "Our priority has been to build a technical team that can stay on top of technology. We have always invested our profits back into new technology and new directions, which has paid off."

Superior Technology.
Superior Service

Today, TechWorks is a leading supplier of Apple Macintosh and PC memory products, as well as an extensive line of performance-enhancement products. Frost has been honored locally by Ernst & Young as Entrepreneur of the Year, and TechWorks has been listed by *Inc.* magazine as one of the 35 fastest-growing privately held companies for three consecutive years. Its products have received numerous awards for excellence in the computer industry.

The cornerstone of TechWorks' performance-enhancement product line is computer memory. The company offers a line of memory modules for every Macintosh model that Apple manufactures— and as new models are released, TechWorks is consistently early to market with supporting memory modules. Its products support a wide variety of machines, from Macintosh PowerBooks and New-tons to popular IBM and compatible products.

TechWorks made headlines in 1991 when it introduced Grace-LAN Network Manager, a software system that allows MIS managers to remotely collect information about problem computers. One of the first products of its kind, Grace-LAN quickly became a leader in the network management arena. TechWorks has since expanded its GraceLAN product line and introduced several upgrades that have enhanced the power and productivity of the popular software line. The company also develops PC video graphics accelerator cards and connectivity hardware such as TechNet LocalTalk connectors, Ethernet boards, and Hubs.

Every TechWorks product receives the company's "outrageous"

customer service guarantee, which includes unlimited toll-free techni cal support, a lifetime warranty, a 30-day money-back guarantee, and a 24-hour replacement policy. In addition, all of the company's prod ucts are assembled at its Austin

manufacturing facility, a strict, quality-controlled environment that uses state-of-the-art surface-mount technology.

"It's simple," says Frost. "We want to be the best in the business at customer service. Our philosophy is to have zero unhapp customers."

To that end, TechWorks contin ues to seek new products and technologies that can help custom ers make their computer operation more productive. In early 1994, fc example, the company acquired National Design, Inc., an Austin-based manufacturer and marketer of the highly touted Volante graph ics accelerator cards.

"Our products are only as good a our people, so we are looking for innovative thinkers who want to work in an atmosphere where the can make a difference," Frost say "Those are the people who will make sure this company continue to be successful."

ALL TECHWORKS PRODUCTS ARE ASSEMBLED AT THE AUSTIN MANUFAC-TURING FACILITY, A STRICT, QUALITY-CONTROLLED ENVIRONMENT THAT USES STATE-OF-THE-ART SURFACE-MOUNT TECHNOLOGY (BOTTOM).

EVERY PRODUCT RECEIVES THE COM-PANY'S "OUTRAGEOUS" CUSTOMER SUP-PORT GUARANTEE, WHICH INCLUDES UNLIMITED TOLL-FREE TECHNICAL SUPPORT (BELOW).

PHOTOS BY BILL ALBRECHT

Austin Trust Company

A USTIN TRUST COMPANY IS THE "NUMBER ONE" TRUST company in Texas—literally. ◆ When state law granted the Texas Department of Banking the authority to oversee trust companies, Austin Trust Company was the first to be chartered

by the state. Its charter number: -001. The company also earned the highest rate of compliance from the Department of Banking for its account administration, supervision, and operations. Once again, number one.

Founded in 1987, Austin Trust acts as a fiduciary in many types of trust, estate, and custody relationships. The company manages approximately $150 million for its more than 350 clients, a list that includes individuals and businesses in Texas and across the nation.

Broad Range of Professional Trust Services

Founder and CEO William J. Hudspeth, Jr., attributes the company's rapid growth, in part, to the

extensive line of services offered by Austin Trust Company. These services include management of living trusts, testamentary trusts, life insurance trusts, guardianships, trusts in lieu of guardianship, estate administration, individual retirement accounts and Keogh plans, escrow accounts, and custody accounts. For business clients, the company provides a full range of employee benefit plans.

Austin Trust Company also acts as an agent for individual executors and trustees. "Our expertise in trust and estate areas enables us to assist trustees or executors with their administrative duties and to provide a detailed listing of assets and

daily transactions," Hudspeth says.

The company works with clients to set clear investment objectives and guidelines, and then manages clients' portfolios to meet their financial needs. Austin Trust Company uses investment advisory services from several companies, including Goldman, Sachs & Co. and Donaldson, Lufkin & Jenrette Securities Corporation. Through its affiliate, Thornhill Securities, Inc., Austin Trust Company offers additional investment research and security trades at costs competitive with discount brokers.

Local and Straightforward

Austin Trust Company offers several advantages over trust departments at banks, according to Hudspeth, and one of the most important is local control. The only locally owned private trust company in the capital city, its seven officers have more than 85 years of combined trust experience. The company has an 11-member board of directors and a 12-member development board, both of which include distinguished Texans. "We make decisions locally and, therefore, more quickly," Hudspeth says.

"We're not a branch of an out-of-state holding company—there's not much bureaucracy here. We're also accessible to our customers and provide services at straightforward, reasonable rates, with no hidden fees."

The staff's longevity and experience also translate into a direct benefit. "We pride ourselves on paying attention to our clients— listening to their concerns and caring about their satisfaction," Hudspeth says.

For Betsy L. Cotton, vice president and trust officer, that sums up why she chose the personal trust administration business. "I remember one client, an elderly woman with no family in Austin, who had to move out of her apartment and into a senior medical unit," says Cotton. "She was a very independent woman and didn't want anyone to think she had to rely on them. During one of my visits, she said to me: 'I don't know what I would do if you weren't here.' Every so often you're reminded that your clients really do need you. That's what makes it all worthwhile."

FROM LEFT: MEMBERS OF THE AUSTIN TRUST COMPANY TEAM INCLUDE DAVID E. REDDING, TRUST ADMINISTRATION OFFICER (SEATED); KRISTIN L. BERLY, TRUST OPERATIONS OFFICER; MARY ELLEN BOBB; BETSY L. COTTON, VICE PRESIDENT AND TRUST OFFICER; KEY M. HILL; WILLIAM J. HUDSPETH, JR., CHAIRMAN AND CEO; VALERIE A. ENGLAND, VICE PRESIDENT AND TRUST OFFICER; CARLA J. BUTTON; DAN M. REMICK, VICE PRESIDENT AND TRUST OFFICER (SEATED); AND MARTY ROSENFIELD (SEATED).

FAR LEFT: TEAM MEMBERS AT THORN-HILL SECURITIES, AN AFFILIATE OF AUSTIN TRUST COMPANY, INCLUDE (FROM LEFT) MARY ELLEN BOBB; FELDER "SCOOP" THORNHILL, CHAIRMAN AND CEO (SEATED); TOM YOUNG, PRESIDENT; AND WILLIAM "TUDEY" TETEN.

Doubletree Hotel Austin

EVERY STAY AT A DOUBLETREE HOTEL BRINGS A FEW SURPRISES, because every hotel in the chain is different—a unique reflection of its home city. Yet while the decor and cuisine vary from place to place, guests will always find luxury accommodations, attentive

THE DOUBLETREE HOTEL AUSTIN HAS 350 ROOMS, INCLUDING 20 SUITES AND 120 NONSMOKING ROOMS.

BUSINESS AND LEISURE TRAVELERS CAN RELAX ON THE TERRACE BY THE TROPICAL WATERSCAPE (RIGHT).

service, and, of course, Doubletree's famous chocolate chip cookies.

For many guests, Doubletree has become synonymous with some of the world's best chocolate chip cookies—giant, cakelike treats packed with chocolate chips and nuts. Guests receive two on the first day of their stay, and most buy at least a few extra to take to friends or family, or perhaps to enjoy during the trip home. The cookies have been a fixture at Doubletree since 1986, when the company president sampled them at a deli in Atlanta. He promptly fell in love with them, bought rights to the recipe, and directed every Doubletree location to bake the cookies daily, ensuring a fresh and steady supply for guests.

An Austin Flavor
At the Doubletree Hotel Austin, guests can munch their cookies in the traditionally styled Spanish Colonial lobby, while relaxing on the terrace by the tropical waterscape or admiring the hotel's magnificent Spanish antiques, or even in one of the 350 luxury rooms and suites.

"This hotel is unique to Austin,"

says Rick Phegley, director of marketing. "We hope that when people who have never been to Austin stay at the hotel, they will feel like they have gotten to know something about the community."

For those who want to learn even more about Austin, Doubletree is just 10 minutes from downtown, Robert Mueller Airport, the University of Texas campus, and the State Capitol. Located at the intersection of Interstate 35 and U.S. Highway 290, the hotel is even closer to some of the city's best shopping and most popular restaurants.

"Our area has become known as 'restaurant row' because there are

so many popular restaurants along this part of the interstate," says Phegley. Doubletree guests are right next door to such popular dining spots as Pappadeaux and Pappasito's. For those who want to venture farther afield, the hotel provides free transportation within two miles. Free transportation to the airport is also available.

But guests don't have to leave the premises for fine dining. With the Courtyard Cafe on-site, plus full room service, Doubletree can introduce guests to local culinary treats. The casual Courtyard Cafe specializes in American cuisine with a Texas twist, including mesquite-grilled meats and fish, fajitas,

GUESTS RECEIVE A WARM WELCOME IN THE TRADITIONALLY STYLED SPANISH COLONIAL LOBBY.

nd Southwest-style salads. The estaurant overlooks the multilevel courtyard with its lush, tropical oliage and waterscapes.

Built around a massive wood-burning fireplace is Courtyard Lounge, a comfortable spot for relaxing, meeting friends, watching the wide-screen television, or playing a game of pool.

Events to Remember

While hotels are designed primarily for out-of-towners, the Doubletree is familiar territory for many Austinites because of its popularity as a meeting facility. With more than 21,000 square feet of meeting space and the city's third-largest ballroom, the hotel hosts everything from small seminars and corporate retreats to international conventions.

Major local employers such as Apple Computer, Inc. rely on the Doubletree to provide space for corporate meetings. With seven permanent boardrooms located on the concierge floor and plenty of flexible meeting space, the hotel can accommodate almost any meeting need.

"We host meetings for many local groups," says Phegley. "They like to come here because of our convenient location, free covered parking, flexible meeting space, and, of course, the hotel's atmosphere. But we also host national and international groups."

The Doubletree Hotel Austin is equally renowned for its elegant wedding facilities. "The ambience of our building really lends itself to weddings," says Phegley. "We've had ceremonies on-site, as well as receptions and rehearsal dinners. Most people are glad to have their wedding guests stay here because they know they'll be treated well."

Superior Service

Guests at Doubletree Hotels nationwide have come to expect more than cookies, and the Austin hotel's reputation for exceptional service draws many regular customers. A guest services manager, for example, is always on duty in the lobby to help guests with any need—from transportation to finding the right souvenir. The Doubletree staff is friendly and accommodating, often greeting guests by name.

The hotel has 350 rooms, including 20 suites and 120 nonsmoking rooms. Special concierge services are available on the sixth floor, where guests are also treated to a complimentary Continental breakfast and evening reception, newspapers, plush robes, and turn-down service. For additional security, the sixth floor requires guest key access.

Austin's Doubletree takes its definition of "service" the extra mile through its participation in the Rooms at the Inn program. The hotel frequently makes rooms available to family members of hospital patients, especially those who cannot afford to pay for accommodations. "We work with the program to make space available when we can," says Phegley. "We believe in this program because it helps people in need and gives all of us at the Doubletree Hotel Austin a chance to make a contribution that really counts."

Buffington Homes, Inc.

FOUNDED IN 1987, BUFFINGTON HOMES IS ONE OF AUSTIN'S MOST experienced home-building companies. The firm's founders brought more than 135 years of local experience—and responsibility for the construction of more than 22,000 homes—to the new

company. Their expertise, coupled with a commitment to quality design and construction, has quickly made Buffington Homes one of Austin's leading home builders.

Buffington sells about 500 homes each year in more than a dozen neighborhoods in the Austin area, including Round Rock, Cedar Park, Pflugerville, and Lakeway. With homes priced from $90,000 to $300,000 and the ability to provide modified custom building services, Buffington has something to offer virtually every home buyer in the area. "We see a lot of local home buyers and a lot of people moving in from out of town," says President Tom Buffington. "It's especially nice to show our homes to newcomers because they can often buy more home here—frequently about 20 percent more than in most cities."

Pride in Every Home

"We want the person buying the $90,000 house to have the same feeling of quality and satisfaction as the one buying the $300,000 house," Buffington adds. "We use the same top-quality construction in every house. All of our homes have extra design features that make people feel good about living there. We always keep in mind that we're not just building a house but a lifestyle for a family."

Buffington homes are known for their roomy floor plans, efficient use of space, convenient locations, and special touches such as high ceilings and crown molding. Kitchens, often considered the heart of the house, get special treatment from Buffington, with skylights, center islands, and other amenities to make them bright and inviting.

While every home has certain standard touches, each is also a reflection of the owner's personal tastes. Buyers get an extensive catalog listing over 200 options and upgrades—from carpeting and tile to door knobs, mantel styles, and built-in bookshelves. Since the options are prepriced, buyers know ahead of time exactly what they will cost. For people who have a difficult time making so many choices, Buffington's sales counselors and design staff can help them select the appropriate finishing touches.

Choosing the Right Neighborhoods

Starting a home-building company in 1987 may have seemed a bit risky to many people. Real estate prices in Austin were dropping, and builders were struggling to stay in business. Yet Buffington and his partners, Ted Kirkpatrick and James Giddens, were willing to take the risk. All three had been key employees of one of the area's largest home builders and had learned a great deal about surviving in a tough market.

"We were able to build the company the right way," says Buffington, "by staying away from risky ventures and just taking what the market would give us." According to Giddens, that meant acting on their instincts about what was right for the Austin market. "We know firsthand what home buyers look for," he says. "The right neighborhood. The ideal floor plan."

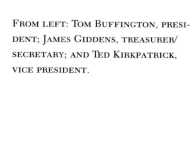

As a result, Buffington has been choosy about what and where it builds. The company seeks out friendly, attractive neighborhoods with plenty of amenities so that families can feel comfortable living there for many years. "We've always been selective about where we build," notes Buffington. "I won't go into a neighborhood where I wouldn't want my kids to grow up."

A Builder to Count On

Just as noteworthy as the special touches in a Buffington home is the company's commitment to its product—and to Austin's future.

sors KLRU public television programming, Blue Santa, and other local groups.

"We are here to stay," says Buffington, an Austin resident for 25 years. "All of us have been in the Austin area for more than 20 years, and we are in business for the long haul. We believe in doing our share to make this community a better place."

According to Kirkpatrick, Buffington Homes takes pride in every home—and in the people who build them. "I've never worked with people more committed to building the right way," he says.

ployee—from site supervisors to customer support representatives—is empowered to correct problems whenever they occur. "If a problem arises, we'll get it fixed right away," stresses Buffington. "Customers can get me on the phone if they need to work something out. We believe in doing what we say we'll do, when we say we'll do it."

While Buffington Homes is still in its first decade of business, Tom Buffington envisions generations of children growing up in the homes he and his partners build. "We have already sold homes to two genera-

That commitment is illustrated by involvement with local organizations such as Habitat for Humanity; every year, the company gives employees time off work to help construct new homes for needy Austinites. Buffington also spon-

"We build homes as if we were going to live in them ourselves." And they mean it. All three partners live in Buffington homes.

For buyers, the company's pride translates into a cooperative, can-do attitude. Every Buffington em-

tions of some families, and we hope to make it three generations," he says. "There's a certain amount of honor in building homes where families grow up, and we take it very seriously."

KITCHENS GET SPECIAL TREATMENT FROM BUFFINGTON (ABOVE), WITH SKYLIGHTS, CENTER ISLANDS, AND OTHER AMENITIES TO MAKE THEM BRIGHT AND INVITING.

Guest Quarters Suite Hotel

GUEST QUARTERS SUITE HOTEL HAS BEEN RECOGNIZED AS ONE of Austin's finest hotels since it opened in 1987, and the American Automobile Association's prestigious four-diamond ranking assures travelers of superior service and value. Unlike the city's

other four-diamond hotels, however, Guest Quarters combines the services of a luxury hotel with the convenience of a suite hotel.

"We are the only all-suite property in Austin that offers a full-service restaurant, room service, and meeting facilities, plus all the amenities visitors expect in a luxury hotel," says General Manager John "Rusty" Wallace.

Convenience and Luxury
Guest Quarters' 189 spacious suites average 700 square feet—the average size of a one-bedroom apartment—and feature views of the State Capitol, downtown Austin, the University of Texas campus, Town Lake, or the Hill Country. All suites include a separate living room, a dining area, a full kitchen, an oversized bathroom, two television sets, and two or three telephones, making them especially attractive to long-term guests.

The 15-story hotel also offers six floors of nonsmoking rooms, ample accommodations for guests with disabilities, and a concierge floor with enhanced service and security, including complimentary breakfast and keyed elevator access. Other amenities include an outdoor pool and landscaped sundeck, whirlpool, sauna, fully equipped exercise room, and guest library that offers reading material ranging from recent best-sellers to children's classics. Flexible meeting and banquet rooms can accommodate groups of up to 250 for company meetings, seminars, wedding receptions, and a variety of other functions.

Many Austinites know Guest Quarters by the arch that makes the hotel a landmark on the city's skyline. Equally distinctive is the popular 15th Street Cafe and Lounge. Featuring an innovative blend of Southwestern and Italian

GUEST QUARTERS HAS BEEN RECOGNIZED AS ONE OF AUSTIN'S FINEST HOTELS SINCE OPENING IN 1987. ITS 189 SPACIOUS SUITES FEATURE VIEWS OF THE STATE CAPITOL, DOWNTOWN AUSTIN, THE UNIVERSITY OF TEXAS CAMPUS, TOWN LAKE, OR THE HILL COUNTRY.

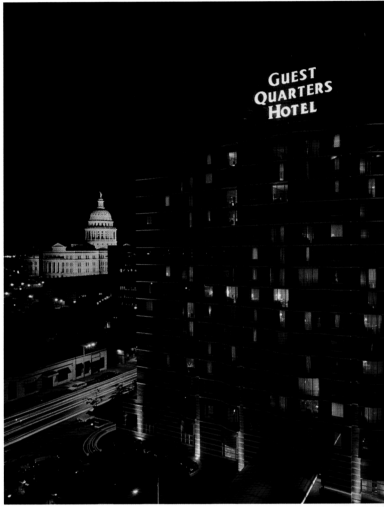

cuisine, the restaurant has become a favorite Austin setting for power breakfasts, business lunches, and quiet dinners.

Making a Mark in Texas
Guest Quarters is well known in many parts of the country. The chain has more than 30 properties in major cities throughout the eastern United States, Florida, Illinois, and California. With hotels already established in Houston and Austin, the chain is planning to continue its expansion into Texas because of the state's robust business climate and popularity among vacationers, says Wallace. Guest Quarters' unique combination of amenities attracts a

wide variety of guests ranging from business executives to vacationing families.

"We are especially popular among people who know they will be in town for several months," notes Wallace. "Many of our guests are legislators, lobbyists, judges, and University of Texas professors. We make them feel at home rather than like they are staying at a hotel."

He adds, "We pride ourselves on getting to know our guests, whether they are staying with us for a day or a year." To that end, each employee wears a nametag imprinted with his or her first name and hometown. In addition to being a good conversation starter, the tags help to create

informal, homey atmosphere. And each employee's job description contains a pledge to help out wherever needed. Says Wallace, "When we're busy, you're as likely to find me parking cars or bussing tables as you are to find me in my office."

Beyond the Call of Duty

Guest Quarters operates according to 500 service standards, and every employee carries a "10 Commandments of Guest Service" card. "But there is only one rule that matters," explains Wallace. "Every employee is responsible for making sure that nobody walks out of this door

dissatisfied with their experience."

It is not unusual at the Guest Quarters Suite Hotel to see a bell captain lending his shirt to a guest whose dry cleaning wasn't returned on time, or to see a front desk clerk hemming a guest's jacket before an important meeting. "One of our favorite customer-service stories happened recently when a bellman overheard some guests talking on the way back to their room at about 2:00 in the morning," recounts Wallace. "They wanted to make muffins, but they didn't have any eggs and it was too late to go to a grocery store. Without saying anything to them, the bellman opened

the kitchen, got some eggs, and took them to the room. The guests were surprised and thrilled."

Guest Quarters Suite Hotel is also concerned about making sure its employees are satisfied. Staff members are encouraged to become involved in community activities such as Adopt-A-School and other nonprofit organizations. At work, employees are encouraged to identify and solve problems rather than ignore them. "We also discourage class distinctions," says Wallace. "We all go by our first names here, because this is a partnership."

Guest Quarters' most recent annual employee survey revealed that an astounding 100 percent of its staff members enjoy their jobs. At the same time, the hotel achieved a remarkable 98 percent guest satisfaction rate and exceeded its profit projection by 12 percent. The Austin hotel was named Guest Quarters' Hotel of the Year in 1991 and has consistently received more favorable guest comments than any other hotel in the chain.

"We have one simple goal: to provide excellent service," says Wallace. "If we can do that, we will succeed. I think we are succeeding."

ALL SUITES FEATURE A SEPARATE LIVING ROOM, A DINING AREA, A FULL KITCHEN, AN OVERSIZED BATHROOM, TWO TELEVISION SETS, AND TWO OR THREE TELEPHONES.

AMENITIES INCLUDE AN OUTDOOR POOL AND LANDSCAPED SUNDECK (LEFT), WHIRLPOOL, SAUNA, FULLY EQUIPPED EXERCISE ROOM, AND GUEST LIBRARY.

EMC Automation

ALL ELECTRONIC DEVICES—FROM SIMPLE CALCULATORS TO sophisticated electronic guidance systems—generate electromagnetic fields at different levels. These fields can interfere with another device operating in the same environment. As

electronic products have become a major sustaining force worldwide, the interference must be controlled for proper operation and harmonious coexistence of these devices.

Since the level of interference varies according to the type of environment, regulating agencies have defined electromagnetic compatibility (EMC) requirements to ensure proper operation in the environment in which a device is designed to operate. The regulations apply to the levels of emission from electronic devices, as well as their immunity levels.

FROM ITS HOME BASE ON TECHNOLOGY BOULEVARD IN AUSTIN, EMC AUTOMATION HAS BECOME A LEADING SUPPLIER OF EMC TEST SYSTEMS IN THE UNITED STATES, EUROPE, AND ASIA.

EMC'S STATE-OF-THE-ART EQUIPMENT, SUCH AS THIS IMMUNITY TEST SYSTEM, HELPS CUSTOMERS MEET VARYING EMC REGULATIONS BEFORE THEIR PRODUCTS REACH THE MARKET (BELOW).

"All electronic devices should be compatible in the electromagnetic environment in which they are working," says R. "Joe" Sivaswamy, founder and president of EMC Automation. "We specialize in the manufacture of automated testing systems that help our customers test their products' compatibility with their environment."

EMC Automation is a leading supplier of EMC test systems in the United States, Europe, and Asia. Its customers are involved in the automobile, computer, medical products, aerospace, military, telecommunications, and commercial electronics industries, among others. These customers share a need to test their products in order to meet varying EMC regulations before the products reach the market. Qualifying products during the design stage is very important: Correcting a problem after the product is designed can be very costly, sometimes leading to complete redesign.

Sivaswamy, who began his career as a satellite design engineer, emigrated from India in 1985 with his wife Margie. EMC Automation was founded in 1987, with Joe putting his two decades of experience to work as president. Margie, who holds a master's degree in psychology, has helped with the

business from the start. Today, she takes care of the business administration and accounting.

Joe and Margie are well supported by Robert Sutton, vice president of systems, and Murali Ranganathan, vice president of software, both experienced in the EMC field. "Our strength is our engineering expertise," says Joe. More than 50 percent of EMC Automation employees are qualified engineers.

In 1992 the company became the first to introduce EMC testing software that runs under Microsoft Windows.™ Several competitors have since followed that lead.

Although EMC Automation is a relatively small company, it looms large in the worldwide EMC testing market. More than half of its revenue comes from outside the United States, and the company is a leading supplier of specialized systems to meet the EMC regulations of the European Community countries.

"Many American companies are already testing their products to meet EC standards so that they can continue to sell products to European customers," notes Joe. "In the future, we expect the United States to impose similar regulations, as well. When that time comes, we hope to have a good share of the market, as we are already well established in the field."

He adds, "The EMC field is becoming more and more important with the increase in dependence on electronic devices. As more complex devices are developed, the problems due to interference are also becoming complex, forcing stricter regulations for EMC testing. This is going to increase the demand for our services and products."

Horizon Savings Association

WHEN DOUGLAS KADISON DESCRIBES THE BUSINESS PHILOSophy of Horizon Savings Association, he chooses words rarely applied to financial institutions: nimble, flexible, and innovative. But there's one word the thrift's president doesn't like to use, and that word is "no."

"We hate saying no. We'd always rather find a way to say yes," Kadison attests. "We may not be able to structure a loan exactly the way a customer wants, but we can present options." Since opening in 1987, Horizon Savings has become a leader in "presenting options" to small-business, interim construction, and commercial real estate borrowers in Austin.

Satisfying Unmet Needs

Unlike traditional savings and loan organizations, Horizon specializes in making commercial loans that are hard to get at most banks. Horizon, for example, has ongoing relationships with most of the area's large builders and is financing several residential developments.

"We're about the only ones in town making these loans," says Charles S. Nichols, Jr., Horizon's executive vice president, "so everyone comes to us. That allows us to pick the best projects."

Horizon has resisted the popular trend of purchasing failed savings and loan associations or buying securities to achieve rapid growth. Rather, the thrift's impressive performance has been fueled by its proven ability to make small-business and commercial loans. Horizon is the only thrift institution in Austin active in Small Business Administration lending and is a certified SBA lender. For the September 30, 1993, government year end, Horizon was the largest SBA lender in its district.

Truly Local in Focus

Horizon's founders—Kadison, Nichols, and Paul Antrim—have been a team since 1978, when they worked together at a local mortgage banking firm. They went into business together as mortgage bankers in 1984 and opened the newly chartered Horizon Savings Association in 1987. All three founders are involved in the thrift's day-to-day operations, and they remain among the largest stockholders. "Our long relationship provides synergy since Charles Nichols is a residential and interim expert and runs that area of the bank," says Kadison, who oversees the commercial area. Antrim serves as Horizon's chief financial officer.

"We have over 110 stockholders, and except for four or five, they all live in Austin," notes Kadison. "Our lending decisions are made locally, and all of our lending is done here."

According to Antrim, Horizon has almost $80 million in assets, with seven Austin locations. Horizon offers full banking services including personal and commercial checking accounts; automatic teller cards; savings accounts; certificates of deposit; and business, commercial, and personal mortgage loans. The thrift recently announced a new credit card division after previously selling its successful credit card operation in 1990.

Antrim, Kadison, and Nichols are proud of Horizon's nontraditional approach to banking. For example, Horizon became the first

savings and loan in Texas to offer Sunday hours.

"We are not conventional," says Kadison. "If we see a good opportunity, we can take it right away. We don't have to wait for clearance from corporate headquarters, because we're it. We are always looking for niches where the community needs services that are a good fit with our knowledge and resources. We try to provide those services with premium results at a fair price. That's what I consider a win-win situation for us, our customers, and the community."

ABOVE, FROM LEFT: BRANCH MANAGERS LORENA GOLDSBERRY, LOU CLARK, CARA BOYD, JOEL CAVNESS, AND KELLY HOLT HELP DELIVER HORIZON'S BRAND OF PERSONAL, FRIENDLY SERVICE.

TOP LEFT: OFFICERS NANCY NICHOLS AND MARK MONROE CONFER WITH A SMALL-BUSINESS LOAN CUSTOMER.

TOP RIGHT, FROM LEFT: FOUNDERS CHARLES NICHOLS, PAUL ANTRIM, AND DOUGLAS KADISON PLACE A PREMIUM ON OFFERING FLEXIBLE, INNOVATIVE SOLUTIONS FOR HORIZON CUSTOMERS.

PCA Health Plans of Texas, Inc.

PCA HEALTH PLANS OF TEXAS IS THE LARGEST PROVIDER OF comprehensive managed health care programs in Central Texas. The company serves commercial members enrolled through employer groups and individuals enrolled through government-sponsored Medicare and Medicaid programs.

PCA Health Plans' parent company, Physician Corporation of America, was established by E. Stanley Kardatzke, M.D., a practicing family physician. The company operates health plans in Georgia, Florida, and Texas, and as of January 1, 1994, serves approximately half a million members enrolled in a variety of plans. What sets PCA apart is that it was founded and is largely managed by physicians. PCA Health Plans of Texas and PCA's other health plans maintain one of the highest physician medical director-to-patient ratios in the industry. This level of physician involvement sets PCA Health Plans apart from its competitors.

"We believe that physicians are the cornerstone of any health care plan," says Donald Gessler, M.D., president and CEO of PCA Health Plans of Texas. "For example, we offer our members a larger choice of physicians than any other HMO in the area, and we complement that network with a higher number of physicians on staff. That way, an attending physician can call and talk to one of our physicians whenever there is a question."

Comprehensive Care with a Personal Touch

The company came to Austin in 1986 when it acquired a local HMO and has since become the area's premier managed care provider. PCA Health Plans of Texas represents more than 2,000 employer groups and is the only Medicare and Medicaid HMO in Travis County. PCA offers a full range of health plans designed to meet the specific needs of its clientele.

"In addition to our HMO, we offer a PPO, self-insurance, managed indemnity plans, and life insurance," says Gessler. "We can customize services to virtually any business. We believe that PCA Health Plans will become the carrier of choice because we offer a variety of plans that provide cost-effective, comprehensive, quality care."

To provide this array of services in a more personal atmosphere, PCA Health Plans takes a modern approach to the traditional family-doctor style of medicine. It relies heavily on family physicians to diagnose and treat most health care problems. When specialty care is required, the family physician makes the referral.

"Primary care physicians can take care of 80 to 90 percent of the problems that most people present to their doctors," notes Gessler. "They are the front line of our program because they know their patients and they know the consulting physicians."

More than 1,000 local physicians participate with PCA Health Plans, giving Central Texas members a wide range of choices. Participating physicians meet strict credentialing and practice quality requirements and are measured against outcom

PCA HEALTH PLANS RELIES HEAVILY ON FAMILY PHYSICIANS TO DIAGNOSE AND TREAT MOST HEALTH CARE PROBLEMS (BELOW RIGHT).

PCA HEALTH PLANS IS LARGELY MANAGED BY PHYSICIANS SUCH AS TEXAS PRESIDENT AND CEO DON GESSLER, M.D., AND FLORIDA PRESIDENT AND COO NEIL NATKOW, D.O. (BELOW).

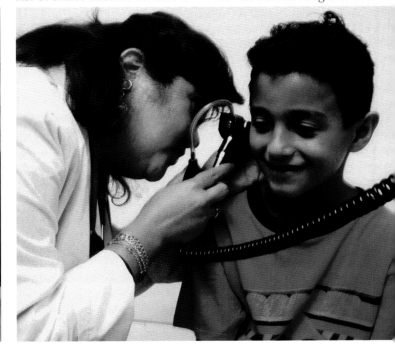

anagement criteria to uphold CA's standards of care. Gessler lieves members are far better off an patients who don't have the me support system when they oose a physician.

"Some people worry that their oices will be limited when they n an HMO, but anyone who ks at our list of physicians sees at's not true," he says. "We have kinds of doctors—all ages, per-

relationship with their physician. It also is one of the most effective methods for reducing medical costs because it eliminates unnecessary visits to expensive consultants. This is just one way PCA Health Plans is leading the health care industry.

PCA Health Plans also covers a variety of auxiliary health services, such as home health care, that allow patients to receive the appropriate level of care at the lowest cost. "We

and inflate costs. PCA Health Plans also has worked to become one of the most customer-friendly HMOs by writing policies that clearly spell out what services are covered and by handling questions quickly and courteously.

While the prospect of health care reform has many in the managed care industry worried about the future, Physician Corporation of America is growing ever stronger.

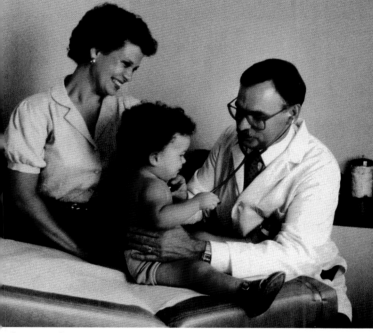

alities, and approaches to medi- e—but each one meets high ality standards. When you pick a me out of a phone book or get a ommendation from a friend, you n't really know whether the doc- is a good practitioner. We base r recommendations on measur- le standards like education, train- , and positive outcomes for tients."

While PCA Health Plans re- ires high standards, it does not tate how its physicians practice. ds Gessler, "We don't control w they practice medicine. They what they think is right for their ients."

Leader in Cost Containment

lying on primary care physicians ws members to build a strong

work to reduce hospital bed days because staying in a hospital can put a patient at risk for other infections," Gessler explains. "With home health care, many people recover more quickly and comfort- ably in their familiar home environ- ment. This is something we've known for years that the rest of the medical establishment is just now catching on to."

The company also employs a staff of registered nurses and physician medical directors to perform case management reviews when pa- tients are expected to incur signifi- cant medical costs. For example, hospitalized patients undergo case review to ensure that they get the appropriate care without dupli- cated, unnecessary, or invasive pro- cedures that complicate recovery

Using Austin as its Texas base, PCA Health Plans of Texas has expanded into other major metropolitan areas, including Houston, San Antonio, Waco, and Dallas-Fort Worth.

According to Gessler, Physician Corporation of America and PCA Health Plans of Texas are prepared to adapt to any changes in the nation's health care system. "We have proven people, a proven sys- tem, and a proven reputation for service," he explains. "Whatever happens with health care reform, Physician Corporation of America is positioned to succeed."

PCA Health Plans serves families in such Texas cities as Austin, Houston, San Antonio, Waco, and Dallas-Fort Worth. The company also maintains one of the highest physician medical director-to- patient ratios in the industry.

Franklin Federal Bancorp

ONE LOOK AT FRANKLIN FEDERAL BANCORP MAKES IT CLEAR that, in banking, new trends in customer satisfaction and innovative community investment have become the keys to success. With more than $1.5 billion in assets, Franklin Federal

RICK PATRICK

is the largest financial institution headquartered in Austin. The five-year-old company has 13 locations—11 in the Austin area and two in the Rio Grande Valley.

"First and foremost," says President and Chief Executive Officer Joe Matlock, "a Texas bank should be focused on meeting customer needs—thus our slogan: 'What a Texas Bank Should Be.' " That focus has been a priority at Franklin Federal, and it's paying off. In a recent survey, 96 percent of current customers expressed overall satisfaction in their banking relationship with Franklin, a figure Matlock calls "extraordinary for a banking organization." He attributes the high level of satisfaction to the way bank employees respond to the public. The tellers, for example, know most customers by their first names. "I get letters all the time complimenting our people," says Matlock.

Innovating to Meet Customer Needs

There's more to customer satisfaction, however, than friendly service: A bank must be prepared to adapt every program, service, and feature to meet customer needs. "We're structured for change," Matlock says. "We're able, willing, and nimble enough to change to better serve our customers."

For example, Franklin Federal was the first bank to offer mutual funds and annuities in Austin. In another innovative move, the bank established a "Money Market" in the Fiesta supermarket in 1993. The first in-store banking location in Austin, the Money Market offers all the services of a traditional branch bank. Customers can open checking or savings accounts, apply for loans, check rates on certificates of deposit—*and* shop for groceries.

According to Matlock, this unique branch is a direct response to community needs. "Our studies showed that in Austin, with its large population of students and two-career families, this kind of service would be appreciated," he says. "Both old and new customers love it. Its success has exceeded our expectations."

Committed to the Community

Going beyond the concerns of individual customers, Franklin Federal also takes the needs of the community to heart. The bank has exceeded compliance guidelines of the Community Reinvestment Act, which requires that banks address the needs of their community. The federal Office of Thrift Supervision has awarded Franklin Federal the "outstanding" rating during every ranking period since the bank was founded in 1988. It is the only financial institution in Austin to

earn that distinction.

In a 1992 article, the *Austin American-Statesman* noted that Franklin Federal not only ranked near the top in Travis County for jumbo mortgages, but that it also made more affordable housing loans—$3 million total—than any other bank in Austin during the preceding 18-month period. Matlock is proud of the fact that Franklin Federal makes its lending decisions locally.

"It's how you serve customers and the products you offer that count," Matlock insists. "The bank that is superior in these areas is the bank that will succeed beyond the year 2000." Franklin Federal Bancorp is poised to do just that and, continuing its focus on customer satisfaction, plans to grow with Austin well into the next millennium.

THE BANK'S LEADERSHIP INCLUDES (FROM LEFT) TED PIGOTT, SHARON KINCAID, RICK BURCIAGA, TIM IRVINE, AND JOE MATLOCK.

FRANKLIN PLAZA (BELOW) ACCENTS THE DOWNTOWN AUSTIN SKYLINE AT NIGHT.

▼ DAVID GRIMES

MaxServ

WHEN A HOUSEHOLD APPLIANCE STOPS WORKING, MOST consumers are unsure about what to do. And, as appliances get more complicated, even service technicians sometimes need a helping hand when they come across tricky problems.

Thanks to Austin-based MaxServ, consumers and technicians across the nation can get expert repair advice by telephone.

Each year, MaxServ answers more than 4 million calls about laundry and kitchen appliances, lawn and garden equipment,

personal computers, consumer electronics, hardware and tools, heating and air-conditioning equipment, garage door openers, exercise equipment, vacuum cleaners, sewing machines, and home office products.

"MaxServ's strategy," explains Charles F. Bayless, president and CEO of the publicly traded company, "is to become the information clearinghouse for the household products repair industry by providing comprehensive solutions to information delivery problems." The company's service package, called StreamLine℠ is used by manufacturers and retailers who want to contract their repair and customer service information management functions to a reliable and knowledgeable vendor.

"Supertechs" to the Rescue

The company's "supertechs"—experienced repair technicians armed with personal computers

instead of tools—offer a variety of services that range from guiding consumers through simple repairs to scheduling service calls. They can assist technicians in fixing unusual problems or identify the parts necessary to complete a repair. In addition to providing part numbers,

MaxServ can actually order parts for consumers or technicians.

The company has arrangements with Sears, Roebuck & Co., Frigidaire Co., and The Signature Group (a subsidiary of Montgomery Ward), and is negotiating with other manufacturers and retailers to provide centralized customer service and repair scheduling. "We help the consumer," says Bayless, "by providing the right information at the time of need."

MaxServ maintains the repair industry's largest and most complete library of technical, parts, and operational literature covering more than 400 brands of products. Callers have immediate access to this current information. MaxServ also helps the appliance companies by eliminating unnecessary warranty repair calls and ensuring that repair technicians have the right parts when they arrive at a customer's home. In some cases, Maxserv can even tell a technician

where in his truck a certain part can be found.

Growing Through Innovation

MaxServ moved to Austin in 1989 with eight employees. By 1994 the company had 400 Austin employees (525 nationwide) and is generating $1.5 million in revenue each month. MaxServ is maintaining its position in the market by developing new technology to meet growing customer needs.

The company recently developed Genuine PartFinder™ software, an electronic catalog that includes updated parts information and digitized images of parts for Amana, General Electric, Sears, and Whirlpool appliances. Previously, suppliers and repair shops relied on unwieldy microfiche and catalogs.

MaxServ has not stopped short in its efforts to make household appliance repair information more widely available. "We believe we are in a unique position to accomplish our objectives," Bayless says, "and we look forward to a bright and exciting future."

MaxServ recently developed Genuine PartFinder™ software, an electronic catalog that includes updated parts information and digitized images of parts for appliances (above).

Each year, the company answers more than 4 million calls about laundry and kitchen appliances, lawn and garden equipment, personal computers, consumer electronics, heating and air-conditioning equipment, hardware and tools, garage door openers, exercise equipment, vacuum cleaners, sewing machines, and home office products.

Conquest Airlines

WHEN DEREGULATION HIT THE AIRLINE INDUSTRY IN 1978, major air carriers responded by cutting service to many small and mid-sized cities. For these regional business centers, the loss of air service was damaging. ◆ Austin-based Conquest

Airlines has since renewed service to many of these cities, offering economic vitality to the community and comfortable travel for residents.

"We're an economic engine for the communities we serve," says Alex Besterman, marketing director for Conquest Airlines. "Air service means access, and access means business and a higher quality of life." From its corporate headquarters in Austin, Conquest now offers direct air service to cities in several states and Mexico. The

CONQUEST AIRLINES' TEXAS EXPANSION INCLUDES SERVICE TO SUGAR LAND MUNICIPAL AIRPORT (RIGHT) IN THE GROWING SOUTHWEST AREA OF HOUSTON.

CUSTOMER SERVICE, DEPENDABILITY, AND LOW-COST, DIRECT AIR SERVICE HAVE BEEN HALLMARKS OF THE AIRLINE SINCE ITS FIRST FLIGHT IN 1988.

airline provides a satisfying alternative to the congestion of larger airports or exhausting trips by car.

Finding a Niche

By concentrating on underserved markets and targeting business travelers, Conquest has carved out a niche in the crowded skies. Founded in Beaumont in 1986 by brothers Rafael and Victor Rivas, the airline made its inaugural flight on April 13, 1988, with 13 passengers. In less than a year, Conquest had issued its first public offering, added 40 daily flights, and begun service to additional Texas cities. The company moved its headquarters to Austin in 1989.

From those beginnings, the airline has never wavered from its commitment to quality and a business strategy of convenient, point-to-point, low-cost travel. Conquest saves travelers time and money. On average, passengers save nearly half the ticket price of major airlines and spend only half the total travel time.

Service, Safety, and Growth

From the airline's start in 1986, motivated employees and a commitment to customer service have been a hallmark of Conquest. Pilots, flight attendants, maintenance managers, and service agents have built an airline with one of the best

records in the industry. As a result, tens of thousands of passengers now choose Conquest on a regular basis.

In 1992 the airline registered a 15 percent increase in passenger traffic over the previous year. Because Conquest has successfully established new service to underserved markets and restructured flights to better serve travelers in existing markets, interest in the airline continues to grow. With the healthy growth pattern in place, the company is moving forward with plans for air service to additional cities.

Recently, the airline began service to Sugar Land in the Houston market. Because of traffic congestion around other Houston airports and the continuing growth of the Sugar Land area, the new service has been enthusiastically received.

Conquest also plans to initiate service with 737 jets bearing the Conquest logo. To begin in 1994, this latest expansion effort opens a new chapter for the airline.

Conquest Airlines is now a significant transportation partner for many cities and major companies across the United States. For thousands of future business and leisure travelers who choose Conquest, the sky is literally the limit.

GLG Energy, Inc.

GLG ENERGY, INC. AND ITS ASSOCIATED AND AFFILIATED companies are engaged in the exploration, production, development, and acquisition of oil and gas properties throughout the United States. GLG's business is conducted from its principal

office at 400 West 15th Street in Austin.

The company's activities are currently conducted from the Gulf of Mexico on the south to the Canadian border on the north, and to offshore California on the west. Foreign operations are active and/or under review in the United Kingdom, Russia, and South America.

GLG is active in eight major areas in the United States and, since inception, has been involved in the drilling of several hundred wells. The highest number of producing wells ever owned by the company exceeded 900, with GLG operating approximately 47 percent of those wells. Likewise, the company's highest gross production exceeded 25,000 barrels of oil equivalent (BOE) per day in 1992. Since that time, GLG has sold off a substantial amount of its domestic onshore and offshore production and has concentrated its efforts toward lower-risk, semiproven exploration, development drilling, secondary and tertiary projects, and acquisitions.

GLG Energy will also continue to pursue other energy-related business opportunities, such as natural gas and crude oil pipelines, hydrocarbon processing plants, liquefied natural gas (LNG) and liquefied petroleum gas (LPG) plants, and environmental remedial services.

A Solid Business Strategy

The company's business strategy is to increase its proven reserves and production rates by continuing to develop its long-lived oil fields and to use cash flow generated by these resources to fund its development program, as well as to finance its exploration program and any reserve acquisition opportunities

▶ PLG LTD.

that may arise.

GLG and its partners currently plan to spend an aggregate of approximately $5 million on development and exploration activities, although the actual amounts spent will be influenced by numerous factors, including many that are outside of the company's control. In accordance with this strategy, GLG Energy may acquire additional oil and gas properties, which may include additional working interest in properties in which the company already holds interest. Further acquisitions may be under-

taken to diversify GLG's reserve base in order to lengthen the average life of its reserves and improve profitability. In the past, the company's merger and acquisition activities have ranged in value from a few thousand dollars to as much as $875 million per transaction.

The principals of GLG Energy look to the future with the same enthusiasm that has served them well over the past 40 years of their participation in the U.S. oil industry.

GALE L. GALLOWAY IS CHAIRMAN AND CHIEF EXECUTIVE OFFICER OF AUSTIN-BASED GLG ENERGY, INC.

National Market Share, Inc.

WITH SATISFIED CUSTOMERS LIKE PIZZA HUT, SEARS, IBM, American Express, and former President George Bush, National Market Share, Inc. is known for providing sophisticated database marketing services to corporate America

as well as the occasional high-level political campaign.

"Our client list is an indication that what we do works," says company President James F. Shearer.

State-of-the-Art Service
Founded in 1989, National Market Share serves companies that have large databases—usually millions of records—by matching high-tech telecommunications technology with a staff of trained operators to deliver timely, important information for clients.

NATIONAL MARKET SHARE IS HEADQUARTERED AT 6200 LA CALMA IN AUSTIN (RIGHT).

"OUR OVERRIDING PHILOSOPHY," SAYS PRESIDENT JAMES F. SHEARER, "IS THAT IT IS POSSIBLE AND AFFORDABLE TO SPEAK WITH MILLIONS OF HOUSEHOLDS AND BUSINESSES TO FIND OUT WHAT SPECIFIC PRODUCTS AND SERVICES THEY ARE BUYING AND WHEN—ALL ACCOMPLISHED WITH THE QUALITY OF A PERSONAL TELEPHONE CALL."

Headquartered in Austin, the company has additional administrative offices in New York City and regional information centers in Austin, St. Louis, Des Moines, and Grand Rapids. National Market Share maintains a full- and part-time staff of more than 600 employees, and during presidential election years, the company swells to as many as nine information centers and 1,800 employees.

National Market Share and its parent company, Campaign Telephone Ltd., have contacted 60 million American households and will add approximately 35 million in 1994. Depending on the client and the project, the information garnered from these contacts might include a list of department store customers in the Midwest who are interested in carpet-cleaning services, Hispanic families in the market for a new car, or the locations of companies that accept a particular credit card.

National Market Share continually upgrades to the latest technology. Now, for example, operators never touch a phone—everything from dialing through recording responses is done via computer. And with "predictive dialing" software developed for the company, computers even monitor the operators, measuring how much time they spend talking and predicting when they'll be ready for the next call.

Friendly Marketing to Diverse Audiences
National Market Share's niche is outbound telephone applications for database marketing. Clients rely on the company for such diverse purposes as targeting specific groups, generating leads, developing new databases, providing customer service, supporting ongoing media campaigns, generating product orders, developing grassroots support, compiling research, and enhancing promotions.

The company's primary mission is to provide clients with revenue-generating information in a cost-effective manner. "Our overriding philosophy," says Shearer, "is that it is possible and affordable to speak with millions of households and businesses to find out what specific products and services they are buying and when—all accomplished with the quality of a personal telephone call."

He adds, "We're becoming a replacement for traditional direct mail. Nationally, the response rate for direct mail alone has dropped so drastically that clients have found a phone call alerts target customers to what's in their mailbox."

Shearer is concerned about the public perception of telemarketers and hopes National Market Share is dispelling some of the bad press. "We design scripts that allow our targeted households to get off the phone within 15 seconds if they're not interested. We're sensitive to the public's privacy."

A longtime Austinite, Shearer says the local employee pool compares favorably to any major U.S. city. "We've patterned our expansions on seeking cities similar to Austin," he explains. "The fact that it's a state capital, combined with the presence of a major university, enhances our work force."

Reedie-York & Associates, Inc.

A S MILLIONS OF AMERICANS EXPERIENCE CAREER CHANGE, new ways of looking at work are required. For many people today, jobs in a traditional sense are in limited supply; however, there is work. Helping people see career choices through new erceptions is the mission of eedie-York & Associates, Inc., ie only locally owned, full-service areer transition management firm i the Austin market.

According to President Norman York and Executive Vice President Lynette Fairey York, their ersonal experiences with career hange and their longtime knowl-dge of the local market help more an 80 percent of the firm's candi-ates remain in Austin when they xperience job loss or retirement, hether voluntary or involuntary.

"When this office was opened in 989," says Lynette, "there were many local firms that provided bits d pieces, but we brought a com-rehensive, personalized approach at includes helping each person in self-knowledge and the skills eeded to be successful in today's ghly competitive job market. Of qual importance is the office sup-rt we provide individuals as they induct their campaigns."

orking with the Whole Person

Ve work with the whole person," ites Lynette. "We use a Ph.D. ychologist to help the candidate d spouse deal with the trauma of ange while we begin the process helping each person acquire the ills that he or she will need for ccess. A key feature of our work day is helping women in transi-n address the special needs and ues that are likely to have an npact on them as they deal with ange both within and without the ganization."

"Because nearly three-quarters the executives and managers who se their jobs do so because of ues of 'fit' and interpersonal compatibility, many related prob-ns can be solved through remedi-ion if the effort is initiated early ough," says Norman. Reedie-rk & Associates conducts such

◀ DON ROGERS PHOTOGRAPHY

PRESIDENT NORMAN J. YORK AND EXECUTIVE VICE PRESIDENT LYNETTE FAIREY YORK ESTABLISHED REEDIE-YORK & ASSOCIATES IN 1989.

remedial programs to help save otherwise valuable employees who would lose their jobs at a significant direct and indirect cost to the organization.

Personalized and Flexible

"We are affiliated with the other offices of Reedie & Company in Dallas, Houston, and San Antonio, plus a network of high-quality, independent firms nationwide," says Lynette. "Because we do not operate under the control of centralized corporate policy, we are free to tailor each program to suit the specific needs of the individual."

As the population ages, people must prepare for extended living by taking personal responsibility for their financial, physical, social, emotional, and spiritual health. Says Norman, "Since effective liv-ing is associated with purpose, and because most people derive much

of their purpose from work, we place work at the center of our long-life planning program that serves as an alternative to tradi-tional retirement planning."

"We believe the quality of our work rests with the understanding and experiences of our staff," says Lynette, who is a native of Austin with lifelong ties to the business community. "No one works for us who has not had practical experi-ence with the realities of career change. This helps us all have empathy for both our clients and our candidates."

Adds Norman, "Few experiences in life create so great a threat as the change associated with career tran-sition, regardless of its nature. We have built our business on our commitment to helping the people we serve meet the challenge of change and emerge as winners in the process. We think that makes us who we are."

Tivoli Systems, Inc.

TIVOLI SYSTEMS HAS A PROBLEM MOST BUSINESSES WOULD ENVY. When the company was founded in 1989 by former IBM Austin software developers, they chose the name "Tivoli" thinking that they would eventually find a more descriptive name. According to President and Chief Executive Officer Franklin Moss, the founders never dreamed the company would experience such growth that they would never have a chance to choose a different name.

A New Approach to Managing Computers

Tivoli is the first company to succeed in the new market for software designed to manage distributed computer systems.

Moss explains, "The world is moving toward a radically different style of computing. Networks of smaller, powerful computers are now handling a lot of the work that large, mainframe computers used to do. Companies can reduce their computing costs by linking together these smaller computers. But there's a problem: managing networked systems is much more difficult and expensive than managing a centralized mainframe or other large computer."

During its first five years, Tivoli has revolutionized the way businesses manage these sophisticated distributed computer systems—so called because they distribute databases, applications, and services like electronic mail over physically dispersed computers from many different vendors. "If organizations tried to manage these distributed environments the way they managed their centralized systems, they'd be stuck using a different management tool for each type of computing resource on each brand of computer," says Moss. "System managers would have to master a whole array of different tools. The larger the network, the more difficult—and eventually impossible—it would be for system managers to keep up."

The Tivoli difference is an innovative software framework based on

the latest object-oriented technology. This framework "lives" on the networked computers and represents the various computing resources as objects on the system manager's computer screen. System managers manage the objects, and the objects manage the underlying details. The Tivoli Management Environment (TME) is a set of software tools that use the framework and the objects to perform various tasks.

Tivoli's elegant, simple, and practical approach has become very popular with customers. Today, more than 150 leading customers worldwide use **TME** to manage more than 50,000 networked computer systems combined. Tivoli's customers include GTE Telephone Operations, the largest U.S.-based local telephone company, and Charles Schwab & Co., a leading discount stockbroker. In addition, the framework has been broadly adopted by industry standards groups and has been endorsed by leading client/server systems ven-

dors, such as Sun Microsystems, IBM, and Hewlett-Packard.

Reducing Cost and Complexity

Tivoli software dramatically reduces the cost and complexity of managing distributed computer systems.

Using Tivoli software, system managers can easily perform a variety of formerly complex tasks. These tasks include adding new computers to a network, distributing software, monitoring a remote computer for trouble conditions, rerouting print jobs among printers, and managing electronic mail systems. System managers can perform these tasks without leaving their desks and can delegate tasks among their staff without risking hazardous security holes.

"This is a much more realistic management approach," says Moss. "To add a new computer to the network, the system manager can simply 'drag and drop' a picture of the computer to a window on his computer screen that represents a network. Before, the system man-

Moss was familiar with the business world's need for ways to manage distributed computers when he arrived at Tivoli in 1991. A former vice president at microcomputer software company Lotus Development Corp., Moss was the driving force in bringing the Lotus 1-2-3 spreadsheet to UNIX and other non-PC platforms. He also helped customers deploy Lotus software on large, organization-wide networks.

"I joined Tivoli because I saw that the company had both the technology and the opportunity to

software, Tivoli has opened up the links to the framework to encourage others in the software industry to develop complementary applications. The company wants to ensure that customers have a wide variety of TME and TME-like management applications available—from Tivoli and others. By growing the market for distributed systems management applications, says Moss, Tivoli will grow its own share of the market.

Tivoli currently has a staff of more than 120 and serves customers through regional sales offices in

TIVOLI SOFTWARE SUPPORTS A VARIETY OF CLIENT/SERVER ENVIRONMENTS.

ger would have had to type many, many lines of complex computer commands and run out to the actual site to do it."

Because it simplifies the management process, Tivoli software allows organizations to manage growing networks of systems with fewer people and lower budgets, to retain centralized control, to protect security, and to more easily add new computers and other resources to accommodate their growing businesses.

grab an early lead in a booming market," says Moss. "By the end of 1995, organizations will be spending as much as $1 billion a year on software for managing distributed computers. Todd Smith and the other Tivoli founders invented some breakthrough technology, but we also have the skills to turn it into solutions for customers. We put an early stake into the ground in this market. Our position can only grow as the overall market grows."

In addition to selling its own

the United States and a dozen distributors in Europe and the Far East. For a small company, Tivoli has already made a great impact. But Moss doesn't intend for Tivoli to stay small long. "Tivoli will be a major player in the global software economy by the end of the decade," he avows. "Our goal is to create a company that is well respected, provides an important product to customers, and does this very well."

International Biomedical, Inc.

I N 1973 A.J. SEGARS FOUNDED A SMALL MEDICAL EQUIPMENT company that, in just 20 years, has become an industry leader in physiological monitoring equipment. It is not surprising, though, that Segars, a father of nine, devotes much of his company's capital and

research to developing products for critically ill and injured infants. Thanks to his vision, International Biomedical, Inc. has become the world's leading manufacturer of neonatal transport systems for use in aircraft and ambulances.

In the beginning, the company served as a manufacturers' representative and marketed electronic medical devices for the hospital and home health care markets. Segars expanded into manufacturing in 1980 when he acquired a firm that produced radiation-resistant gloves for physicians and technicians.

Headquartered in Austin since 1990, International Biomedical today manufactures, sells, and services medical products for use in a variety of health care fields. Its staff of 70 work out of three offices spread across Texas, but Austin is the company's nerve center. The headquarters on Cross Park Drive houses administration, research and development, engineering, and most manufacturing.

Growth Through Innovation and Acquisition

"We are constantly looking at the direction the medical industry is going and identifying new products that present a good opportunity for our company," says Executive Vice President William P. South. "We have a large research and development program for new products, and we are in an aggressive acquisition mode looking for companies that fit our mission."

International Biomedical acquired its transport incubator division, Airborne Life Support Systems, in 1983 and began manufacturing the transportable, self-contained units that provide a protected environment and allow medical personnel to sustain and monitor critically ill infants during

transport. The company expanded the existing product line with the introduction of an incubator for use by hospitals to transport infants in-house.

Continuing its commitment to newborns, International Biomedical acquired Arvee Medical, Inc. in 1992 and began manufacturing its Arvee Sleep Apnea Monitors. This state-of-the-art equipment, de-

signed for use with newborns at risk of sudden infant death syndrome, records an infant's vital signs including heart rate and respiration. The caregiver is alerted by an audible alarm if a monitored parameter deviates from the prescribed physiological limits. The monitor's recordings can even be loaded into a computer for analysis by a physician.

International Biomedical also owns Narco Bio-Systems and manufactures physiological recording systems, motility measurement systems for esophageal diagnostic procedures, and ambulatory pH data recorders under the Narco brand

name. The widely used Narco Bio-Systems Physiograph® the world's most complete physiological recording system, is used to teach physiology to pre-med and medical students and gives them hands-on experience in monitoring vital physiological parameters.

"This line of products is so popular," says South, "that people use the term Physiograph® generi-

cally to describe all physiological recording systems. Most of them don't realize that it's our brand name."

After two decades of growth and progress, International Biomedical has become one of the most innovative and financially stable companies in the industry. Looking to the future, it hopes to continue to offer state-of-the-art medical technology to patients across the nation and at home in Austin.

HEADQUARTERED IN AUSTIN SINCE 1990, INTERNATIONAL BIOMEDICAL IS LED BY PRESIDENT AND CEO A.J. SEGARS (LEFT) AND EXECUTIVE VICE PRESIDENT WILLIAM P. SOUTH.

Strasburger & Price, L.L.P.

FOR MORE THAN FIVE DECADES, CLIENTS HAVE RELIED ON Strasburger & Price for all types of legal representation. Established in Dallas in 1939, the firm opened a full-time Austin office in 1990 after merging with Armbrust & Brown, a respected local

firm with nearly 20 years of legal experience.

One of the largest law firms in the Southwest, Strasburger & Price serves more than half of the Fortune 500 companies among its 9,000 national and international clients. In addition to its Austin and Dallas locations, the firm has offices in Houston and Mexico City.

"Our clients benefit from the depth of a large law firm," explains Hal L. Sanders, managing partner of the Austin office. "They have access to extensive legal talent and resources on short notice. At the same time, clients are personally served by a lawyer who knows their business and concerns."

Diverse Practice Areas

The two dozen attorneys in the Austin office provide a variety of services, including the capital city's leading real estate and land use practice; corporate, taxation, and estate planning services; legislative and administrative representation before state and local governments; and litigation in federal and state courts in Central, South, and West Texas.

Strasburger & Price has helped numerous companies locate and develop plant and office sites in Central Texas. Likewise, the firm developed the foreign trade zone for the Austin-Round Rock corridor and has negotiated special location incentive packages with local governments. The Austin office also has developed expertise in dealing with all aspects of endangered species, water quality, air quality, solid waste, land use, and other environmental issues.

Business law and litigation have been strengths of Strasburger & Price throughout its history. Representing a variety of entrepreneurs, partnerships, privately and publicly

held companies, and governmental entities, the Austin office continues that legacy.

Strasburger & Price is also well known for its representation of domestic and foreign automotive manufacturers in all aspects of business, including administrative proceedings; business litigation; and trademark, environmental, tort, and product liability matters. Its attorneys are experienced in a variety of alternative dispute resolution techniques, including mediation and arbitration.

Because some tasks can be performed in a more cost-effective manner by nonlawyers, Strasburger & Price has developed one of the nation's largest legal assistant programs. The firm also employs a network of computer programmers, technicians, and research assistants to complement its traditional support personnel.

"We emphasize accessibility, responsiveness, and efficiency," says Sanders. "Matters are addressed quickly so that we can provide direct, timely responses and minimize legal costs."

A Strong Presence in Austin

The Austin office of Strasburger & Price also makes its presence felt through community involvement. "We encourage our lawyers to dedicate time to their chosen causes, and the firm lends its financial support," explains Sanders.

As a result, Strasburger & Price provides pro bono legal representation, volunteer time, and financial support to numerous civic, educational, environmental, social service, and health organizations. Several of the firm's attorneys volunteer at the University of Texas School of Law and provide continuing legal education for other attorneys.

"Whether in the area of community service or complicated legal matters, our real strength is the quality of our attorneys," explains Sanders. "Our lawyers have outstanding academic credentials and the ability to listen, assess, and communicate. They are committed to providing quality legal advice, regardless of the problem."

THE AUSTIN OFFICE HAS DEVELOPED EXPERTISE IN DEALING WITH A VARIETY OF ENVIRONMENTAL ISSUES (TOP).

THE FIRM'S NETWORK OF COMPUTER PROGRAMMERS, TECHNICIANS, AND RESEARCH ASSISTANTS HELPS ENSURE ACCESSIBILITY, RESPONSIVENESS, AND EFFICIENCY FOR CLIENTS (BOTTOM).

Summagraphics Corporation

AUSTIN-BASED SUMMAGRAPHICS CORPORATION HAS LONG been respected for the quality and reliability of its digitizers, plotters, scanners, and other computer peripherals. Today, the company is receiving praise—and new customers—as it emerges

on the forefront of graphics technology.

Summagraphics' most recent innovation, SummaChrome,™ lets users print large-format color images with photographic quality directly from their computers. Introduced in 1993, the large-format color printer system was hailed as one of the best new graphics hardware products of the year. It represents a landmark in hard-copy imaging, an industry estimated to eventually reach the $1 billion mark in yearly sales.

SummaChrome printers employ a breakthrough in technology called thermal wax transfer to produce large-format paper prints with vivid colors in just 20 minutes—far less time than traditional means such as offset printing. The resolution, 406

dots per inch, is considerably finer than previous applications of thermal wax technology for small-format printers, which have been used for color transparencies and product bar coding.

Summagraphics used its expertise in building pen plotters—computerized drafting devices—to develop SummaChrome's revolutionary two-inch printing head. With ultraprecise controls, the printing head transfers the image to paper by traveling back and forth across the surface in 12 swaths for each color of wax, yielding the highest quality, lowest cost hardcopy color image available.

THE SUMMACHROME™ IMAGING SYSTEM, THE INDUSTRY'S FIRST LARGE-FORMAT, THERMAL WAX TRANSFER COLOR PRINTER, CREATES HIGH-QUALITY PRINTS OF COMPUTER-GENERATED GRAPHICS OR SCANNED PHOTOGRAPHS (RIGHT).

FROM LEFT: SUMMASKETCH® III, THE INDUSTRY STANDARD AND THE WORLD'S BEST-SELLING DESKTOP TABLET, IS USED FOR INPUTTING GRAPHICAL DATA INTO COMPUTERS.

THE T-SERIES OF HIGH-PERFORMANCE VINYL CUTTERS PRODUCES CLEANER, MORE PRECISE CUTS FOR CUSTOMERS IN THE SIGN INDUSTRY.

THE SUMMAGRAPHICS HIPLOT® SERIES—USED TO OUTPUT HIGH-QUALITY PLOTS FOR ARCHITECTURAL, ENGINEERING, CONSTRUCTION, AND MAPPING APPLICATIONS—INCLUDES THE INDUSTRY'S FASTEST MULTIPEN PLOTTERS.

Known for Quality and Innovation

With the introduction of Summa-Chrome, Summagraphics continued its tradition of developing innovative computer input and output devices. Shortly after its founding in 1972, the company developed the first handwriting digitizer—a device that converts handwriting into digital code for entry into a computer. From that beginning, Summagraphics developed a series of increasingly versatile and sophisticated products for use in manufacturing, engineering, computer-aided design, and other industries.

Summagraphics came to the capital city in 1990, when it acquired Houston Instrument, a division of

Ametek, Inc. In 1993 the company moved its corporate headquarters and domestic manufacturing capability to Austin. About 170 of its 310 employees are now based in the city, with the remainder in an office in Connecticut and a distribution/engineering/manufacturing center in Belgium.

With the arrival of President Michael Bennett in April of 1993, Summagraphics began aggressively developing new products to expand its markets. SummaChrome is just one of the breakthrough products developed or released under his leadership. The company recently introduced its first desktop graphics tablet with a cordless pressure-sensitive stylus and is currently pushing ahead with new technology for inputting graphic design information into computers. Bennett promises that more innovations will soon follow.

"All we have done since I've been here is push the accelerator to the metal," he says. "We don't plan to let up any time soon."

ATS Travel

W HETHER A TRAVELER HAS TO JET ACROSS THE COUNTRY for a business meeting or wants to celebrate a wedding anniversary with a cruise up the coast of Alaska, Austin's ATS Travel promises professional assistance and the lowest

possible fares. In business since 1991, ATS Travel has rapidly become a major player in Austin's busy travel industry.

Traveling to the Top

ATS Travel's owner Mitchell Esmond has been in the travel business for more than 15 years. He built one of California's largest travel agencies in his hometown of Newport Beach, and when he sold that company in 1987, he took a four-year vacation and traveled around the world—twice.

On a weekend trip to Austin, Esmond fell in love with the city and relocated without plans to re-enter the travel industry. He was drawn back, however, and was soon recruited to help a small agency increase its market share. He eventually bought the company.

Since Esmond took over, ATS Travel has grown from one employee to a staff of 40 in three Austin offices. The agency advertises nationally, sponsors its own half-hour television show, and has satellite offices in cities including Atlanta, Tacoma, Cincinnati, and Las Vegas. Esmond attests that ATS is on its way to becoming the number one travel agency in Austin.

"The public is extremely fond of travel," Esmond says. "It's not a totally recession-proof business, but vacations are so important to Americans that they will sacrifice to take them."

Resources and Expertise

The bottom line—and the biggest reason for ATS Travel's success—is that the company guarantees the best price for business or pleasure travel. The company's investment in technology backs up the lowest-price promise: A software package called "Fare Assurance" constantly

checks reservations for savings opportunities, traveler preferences, and accuracy. "We saved clients $40,000 in one month on reservations that were already made, and some that were already ticketed," Esmond says. "We're one of the few agencies in town with that kind of capability."

ATS Travel also takes advantage of partnerships to save money for its clients. For example, the firm works with Cruise Consortium, a national group of travel agencies that specializes in selling cruise vacations. Thanks to the consortium's combined buying power and industry knowledge, ATS can offer highly competitive cruise fares, extensive ship selections, and specialized service.

Esmond, a veteran of over 50 cruises, enjoys sharing his personal experience with clients. In addition, an extensive video library with informative tapes about more than 300 cruise lines and destinations helps vacationers make decisions about where to go.

The company also is associated with Hickory Travel Systems, Inc., a $3.5 billion travel agency network with members worldwide. Through this relationship, ATS is able to provide services that are competitive with national "mega-agencies," including savings of up to 37 percent at more than 900 properties in 200 markets and more than 50 countries, a 24-hour reservation center, and an international rate desk offering fares averaging 10 percent less than those quoted by carriers.

Esmond attributes his success to his love of the travel business. "You are dealing with people's dreams," he explains. "Sometimes they've planned these trips for 20 years—and that's what makes it really fun."

ATS Travel has been a part of the growing Austin community since 1991.

Oppenheimer Environmental Company, Inc.

IMAGINE POURING A FEW DROPS OF CRUDE OIL ONTO THE SURFACE of an aquarium, adding a tiny amount of microbe-laced powder to the oil, then watching the fish survive, even thrive, by eating the converted oil. It's possible! ◆ Thanks to the pioneering work of oceanographer and microbiologist Dr. Carl Oppenheimer, Jr., students of all ages are learning a vivid and valuable lesson—that nature, through microbes, has the resources to heal and sustain itself.

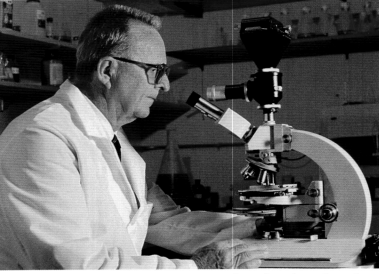

uct eliminates contamination rather than just moving it to another site.

The Oppenheimer Formula™ is produced and marketed by Oppenheimer Environmental Company,

"The Oppenheimer Formula™ is a natural and environmentally safe product that has been thoroughly tested and found to be extremely effective, yet entirely harmless to the environment," Daphne

CLOCKWISE FROM ABOVE:
DR. CARL OPPENHEIMER, JR., A MUCH-HONORED AND RESPECTED PROFESSOR EMERITUS OF MARINE SCIENCE AT THE UNIVERSITY OF TEXAS, DEVELOPED THE OPPENHEIMER FORMULA,™ A SPECIAL MIXTURE OF NATURALLY OCCURRING MICROBES USED TO ACCELERATE OIL SPILL CLEANUP ON WATER OR SOIL.

JENNIFER NEVE AND TRISH HILL SUPERVISE PRODUCTION AT THE COMPANY'S AUSTIN FACILITY.

OPPENHEIMER AND HIS WIFE DAPHNE ARE COMMITTED TO A CLEAN, HEALTHY ENVIRONMENT.

PHOTOS BY KELLY HOUSTON

"Hydrocarbons have always been and always will be a part of our environment," says Oppenheimer, a much-honored and respected professor emeritus of marine science at the University of Texas. "Nature takes care of itself. Naturally occurring microbes metabolize the hydrocarbons and turn them into food. That's why fish can survive with no additional food. It works in the oceans just like it works in an aquarium. The problem is that mankind is now upsetting nature's balance by putting more hydrocarbons into the environment than nature can compensate for."

After 40 years of research into marine systems from the Gulf of Mexico to the Mediterranean Sea, Oppenheimer learned how to give nature a needed boost and developed The Oppenheimer Formula,™ a special mixture of naturally occurring microbes used to accelerate oil spill cleanup on water or soil. Unlike many other treatment methods, the Oppenheimer prod-

Inc., which was established in 1991 by Oppenheimer's wife, Daphne. "I run the company while Carl works on the next generation of bioremediation products," says Daphne.

Cleaning Up Pollution

The microbes are packaged as a highly concentrated, gray powder—about 100 billion microbes per gram—with a five-year shelf life. When needed, the powder is spread or sprayed onto the contaminating material. When water is added, the microbes come to life, consuming the hydrocarbon molecules and converting them to harmless natural substances. The process is called bioremediation.

stresses. "This company was founded to help clean up man's pollution on Earth, and that will always remain our goal."

Much of the Earth's pollution is caused not by major oil spills but by small daily accidents—such as the 20 million gallons of oil that are drained from or leak from cars into Texas sewers and onto Texas street each year. As a result, Oppenheimer Environmental also markets microbes for home use, so that even the smallest leaks don't contribute to the overall problem.

"One of our main objectives is to educate the public about the benefits of bioremediation," says Robert Neve, director of education for Oppenheimer Environmental. "We believe that if all of us—from individuals to large corporations—learn how best to recycle our own pollution, we can make the Earth cleaner and healthier place to live.

Apple Computer, Inc., U.S. Customer Support Center

WHEN APPLE COMPUTER, INC. ANNOUNCED PLANS TO OPEN an Austin office, residents prepared to welcome a major sales center or a regional service hub. In June 1992, however, Apple amazed Central Texans by bringing to Austin a major portion

of its administrative business functions, as well as its entire customer support operation. Approximately 640 employees now work in the Austin office, and a total work force of 700 is projected.

Serving Customers and Staff Nationwide

Austin is now home to Apple's U.S. Customer Support Center, which provides a variety of sales, service, and support functions to Apple's business, education, government, and consumer customers in the United States. Working closely with major Apple sites in several states, it is the chief liaison between the company and its customers. The Austin employees also handle a variety of other functions, ranging from accounting and payroll to travel arrangements for all Apple employees.

"We answer up to 1 million phone calls per month, and we manage more than $4 billion in revenue per year," says Jim O'Neill, site director of Apple Austin. "Every order is administered, invoiced, and collected here. Every customer call Apple receives goes through Austin. Every check we disburse goes through here, and every domestic travel arrangement for Apple employees is made here."

The Austin office continues to thrive. Apple has already outgrown its quarters in the Ridgepoint Business Park and has obtained approval to construct a campus on a 130-acre site located at the intersection of Highway 620 and Parmer Lane.

Austin: The Perfect Home

Because of the center's importance to corporate operations, Apple conducted an exhaustive review of several sites before selecting Austin.

"We had numerous criteria," recalls O'Neill, who participated in the selection process, "and Austin ranked first or tied for first in every category. It has everything we were looking for: central location, competitive business costs, highly skilled labor force, strong educational system, high-technology infrastructure, attractive cost of living, and a very desirable quality of life."

The city's progressive attitude also attracted Apple. "The community values in Austin are compatible with our corporate values. We are concerned with issues of diversity, business support of the community, and environmental matters, and we wanted to be in a community that shares those concerns," notes O'Neill.

As a major corporate citizen, Apple is also aware of its duty to the local community. During its first year in Austin, the company and its employees contributed more than $65,000 in cash and equipment to groups such as Adopt-A-School, AIDS Services of Austin, Austin Children's Museum, Goodwill Industries Coats for Kids, Junior Achievement, Save Our Schools, and the YMCA Summer Camp.

"We encourage our employees to get involved, and we help by contributing to causes they suggest," O'Neill says. "We want to be part of the fabric of the community—not in a superficial sense but by making contributions that really count. That's why we concentrate on causes like education, health, and youth services. They are important to our employees, to our future, and to the future of Austin."

APPLE'S U.S. CUSTOMER SUPPORT CENTER INCORPORATES UNIQUE DESIGN AND COLOR TO FOSTER AN ATMOSPHERE OF PRODUCTIVITY AND INNOVATION.

PHOTOS BY PAUL BARDAGJY

Guaranty Federal Bank, F.S.B.

ONE OF THE LARGEST TEXAS-OWNED AND -OPERATED FINAN-
cial institutions in the state, Guaranty Federal Bank, F.S.B. is also
part of a family of financial services firms that brings extensive
experience and resources to Austin. ◆ Guaranty is part of

Temple-Inland Financial Services
(TIFS), which is owned by Temple-
Inland Inc., a Fortune 200 com-
pany headquartered in the East
Texas town of Diboll. Austin-based
TIFS also includes Temple-Inland
Mortgage Corporation, Lumber-
men's Investment Corporation, and
Timberline Insurance Services—
all of which are leaders in their
industries.

Operating under the TIFS um-
brella, Guaranty Federal Bank and
its three sister companies provide
comprehensive, integrated financial services for both businesses and
individuals.

Deep Roots in Texas

Guaranty was formed in 1992
through the merger of Kilgore
Federal Savings & Loan Association and Guaranty Federal Savings
Bank, both of which were owned by
Temple-Inland. Now headquartered
in Dallas, Guaranty operates 123
banking centers in 78 Texas cities,
servicing more than $8 billion in
assets and more than 470,000 consumer accounts. It is the largest
Texas-owned financial institution
operating exclusively in Texas.

In Austin, Guaranty maintains
eight neighborhood banking centers offering full commercial and
personal banking services. From
checking and savings accounts to
certificates of deposit, consumer
loans, mortgages, and lines of
credit, Guaranty is a one-stop
source for neighborhood banking
services.

his days as a University of Texas
Longhorn.

"What this business really boils
down to is people helping people,"
maintains Saxton. "At Guaranty
Federal Bank, it's my job to ensure
that we bring together an exceptional team of management and
staff who are dedicated to meeting
the needs of friends and neighbors
we proudly call our customers."

Guaranty plays a special role in
the Temple-Inland family of companies, making the dream of home
ownership a reality for many Central Texas families while financing
businesses that help the region's
communities continue to grow.
These have been the core goals of
Temple-Inland's financial services
business.

The parent company, Temple-
Inland Inc., traces its roots to Tom
Temple's Southern Pine Lumber
Company located on the Neches
River in East Texas' Angelina
County. A successful logging company that has expanded into a major
paper and forest products company, Temple-Inland has always
been progressive in its attitudes
toward the environment and its
employees.

Fueling Austin's Future

Austin serves as the headquarters
for many primary businesses of
Temple-Inland Financial Services.
Temple-Inland Mortgage Corporation is the largest TIFS operation in
the capital city, employing nearly
700 people. A national single-family
lender with 60 offices in 22 states,
the company services $9.1 billion
in mortgage loans and is ranked
among the nation's top 30 mortgage
lenders. Temple-Inland Mortgage
offers a full menu of products,
including fixed-rate and adjustable-
rate loans, and has three offices in
Austin—downtown, Northwest

JIM SAXTON, MANAGING DIRECTOR OF
GUARANTY'S CENTRAL TEXAS REGION,
BRINGS MORE THAN 30 YEARS OF HIGH-
LEVEL MANAGEMENT EXPERIENCE TO
THE BANK (BELOW RIGHT).

KENNY JASTROW, GARY COOPER, AND
JIM SAXTON STAND ON THE STEPS OF
THE TEMPLE-INLAND FINANCIAL SER-
VICES HEADQUARTERS IN AUSTIN.

James E. Saxton, Jr., managing
director of Guaranty Federal
Bank's Central Texas region, brings
more than 30 years of high-level
management experience to the
bank, including a term as chairman
of the Texas State Board of Insurance. In addition, he is well known
throughout Austin as a consensus
All-American football player during

ustin, and South MoPac. Kenny astrow, chairman and CEO of mple-Inland Mortgage, is a long-me Austin resident and also serves Temple-Inland's chief financial ficer.

Lumbermen's Investment Corporation has been in business in e capital city since 1954 and is sponsible for some of the most prestigious commercial and residential developments in the Austin area. For example, the company developed Onion Creek residential community and Onion Creek Country Club, the original home of the Legends of Golf tournament that gave life to the PGA Seniors Tour. Other well-known developments include Anderson Mill, Village at Western Oaks, and Buttercup Creek. Lumbermen's also owns several office buildings and the Radisson Hotel in downtown Austin, among other properties. With residential developments in Dallas, Houston, and San Antonio, Lumbermen's is one of the state's busiest developers.

Timberline Insurance Services, under the guidance of President Gary Cooper, is the largest full-service insurance agency in Austin, providing property and casualty coverage for businesses and individuals. The agency is also one of the largest in Texas and among the top 50 in the United States. Because of its national expertise, Timberline provides a depth and breadth of experience unmatched by other area agencies.

Robert Adelizzi, chief executive officer of TIFS and Guaranty Federal Bank, says these companies work together with the parent company, Temple-Inland Inc., to help create good places for people to live and work. "Through Lumbermen's, TIFS prepares land for residential development and sells lots to top Texas home builders," he explains. "Guaranty, in turn, loans money to quality developers and builders, providing funds to develop lots and build quality homes and commercial real estate, which supports growing communities. Our customers can secure their home loans through either the bank or Temple-Inland Mortgage. Guaranty and Timberline then provide these and other customers with a wide range of personal and commercial banking, insurance, and financial planning services."

Adds Adelizzi, "Temple-Inland Financial Services may appear different from Temple-Inland's forest products-related businesses. However, just as our forests hold the promise of tomorrow, so do the banking, mortgage, insurance, and real estate services we provide through our TIFS companies."

Hawthorn Suites Hotel

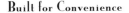

FOR SOME TRAVELERS, CHOOSING A HOTEL IS A MATTER OF finding a comfortable room for a night or two. For others, it's a matter of finding a home away from home for several weeks, or even months. Fortunately for all travelers to the Austin area, there

are three Hawthorn Suites Hotels that combine the comforts of home with the convenience of a hotel.

Unlike standard all-suite hotels, Hawthorn Suites offers apartment-sized accommodations, fully equipped kitchens with name-brand appliances, and special services designed to make life a little easier. For example, guests can drop off a grocery list in the morning, then come home to a fully stocked pantry in the evening.

AT HAWTHORN SUITES, GUESTS ENJOY APARTMENT-SIZE ACCOMMODATIONS WITH SPACIOUS LIVING AREAS, CABLE TELEVISION, AND EXTRA-DEEP CLOSETS FOR STORING LUGGAGE.

"Many people don't have time to shop for groceries, but they want to come home and relax in the evening without worrying about going out to eat," says Lee Leatherwood, suite division director of Shaner Hotel Group. "Our complimentary grocery shopping service means there's one less thing for them to worry about. It's typical of our approach—we find out what our clients need, then develop services to meet those needs."

Built for Convenience

Many of Austin's major companies rely on Hawthorn Suites to provide accommodations for employees who are relocating from other cities or who are in town to work on special projects. All three hotels are conveniently located near down-town and major employers.

Hawthorn Suites South, at 4020 Interstate 35 South, is only five miles from downtown and a short drive from Advanced Micro De-

vices, Lockheed, Motorola, SEMA-TECH, and the area's largest shopping mall, Barton Creek Square. Located at 8888 Tallwood Drive, Hawthorn Suites Northwest is similarly close to downtown and major employers, including Abbott Labs, IBM, MCC, Tandem Computers, and Texas Instruments. The northwest location is also convenient to shopping and ice skating at Northcross Mall. Hawthorn Suites Central, located near the airport at 935 La Posada Drive, is convenient to numerous business centers, the University of Texas, and shopping at Highland Mall.

Austin's Hawthorn Suites Hotels are part of a national chain of 16 properties under common owner-

ship with Hyatt hotels. In addition to Austin, there are Hawthorn Suites properties across Texas in Arlington, Dallas, Richardson, and San Antonio. Nationwide, Hawthorn Suites can be found in Atlanta, Charleston, Chicago, Minneapolis, Orlando, Pittsburgh, and Tulsa.

All seven Texas hotels and the one in Pittsburgh are owned and managed by Shaner Hotel Group, Pennsylvania-based investment

firm owned by brothers Fred and Lance Shaner. The company operates 30 hotels spread across the country from New Hampshire to Arizona, including 12 properties in Texas.

Shaner Hotel Group began investing in Texas hotels in the mid-1980s, when a depressed real estate market made the properties attractive to investors. By combining professional hotel management with extensive capital improvements and an aggressive maintenance program, Shaner has found winning formula.

"We put a lot of effort into improving our hotel properties," says Leatherwood, a hotel management professional who joined

haner Hotel Group in 1992. "We ave what we call 'suite care,' which our preventive maintenance program. Every suite undergoes a omplete review several times a ear in which we take care of any roblems that exist. That way, the ooms stay in good shape, and we revent big problems from occurng. It's an expensive program, ut we believe it pays off in the ng run."

xtraordinary Amenities

Iost Hawthorn Suites units, like partments, feature outside enances for increased privacy and ee parking provided nearby. nlike corporate apartments, hich require guests to take care

of such details as turning on the utilities and providing furnishings, Hawthorn offers large, fully furnished and decorated suites that are ready to occupy. Each unit is at least 550 square feet in size and features a roomy living area, cable television, and extra-deep closets for storing luggage. Most have wood-burning fireplaces. Kitchens feature full-size appliances, including microwave ovens and coffeemakers. Cooking utensils and table settings for four are also included. Each hotel has on-site laundry facilities, and guests can take advantage of valet service for their dry cleaning.

In addition to the complimentary grocery service, guests receive

morning newspapers and are invited to a complimentary breakfast buffet served daily. Monday through Thursday, the hotels offer an evening reception where guests can mingle and unwind. During warm months, the hotels have cookouts one evening a week, allowing guests to get to know one another in a relaxed atmosphere. In their spare time, guests can go for a swim in the outdoor pool, soak in the hot tub, play tennis or basketball on the Sport Court, choose a movie from the video library, or stop by the comfortable lobby lounge to visit with the friendly staff or other guests.

While individual suites are large enough to accommodate a small business meeting, the hotels also provide separate meeting facilities for business travelers. Meeting facilities vary by hotel, but all can accommodate up to 15 people and provide light food service. "This is an extra benefit for our guests," Leatherwood says. "It's a service we provide to make sure that our guests know we are interested in helping them take care of their business."

MEETING FACILITIES FOR BUSINESS TRAVELERS, FULLY EQUIPPED KITCHENS, A COMPLIMENTARY GROCERY SHOPPING SERVICE, AND A RELAXING HOT TUB ARE A FEW OF THE EXTRAS THAT MAKE HAWTHORN SUITES COMFORTABLE AND CONVENIENT.

Ions Incorporated-Austin

A T THE HEART OF EVERY COMPUTER LIES A TINY, YET VITAL component—the silicon chip. Imbedded in each chip can be hundreds of thousands of transistors that allow the chip to perform its task. The design of the transistors and their layout

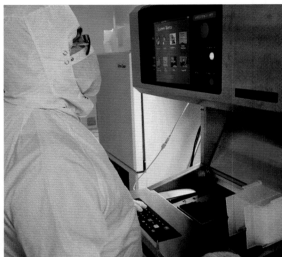

determine the chip's speed, power, and efficiency; consequently, chip "recipes" are among the most carefully guarded secrets in the computer industry.

Ions Incorporated-Austin provides one of the most critical and difficult steps of chip production—ion implantation. In this delicate process, ions (electrically charged atoms) are accelerated to a high energy and implanted into silicon wafers to create and adjust devices in the circuit.

A Pioneer in Industrial Ion Implantation

Ions Incorporated-Austin, founded in Austin in 1991, is the brainchild of Dr. Wesley Weisenberger, a nuclear physicist considered to be one of the early pioneers of industrial ion implantation. While working at TRW Semiconductors in the mid-1960s, Weisenberger became frustrated by the limitations of the existing process capabilities for the advanced microwave transistors his team was developing. He became interested in ion implantation as a possible solution to these problems.

Over the next few years ion implantation became a standard technique in chip production. The process employs large ion accelerators to shoot charged atoms into the wafers. Implanting the precise patterns, usually defined using a photoresist, is much like spray painting through a stencil that allows dimensions smaller than 1/100th the width of a human hair (0.00004 in.). The ions actually change the electrical properties in the wafer, creating transistor junctions. A single wafer may have several million junctions, requiring extreme precision and accuracy in the implantation process.

In the early days of ion implantation, misprocessing and process control were problems for many companies. In Silicon Valley alone more than 1 million wafers were

implanted with the wrong ions in a single year. In addition, production bottlenecks and equipment downtime often made it difficult for companies to meet production quotas. Weisenberger believed he could do better.

In 1978 he opened Ion Implant Services, the first company dedicated to providing ion implantation to semiconductor manufacturers. Located in Sunnyvale, California, it is today the nation's leading provider of ion implantation as a vendor service, working with leading semiconductor manufacturers in Silicon Valley and throughout the United States.

Bringing Quality and Customer Service to Austin

By the 1990s, Weisenberger recognized Austin as an increasingly important player in the semiconductor industry. With more high-tech growth than many other areas, including Silicon Valley, Austin was, he believed, "the most logical place to open a new facility."

Dr. Ken Duerksen, marketing director for Ions Incorporated-Austin, points out another reason for the expansion. "Wes fell in love with Austin," says Duerksen.

"He was delighted when there was a critical threshold of companies here that could support this business."

Today, several Austin-area companies rely on Ions Incorporated, thanks to its reputation for quality control and customer service. The company, for example, picks up and delivers wafers for customer convenience, maintains a sophisticated computer tracking system that monitors every phase of production, and promises timely delivery of implanted wafers—usually within 24 hours.

The company's quality mission is backed by outstanding people, superior equipment maintenance, and state-of-the-art process controls. Ions Incorporated boasts a clean room designed specifically for ion implantation to minimize particle counts within the implanters, and every wafer goes through an extensive series of quality checks. Quality efforts also include empowering employees to think for themselves on the job. This translates into a high-quality product at prices that are often lower than what it costs customers to do the work in-house. Ions Incorporated-Austin and Ion Implant Services have one

of the industry's lowest error rates and have become vital in the success of their customers. That success is of primary importance to Weisenberger, who still holds the philosophy, "When our customers win, we win."

The Austin company is an environmentally sensitive operation as well. The facility has been designed to exceed the environmental requirements and guidelines recommended by one of the toughest "Model Cities" programs, which far exceeds existing municipal laws and requirements.

Many companies with initial reservations about outsourcing ion implantation have become enthusiastic after taking a closer look at Ions Incorporated-Austin. As companies in all industries begin to focus on what they do best and outsource other activities, the semiconductor industry is following suit. And that means a bright future for Ions Incorporated-Austin. As specialists, the firm and its employees perform only one process in the complex operation of silicon chip manufacturing and can stay single-minded in this business. According to Weisenberger, "We do one critical thing, and we do it better."

THE COMPANY'S CLEAN ROOM FACILITY WAS DESIGNED SPECIFICALLY FOR ION IMPLANTATION TO MINIMIZE PARTICLE COUNTS WITHIN THE IMPLANTERS (ABOVE).

AN EMPLOYEE LOADS A SEMICONDUCTOR DEVICE WAFER FOR IMPLANTATION (ABOVE LEFT).

Frost National Bank-Austin

FROST NATIONAL BANK HAS BEEN SERVING CUSTOMERS FOR more than a century. A leading financial institution in South Texas, Frost has 25 locations and is part of Cullen/Frost Bankers, Inc., a Texas-based holding company with $3.5 billion in assets.

The bank entered the Austin market in 1982, and with three branches and $350 million in assets, it has become the city's sixth-largest financial institution. Frost hopes to keep growing with the community by responding to the needs of customers, providing a return to shareholders, and demonstrating good corporate citizenship.

IN THE AFTERMATH OF THE CIVIL WAR, COLONEL THOMAS CLAIBORNE FROST PLANTED THE SEEDS OF WHAT WOULD BECOME FROST NATIONAL BANK.

A PART OF THE AUSTIN COMMUNITY SINCE 1982, THE BANK MOVED INTO ITS RENOVATED QUARTERS IN 1994 (RIGHT).

A Rich Texas History

The seeds of what would become Frost National Bank were planted in the aftermath of the Civil War, when Colonel Thomas Claiborne Frost established a freight business between San Antonio and Indianola. Soon after, his brother John asked the colonel to join his mercantile and auction business. Together with a third partner, they successfully operated Fitch, Frost and Bro. on San Antonio's Main Plaza.

After John's death, Colonel Frost added a new dimension to the enterprise: the wool commission business. He collected and stored area wool producers' goods until market conditions were favorable, making loans to them using the wool stock as collateral. This diversification marked the birth of Frost Bank, which was established in 1868 and received its national charter in 1899.

The new bank continued to grow with the nation through the 1920s, despite the death of Colonel Frost in 1903. In 1928 a merger with Lockwood National Bank, San Antonio's oldest bank, made Frost stronger yet.

In 1929 the bottom fell out of the stock market, and by the close of the decade, nearly 5,000 financial institutions had failed. Frost Bank, however, successfully weathered the Great Depression and has never closed its doors for any reason other than national bank holidays.

But it wasn't until World War II that Frost, like many other American companies, truly began to grow again. Today, the bank is still under the guidance of the founding family: Thomas C. Frost, a descendant of Colonel Frost, serves as chairman of the board, and his four sons all hold positions in the company. Frost National Bank remains faithful to the founder's vision, and its progress can be attributed to the values he instilled more than 125 years ago.

Committed to Austin

"We want to bring traditional Texas banking back to Austin," says Robert Huthnance, president of Frost National Bank-Austin. "That's where we differentiate ourselves. People want to know their bankers again. We believe the two-way relationship between a bank and a customer is central to any community."

Accordingly, Frost continues its commitment to convenience for all of its customers. The bank has been on the cutting edge of industry innovation, including drive-in teller windows, computerized service, and automated teller machines.

The key to offering convenience, though, is assembling a top-notch and knowledgeable staff. To that end, Huthnance has put together a banking team with longevity and experience. "The level of talent on our staff fits well with the high level of education of the Austin community," he notes.

Frost National Bank brings to the capital city a long tradition of commitment to Texas. The bank and its staff look forward to fueling the progress of Austin and its people.

Loye W. Young, P.C.

DURING HIS TIME AS A SUCCESSFUL CORPORATE LAWYER IN A prominent Austin law firm, Loye Young spent several years putting together multimillion-dollar deals for companies and financial institutions all over the world. Despite the challenges and rewards of his busy practice, Young wasn't satisfied. His clients were major corporations, not Austin businesses, and he began to feel out of touch with the city that was his home.

From a Large Firm to Private Practice

So Young decided to make a change. On January 1, 1993, he opened Loye W. Young, P.C., a private practice dedicated to making the high caliber of legal services provided by large firms available to Austin-based businesses.

"Large law firms are designed for Fortune 500 companies, banks, and publicly traded companies," Young says. "In Austin, there is one Fortune 500 company headquarters, a dwindling number of banks, and very few publicly traded companies. The real heart of our economy is privately held, locally based, growing businesses."

A "Family Doctor" Approach

Young designed his firm to serve the specific legal needs of Austin-based businesses, their owners, and executives. Like the legal equivalent of a family doctor, he provides counsel on the issues businesses and their managers are most likely to encounter—including business planning and start-ups, real estate transactions, contracts, and estate planning. When other services are required, he recommends a qualified professional.

A Strategic Approach

Companies are very much like families, with their own attitudes and characteristics," Young notes. "They need comprehensive legal advice, but they rarely need the extraneous long list of services big law firms offer—and they definitely don't need the expense." As a company's counsel, Young develops

HENRY FRIEDMAN

an overall understanding of the business' goals and priorities. "The way I practice law is to find out what's most important to my clients and to help them achieve it," he explains. "It's a strategic approach. It's proactive compared to reacting to a problem or situation. Everything we do relates to the organization's overall strategic or corporate plan for both long-range and short-term goals and objectives."

Young's goal is to work with businesses throughout their life cycles—beginning at birth or even before. "I help them understand how a particular legal situation affects their big picture," he says. "I can minimize their legal expense and exposure by doing things right the first time so they can avoid having to fix them later."

Timely Legal Service

Unfortunately, many business owners consider legal advice an expensive luxury. Young says these businesses learn too late that the costs of forgoing legal counsel can be even greater. "Anyone who is in business needs to seek legal advice before risking significant resources or attracting investors or partners," he recommends. "Otherwise, the business will be in trouble when the unexpected happens."

Loye Young has combined his professional objectives and his religious faith into a business strategy based on honesty and integrity, and his mission statement details his personal commitment to "providing principled, efficient, knowledgeable, and straightforward counsel and assistance."

Young's priority is to help businesses make the right choices. He adds, "Selecting a lawyer you can trust—one with the same outlook you have—is one of the most important choices you will make in business."

LIKE THE LEGAL EQUIVALENT OF A FAMILY DOCTOR, LOYE YOUNG PROVIDES COUNSEL ON THE ISSUES AUSTIN BUSINESSES AND THEIR MANAGERS ARE MOST LIKELY TO ENCOUNTER— INCLUDING BUSINESS PLANNING AND START-UPS, REAL ESTATE TRANSACTIONS, CONTRACTS, AND ESTATE PLANNING.

Worthen National Bank of Texas

WORTHEN NATIONAL BANK OF TEXAS VIEWS AUSTIN AS A solid base for building a community banking organization that is both sensitive and responsive to local businesses, as well as to the individual citizens it has the privilege to serve.

"WORTHEN NATIONAL BANK OF TEXAS IS A SERVICE-DRIVEN, COMMUNITY-ORIENTED BANK," SAYS BILL RENFRO (RIGHT), CHAIRMAN AND CEO OF THE AUSTIN BANK.

The former Union National Bank-Austin took on its new name in June of 1993 when parent company Union of Arkansas Corporation merged with Worthen Banking Corporation headquartered in Little Rock, Arkansas.

Today, Worthen National Bank of Texas has $113 million in assets and more than 75 employees. Worthen boasts six locations in the Austin area: two in the heart of the city and one each in Westlake Hills, Cedar Park, Brushy Creek, and Round Rock.

A New Banking Resource
"Worthen brings to the people of Austin a new banking resource—one with the financial strength of a regional bank that has received national recognition for its financial accomplishments and its unique management style," says Curt Bradbury, chairman, president, and chief executive officer of Worthen Banking Corporation. "Austin is

famous for its traditions, economic vitality, progressiveness, and quality of life. Worthen's commitment is to provide financial services and innovative delivery systems that will contribute positively to the future of a community that already boasts a proud past."

Bill Renfro, a veteran Texas banker and the new chairman and CEO of the Austin bank concurs. "Worthen National Bank of Texas is a service-driven, community-oriented bank. We believe that the many changes in our local banking community leave a profitable place for a bank with the Worthen brand of local autonomy and community focus," he says.

Austin benefits from the additional depth of financial resources, which fuels continued economic growth. Customers benefit from a variety of new and expanded services, including a very low-interest credit card, a complete line of checking and savings packages, credit lines, trust banking, mortgage banking, senior citizen packages, and full-service investment brokerage services.

And why choose Austin? "Austin is a city rich with potential, and it's a great place to do business," Renfro says. "We believe we can make a difference in this community."

Service to Customers and the Community
Worthen National Bank of Texas is a nationally chartered bank headquartered in Austin. "We have a local board of directors, and we are very involved in the things that are important to Austin, such as education, health care, and a safe environment," Renfro explains. The bank has been a leader in support-

ing Austin Adopt-A-School, Seton Medical Center, Boy and Girl Scouts, and the American Heart Association, to name a few.

Attention to customer needs is another value important to Worthen, as evidenced by its mission statement calling for the bank to be "procedurally sound and entrepreneurial in spirit."

"We go out of our way to be flexible," Renfro says. Willingness to customize services to customers needs and to go the extra mile are hallmarks of Worthen's business philosophy. Services such as expanded hours, expert investment and trust services, and innovative accounts are important to the bank's customer base, which is primarily made up of small-business owners and professionals who want to take care of all their financial needs in one place.

In the future, Worthen National Bank of Texas will be seeking new ways to establish a market presence in the Austin area, as well as opportunities for growth in Austin and other Texas markets.

Photographers

RALPH BARRERA is a full-time photographer for the *Austin American-Statesman*. He has a bachelor's degree in journalism and has covered everything from political conventions to Super Bowls to Central America. He has been published in national news magazines and newspapers and has won numerous national and state awards for photojournalism. Barrera is also an avid golfer who competes in national and local tournaments.

REAGAN BRADSHAW, an Austinite since 1961, earned a bachelor's degree from the University of Texas in 1965. He has since opened Reagan Bradshaw Studio. Bradshaw specializes in high-tech and advertising photography and has been recognized for his work with a number of local Addy awards, including a district Addy in 1990. His work was also featured in the books, *Forgotten Texas*, *The Indians of Texas*, and *The Great State of Texas*. Founding president of the Austin/San Antonio chapter of the American Society of Media Photographers, Bradshaw has served on the ASMP national board since 1987.

JOHN CHRISTIAN, originally from Mexico City, studied at the New Mexico Military Institute and at Sam Houston State University, where he earned his bachelor's degree. He has been featured in numerous publications, including *Texas Monthly*, *Journal of American Folklore*, *Popular Photography*, *Heritage Magazine*, *ArtWeek*, *Artes Visuales*, and *Mexico Desconocido*. Specializing in documentary, people, and outdoor photography, Christian has had experience photographing rural Texas and Mexico, including the Huichol Indians of Western Mexico, the Sierra Madre Occidental Mountains, and the mountains, creeks, and rivers of rural Texas.

KAREN DICKEY, originally from Tucson, Arizona, works as a photographer for the Texas Department of Agriculture. She has a bachelor's degree from the University of Arizona and was the photographer for the recent book, *Monkeys of the Mesquite—Social Life of the South Texas Snow Monkey*. Dickey is the chapter treasurer for the Austin/San Antonio American Society of Media Photographers.

LYNNE DOBSON has been a photographer for the *Austin American-Statesman* for seven years. She has a number of specialties, including fashion, sports, and feature photography. Dobson has won a variety of awards for her work and, in both 1983 and 1986, won the Best Photo Essay award from the California Newspaper Publishers Association. She has also received the Best of Show award from the Texas Photographic Society (1989). In addition to Texas, Dobson has worked in Ohio and California.

JAMES A. DUMAS, operator of Spectrum Photography, specializes in commercial, aerial, landscape, event, and portrait photography. In 1993 his work was published in over 50 local and national publications. Tailored to serve Austin businesses, Dumas' firm also has an image bank of almost 3,000 photographs of people, places, and events in the Hill Country, Colorado, and Mexico.

M.L. EDWARDS, an Austinite since 1978, has a fine arts degree from the University of Texas. A self-described "good housewife that went bad," Edwards is a free-lance photographer specializing in environmental portraits. Her portraits, including extensive documentation of the homeless, have appeared in numerous exhibitions and books. She has served on the board of the Texas Photographic Society and continues as an active supporter of the society.

JAY GODWIN, originally from San Marcos, Texas, is the photo editor for the *Austin American-Statesman*. He has a degree in radio/television/film from the University of Texas where he also studied photojournalism. He has been a newspaper photographer since 1975. When not pursuing news photography, Godwin enjoys mountain biking, ham radio, woodworking, brewing, music, boating, reading, orienteering, and, according to Godwin, "whatever seems interesting."

JESSE HERRERA, a native of Monterey, Mexico, has degrees from the University of Illinois at Chicago and UT Austin. Specializing in photodocumentary work, Herrera has had photos published in *Quincenera*, a book about a Hispanic girl's rite of passage, and other publications about Texas history and culture. He has been documenting the religious festivals of a small village in the high-lands of Puebla, Mexico, for the past six years and has begun to incorporate images of the religious customs of Seville, Spain, into his photodocumentary work.

JAMES M. INNES, operator of James M. Innes International Images, specializes in architectural photography as well as international and Austin stock images. He has supplied photography to many area clients, including Motorola, Omni Hotels, NationsBank, Trammell Crow, Majic 95.5, Aetna, Bank One, Franklin Federal, General Electric, Heritage Title, Charter Management, Oxford Commercial, Norwood, and others. Innes has photographed over 500 architectural projects in Texas and has traveled extensively around the world photographing landscapes, seascapes, and cityscapes. He currently has two posters (entitled "Austin at Night" and "Austin at Twilight") and a note card series available in many retail outlets in Austin.

BILL KENNEDY, an associate professor of photography at St. Edward's University, has a degree in photojournalism from UT Austin and, in addition to teaching, has experience in newspaper photography. Kennedy's projects include profiles of Big Bend National Park, neighborhood life in Austin, and a four-year documentary project on the Texas prison rodeo. His work is included in the photography collections of the Humanities Research Center in Austin, the Houston Museum of Fine Arts, the Ansel Adams Estate Trust, and the Center for Creative Photography in Tucson, Arizona, to name a few. Kennedy, in 1991, was appointed as photographer for the Texas State Library System, Archives Division.

DAVID KENNEDY, originally from Nebraska, has a degree in journalism from the University of Nebraska at Lincoln. He has lived in Austin since 1980 and is currently a photographer for the *Austin American-Statesman*. Kennedy enjoys sociology and cultural anthropology photography, and his work has been published in a variety of magazines and textbooks.

LARRY KOLVOORD is a staff photographer for the *Austin American-Statesman*. He has a journalism degree from the University of Texas and specializes in sports and features photography. Kolvoord enjoys photographing all Texas subjects—especially the Hill Country, Big Bend, the Texas Gulf Coast, and the Barton Creek watershed.

GARY LOCKHART operates Blimp Photo/Video Services in Austin. Using a 21-foot, helium-filled, tethered blimp, the company can shoot subjects from 10 to 200 feet above the ground. The completely maneuverable system is silent and offers a real-time view of potential shots on a video monitor worn by the operator. Lockhart and Blimp Photo/Video have provided low-level, close-up aerials for the Texas Department of Transportation, the City of Austin, Motorola, 3M, the Lyndon Baines Johnson Library, *Texas Highways* magazine, and others. Lockhart has also flown the company's blimp inside the Capitol rotunda for an aerial photograph of the state seal embedded in the floor, and inside the AlamoDome for aerial video of a 1993 George Strait concert.

REBECCA McENTEE, an internationally published photographer, is a photographer for the *Austin American-Statesman*. She grew up in several states and spent some time in Japan, where she began art lessons. McEntee graduated from the University of Texas and has since had her work used by The Associated Press and a variety of magazines, newspapers, and agencies.

LARRY MURPHY, a graduate of Southern Methodist University, came to Austin in 1970. He is now the photography supervisor for the UT Office of Public Affairs and also operates Larry Murphy Photography. Murphy specializes in scenic, portrait, fashion, and product photography. He also turns much of his attention to music: Murphy has provided photographs for local musicians that have been used in publicity materials and on album covers.

JULIE NEWTON, a photography professor at UT Austin, was recently named head of the photojournalism sequence. Specializing in ethnography and visual ethics, she has more than 20 years experience reporting and/or editing for three daily newspapers, radio, and television. Newton has served the Texas Photographic Society, the Vision 2000 task force, and the Visual Communications Division of the Association for Education in Journalism and Mass Communication. She has also edited two books and her article "Why Ethics?" was published in the National Press Photographers Association's special report, *The Ethics of Photojournalism*. Newton has been featured in more than 50 exhibitions in the United States and Mexico.

ALAN POGUE, a former army combat medic in Vietnam, has been a resident of the Austin area since 1969. He has a degree in philosophy and has studied Zen Buddhism, Existential Phenomenology, and Martial Arts at a number of international schools. His photography, influenced by his friend, the late Russell Lee, emphasizes documentary and social justice subjects. He has done work for the NAACP, the Mexican-American Legal Defense Fund, and the National Migrant Resource Program. Pogue has won the Dobie-Paisano Award from the Texas Institute of Letters and the Director's Special Citation from the Bureau of Primary Health Care.

RICHARD REYNOLDS, a graduate of the Brooks Institute of Photography, specializes in nature and landscape photography. He spent seven years as chief photographer for the Texas Tourist Development Agency and the Texas Department of Commerce, Tourism Division. He was the photographer for two books, *Texas, Images of Wilderness* and *Green Pastures Cookbook*, and his work has appeared in Sierra Club calendars, *National Geographic Traveler*, *Sunset*, *Southern Living*, *Texas Highways*, *Texas Monthly*, and *Reader's Digest*.

GARY RUSS has a bachelor's degree in photography from St. Edward's University in Austin. His studio, G. Russ Images, specializes in studio product, architecture, and interior photography, and has done work for many notable local companies, including IBM, 3M, Dell Computers, Texas Instruments, Motorola, and Advanced Micro Devices. He has won local and national Addys and is represented by The Image Bank.

PARK STREET was born in 1951 in San Antonio and later attended UT Austin. Before entering photography professionally in 1988 he was involved in real estate, travel consulting, and the management of internationally known guitarist Eric Johnson. His travels have taken him to 52 countries on four continents. Since 1988 his photographs have been chosen for inclusion in books, magazines, posters, and exhibitions, including *Communication Arts*, *Guitar Player*, and *Downbeat* magazines. He has also done work for clients such as Capitol Records, Steck-Vaughn Publishing Corporation, Sherry Matthews Advertising, Hal Leonard Publishing, and United Austin for the Elderly, and Holt, Reinhart, and Winston. Street is currently a board of directors member and the program director of the Austin/San Antonio chapter for the American Society of Media Photographers.

L.J. TINSTMAN, born in Hays, Kansas, currently resides on Lake Travis in Travis County, where she operates LJ Images. Tinstman specializes in nature and the outdoors and has spent much of her time photographing orchids. Her work has appeared in *Birder's World*, *American Orchid Society Bulletin*, and the book *Orchids Simplified*. Under contract with Images West, Tinstman has had work selected for encyclopedias, travel brochures, and textbook covers. She is currently at work on a project for the National Wildflower Research Center photographing a site every two weeks to record vegetation changes.

KEVIN VANDIVIER moved to the Austin area in 1984. He has a bachelor's degree in photography from UT Austin and has been featured in numerous publications, including *Newsweek*, *Time*, *Life*, and *National Geographic World*. He is experienced in both location and news photography. Vandivier's favorite subject is Christianity, and he recently worked as chief photographer for an archeological expedition in Israel.

JENNIFER VANGILDER, a resident of the Austin area since 1987, is both a writer and a photographer. She earned both a bachelor's degree in advertising and a master's degree in journalism at UT Austin. VanGilder has been featured in a number of publications, including *Texas Highways*, and is a board member and the exhibits chair for the Texas Photographic Society.

RICK WILLIAMS, a native of Houston, earned his bachelor's and master's degrees from UT Austin. He specializes in people and product photography for use in advertising, as well as documentary work on West Texas cultures. His work has been used by nationally known clients, including IBM, Motorola, Texas Instruments, former Vice President Walter Mondale, and Senator Bob Krueger, and has appeared in the pages of *Texas Monthly*, *Texas Highways*, *Southern Living*, *Forbes*, and the book *Contemporary Texas: A Photographic Portrait*. Williams' work can also be seen in the permanent collections of the Museum of Fine Arts in Houston, the Humanities Research Center at UT Austin, The Amon Carter Museum in Fort Worth, and the George Eastman House in Rochester, New York.

Index to Patrons